The Changing Role of Fathers

Graeme Russell

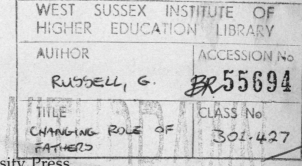
Open University Press

Milton Ke

First published in this edition 1983
by
Open University Press
A division of
Open University Educational Enterprises Limited
12 Cofferidge Close
Stony Stratford
Milton Keynes MK11 1BY, England

British Library Cataloguing in Publication Data

Russell, Graeme
   The changing role of fathers.
   1. Fathers – Australia   2. Child rearing –
   Australia   3. Father and child
   I. Title
   306.8'742   HQ756

ISBN 0-335-10198-4

Printed in Great Britain by
The Thetford Press Limited, Thetford, Norfolk

Contents

Tables

To Susan, Kirstine, Emily and Benjamin, without whom this book would never have been started, but if it had, would have been completed a lot sooner

Preface

This work has benefited considerably from the assistance, support and critical comments of many others. First, there are the contributions of the parents who were interviewed. Without their willingness to participate, to give their time, and to provide information about themselves, this study would not have been possible.

Several people were employed on the project to assist in data collection, coding, and data analysis: Susan Ballinger, Ann Beck, Judy French, Richard Glass, Joanna Greenwood, Margaret Kennedy, Christine Manning, Susan Tindale, and Wayne Sommerville. The assistance given in the latter stages of the project by Judy French was particularly significant.

I have also benefited either from the support, encouragement, or the critical comments and suggestions of: John Antill, Jacqueline Goodnow, Deidre James, Rosemary Knight, Michael Lamb, Alan Russell, Jacqueline Smith, and Peter van Sommers.

Funding for this project was provided primarily by the Macquarie University Research Grant Scheme. This support was particularly significant in enabling this project to get under way. In the later stages, funds from the Australian Research Grants Commission also helped to support the project.

Finally, I wish to acknowledge the contribution that attending academic conferences made. Both the academic and social aspects of these conferences provided the impetus for me to change completely my research interests (previously auditory localization) and begin the work on fathers described here.

1

Introduction

A few years ago I was at home with two four-year-olds — my daughter and a male friend of hers who had come to play. While I was in the process of tidying up after lunch, the boy edged up close to me at the sink and rather cautiously enquired: "Mrs Russell, don't you go to work? *My daddy* goes to work; my mummy stays at home." He obviously had difficulty deciding who I was; my behaviour contradicted his view of the world. I looked and talked like *Mr* Russell, but I was doing what he expected *Mrs* Russell to do. He *thought* he had it all figured out: dads go to work and mums stay at home. That's what his dad did, and what most, if not all, the other dads and mums he had seen did as well. This boy's experience of a man giving him lunch, washing up, and looking after children was probably his first ever encounter with such behaviour from a man, either in person or through the media.

There are very strong pressures within Western industrialized societies for dads to go to work and for mums to stay at home (or at least have the major responsibility for child care). Fathers identify much more closely with their paid work role than their family role, and it is success in the paid work force and the public domain that men depend on for their status. It is not difficult to find examples of how a father's role as an active participant in the paid work force is held in high esteem. Consider the following excerpt from a newspaper article about a football referee (names have been changed). The article was headed: "It's business as usual for football's Mr Cool".

> The hurly burly of the Sydney football season is approaching fever-pitch but for referee Bill Brown life is still very much business as usual. Yesterday, Brown, an area manager for Stevenson & Sons, was working through heaps of paperwork in his office in the city. He spends 10 or 11 hours most days in the office and when he is on the road inspecting the many country branches of

his company, a day can be 12 or 13 hours long. Each Wednesday night Brown attends a Sydney College where he is in the third year of a four-year managerial course. At least one other night of the week is taken up by group discussion with others in the course. "I get home when I can", he said with his typically dry sense of humour. Home is a comfortable three-bedroom house in Lane Cove. Brown's greatest regret is that he cannot spend more time with his wife Jill and daughters Emma 7 and Kate 3. At 32, Bill Brown, the young business executive is clearly going places. Slim, impeccably dressed, with styled collar-length hair and an air of complete unflappability, he strikes one as being more suited to a board room than to the football arena.

It is difficult, however, to find examples from the media and popular culture of men caring for children. There are few models of highly participant fathers and even fewer examples of this model of fathers being given any status. The absence of such models reflects in part the reality — there are indeed few men in Western societies who are highly participant in child care, either in the home or in paid employment (e.g., in child-care centres, pre-schools). But is this the only way in which roles or divisions of labour can or should be organized?

My own interest in fathers and their involvement with their children was prompted in large part by reactions such as that of the four-year-old boy described above. It was the reactions of both children and adults that led me to begin the research project that forms the basis of this book. While the majority of people agree with the four-year-old's view of fathers, my research also shows that a significant minority don't agree. And it is this significant minority — the fathers who have rejected traditional notions of fatherhood and who either share or have the major responsibility for child care — who provide the substance for many of the arguments to be presented here. I have called these fathers *caregivers*, and their families, *shared-caregiving families*. These families are basically of two types:

1. Families in which fathers are not employed in the paid work force and care for the children, and mothers are employed (families that have been popularly but mistakenly termed reversed-role families)
2. Families in which both parents are employed in the paid work force but have organized their work hours/types of jobs to allow the family to have the major responsibility for child care. In all families, however, the father was highly involved in the day-to-day care of his children.

This book aims to question traditional notions of fatherhood (e.g., that the main role of a father is to be the breadwinner, decision-maker, and sometime disciplinarian) and divisions of labour for child care and employment. The alternative view proposed is that fathers and mothers are *equally capable* of taking responsibility for and providing the day-to-day care for their children, right from birth onwards, they are *equally important* to their children, and they have *equal responsibility* for providing the day-to-day care for their children. These arguments are based partly on the burgeoning research findings on fathers now available from several different cultures, but primarily on the presentation of my own findings of a study of Australian traditional and shared-caregiving families. The major topics and issues covered in the book are as follows:

First, what are the current patterns of paternal participation in child care? Data are presented in chapter 3 which describe current levels of father- and mother-involvement in child care and play and the extent to which each parent assumes responsibility for their children. These patterns are examined both in traditional families, in which fathers are employed in the paid work force and mothers are at home as full-time child-carers, and in shared-caregiving families, in which fathers assume a significant responsibility for child care. While the chapter is based primarily on data obtained from Australian families, a comparative analysis of findings from several other cultures reveals the Australian pattern is consistent with those reported by others.

The fourth and fifth chapters examine the question of possible antecedents of paternal participation. Why is it that some fathers become highly involved and others do not? Chapter 4 examines this question within an essentially traditional family framework and explores the possible influences of factors such as maternal and paternal employment status, parental characteristics (e.g., education levels), family characteristics (e.g., number and ages of children), beliefs about parental roles, and the previous experiences of parents. Chapter 5 takes up the question of antecedents for shared-cargiving families and asks what it is about these families that makes it more likely that they will adopt a very radically different type of family pattern?

The focus of chapter 6 is on the question of whether or not fathers and mothers are equally competent in caring for children and providing for their day-to-day needs. Are mothers and fathers equally responsive and sensitive to children? Or is there a fundamental biological difference between males and females that makes it more likely that mothers are especially attuned to children and their needs and that, in turn, children are specially attuned to their mothers?

Chapters 7, 8, and 9 examine the likely consequences of fathers sharing in child care, consequences both for fathers, mothers, and children. What are the likely benefits and costs for *all* family members when fathers are highly participant? The major emphasis in the chapters on fathers and mothers is on data collected in the study of Australian shared-caregiving families, whereas the chapter on consequences for children is primarily based on studies conducted by others in the United States.

Chapter 10, examines the question of the longer-term stability of shared-caregiving families. Most social science research projects of the type described here adopt a fairly static approach to their subject matter, only reporting information on phenomena of interest at *one* period of time. The current approach was vastly different; several of the shared-caregiving families were interviewed two years after initial contact had been made with them. The idea behind doing this was first to see how stable this family pattern is. Was it the case, for example, that many of these families had reverted back to a more traditional family lifestyle, and if so, why? Second, the idea was to explore how these people's views of their lifestyles changed over time. Were families as enthusiastic about shared-caregiving two years later? Had they resolved the problems they reported earlier?

The final chapter presents a summary of the current knowledge about fathers and divisions of labour for child care and attempts to point out the implications for likely further changes in the family. Is it possible, for example, that this type of family form will become much more prevalent in the next twenty or thirty years? What are the likely psychological, social, and economic barriers and facilitators for such a change? The final chapter also takes up the broader issue of the implications of family change for changes in employment patterns. It is argued that a new role for fathers as caregivers is fundamental to any proposals to change current family or work patterns. Parental roles, and especially the marked divisions of labour for child care, constitute probably the most fundamental and pervasive of the differences between males and females in Western industrialized societies and are closely linked to sex differences in work-force participation. Many of the socialization practices adopted in these societies have as their basic assumption that women *will have* the major responsibility for child care for a large portion of their lives (even if they are employed in the paid work force), and that men *will not have* this responsibility. Moreover, this message appears to get through very early indeed, as is illustrated both by the story above of the four-year-old boy's reactions to a father at home and by recent sex-role studies. For example, in one study (Russell and Smith 1979) 450 children were asked what they would like to do when they grew up and left school. A significant proportion of both seven- and ten-year-old girls said that they would like to marry and have a family. Furthermore, there was considerable optimism represented in the responses; for example, "I would like to marry a nice man who makes chocolates." Only seven boys in the entire sample gave marriage and family as their likely occupation or what they aspired to when they left school. They major emphasis of boys was on high status and action-oriented occupations in the paid work force.

This book, therefore, represents a proposal for changes in the accepted roles of men and women, primarily within the home, but, as a consequence, *outside* the home too. Such a proposal may not be seen as being very new or radical at all for a significant minority of people. As the data presented in subsequent chapters show, the range of family lifestyles is quite marked, and some have already adopted a shared-caregiving family pattern. Others, however, might see these proposals, especially the proposals that men take on *equal* responsibility for child care and that women be more involved in the paid work force, as a threat to the family and therefore a threat to the basic fabric of society.

A cry that the family is under threat and needs strengthening is never too far away. This view has been expressed particularly strongly in recent years, especially in relation to the changing roles of women and their increased participation in the paid work force. Employed women have been blamed not only for family breakdown but for a whole range of other "social ills", among the more bizarre of which have been the failure of public telephones to operate (children break them while their mothers are at work) and an increase in head lice (employed mothers haven't the time to keep their children clean and healthy). Such views about mothers are based on beliefs like children need their mothers; there is a unique mother-infant bond; the nuclear family is the basic unit of society; the nuclear family, with marked sexual divisions of labour, is the natural and universal form of the family.

Moreover, there is a strong tendency for people to believe that the institutions they grow up with are *natural* and *necessary* for the stability of society. This is especially true in relation to the nuclear family and sexual divisions of labour. These views are as evident in the statements of politicians (and in their formal policies) and religious leaders as they are in the views of the general public. Tamie Fraser, the woman the former prime minister of Australia is married to, for example, had this to say about the family in a recent public statement: "The family is the basis of a well-integrated society. The Royal Family is a shining public example of the traditional family unit. . . . The pace of life is causing tremendous pressures on modern family life" (*Sydney Morning Herald*, 20 September 1977). Cardinal Freeman, the Roman Catholic archbishop of Sydney, was in basic agreement when in his 1978 Christmas message he said: "History taught that, whenever family life was strong and stable, a nation remained steadfast in its moral and physical growth. Sadly, the pressures of family life today are increasing." Neither of these statements, however, recognizes either the *variety* in family types or the changing nature of the family. In view of the emphasis being placed here on *non-traditional* family patterns, it seems as well to evaluate critically some of the commonly accepted beliefs about the family and family change.

The Nature of the Family and Family Change

Myth: The traditional nuclear family is currently the dominant type of family. While it may be true that the overwhelming majority of children are *at some stage* part of a traditional nuclear family — that is, a family in which there are two parents and only the male is employed in the paid work force — the overwhelming majority of people do not *remain* in such a family structure. A common life-span pattern might be: child in traditional family (eight years); child in a single-parent family (ten years); cohabitation (two years); marriage without children (four years); marriage with children (ten years); lone parent (three years); reconstituted family (ten years); single person living alone (ten years); living with son and his family as grandparent (ten years). Nor is it true to say that the overwhelming majority of families at any particular time are of the traditional type. Cogswell and Sussman (1972), for example, have estimated that in the United States only 30% of families are of the traditional nuclear type, as defined above. Other family types included: single-parent (13%), reconstituted (15%), experimental (8%), nuclear dyad without children (15%). Comparable family patterns also occur in other Western societies such as Australia and the United Kingdom (cf. Rapoport, Rapoport, and Strelitz 1977).

There are other possibilities for variety in family forms. Most analyses of family patterns have emphasized employment structure (mother unemployed vs. employed), parental structure (one vs. two parents), marital status (married vs. cohabiting), and family composition (children vs. no children). Little account has been taken of a further important family dimension – divisions of labour for child care and family work. We do not know the extent to which mothers and fathers share child care and family work, or indeed the extent to which fathers might have the major responsibility in this domain. This omission notwithstanding, the evidence is quite clear in showing that there is a considerable range in family types, and it is a gross oversimplification to assume that what has become known as the traditional nuclear family *is* the dominant type of family.

Myth: The nuclear family and rigid sexual divisions of labour for child care are universal. An argument often heard in support of the belief that the traditional nuclear family is natural is that it is the *universal* form of the human family; that it is the only type of family that has existed in all societies – industrial, hunter and gatherer, and horticulturalist alike. Perhaps it is not surprising the traditional family and sexual divisions of labour have come to be assumed to be universal when it is considered that in the majority of societies mothers have the major or sole responsibility for their *individual* children. But, this is *not always* the case.

Instances of extended family, group, or community-based child care have been found in both pre-industrial and industrial societies. Group child care in traditional small-scale social groups, for example, has been found in the form of communal breastfeeding. In several societies (e.g., Dakota, Alor, Bamenda), children have access to many breasts, making it possible for *all* mothers to participate in food production on a regular basis. Examples of industrialized societies with high levels of group child care or in which community responsibility for child care has a high priority include Russia, China, and particularly Israel on kibbutzim. Nevertheless, while there is group care and community responsibility for children in these industrialized societies, the caregiving role is primarily fulfilled by women. Men take on little responsibility either at home or in the work of community care.

Even so, marked sexual divisions of labour for child care are not universal either. Oakley (1972) reports that in both Arapesh and Trobriand Island societies, fathers share in the care of their infants:

> The Arapesh, for example, consider that the business of bearing and rearing a child belongs to father and mother equally, and equally disqualifies them for other roles. Men as well as women "make" and "have" babies, and the verb "to bear a child" is used indiscriminately of either a man or a woman. . . . The father shares all the routine activities of child care as naturally as the mother. [P. 134]

> The Trobriand Islanders . . . stress the need for the father to share with the mother all the tasks involved in bringing up children. . . . he shares fully in its care: he fondles and carries the baby and holds it on his knees, a task which is his special prerogative rather than the mother's. He cleans it when it soils itself and gives it mashed vegetable food almost from birth. [Pp. 135-36]

The idea of the Arapesh that both men and women "make" and "have" babies stands in stark contrast to attitudes in Western societies. A suggestion of joint involvement in *making* babies can hardly be denied and would cause no unusual reactions, but the idea that both parents "have" the baby does. After reading the report of the Arapesh some years ago, I made a point when talking about recent births to say that the father *had* the baby. This statement was always greeted with laughter, and became the object of further jokes; most thought a slip of the tongue had been made – they couldn't for a moment entertain the idea it was intentional.

More equitable divisions of child care tasks between the sexes have also been found in the highly industrialized society of Sweden. This society represents an important variant because it is one of only a very few societies in which there is social approval, and active encouragement through social policy, for men to take on the role of caregiver. Although only approximately 10% of Swedish fathers take on the primary caregiving role for some period of time, this is a significant group in comparision with other industrial societies. The possible implications of this type of social policy are considered in detail in subsequent chapters.

The idea that the traditional nuclear family and individual mothers having sole responsibility for child care are universal, therefore, can be refuted on several grounds. Most importantly, however, the present analysis indicates that in numerous societies child care is a community responsibility and, in a significant few, men share in these responsibilities too. Further evidence bearing on this issue is considered in chapter 6.

Myth: Family patterns are static. Family patterns are in a process of constant change, changes that are very much related to changes in social and economic conditions. The Industrial Revolution, for example, helped to emphasize the divisions of labour between the sexes. Men, as a consequence of the revolution, spent more time away from the home and less time interacting with their children, and thus probably had less direct influence on them. Before the revolution, sons especially spent a good deal of time with their fathers, and both were in close proximity to the home. Mothers, on the other hand, as a result of the revolution spent more time isolated at home and less time involved in productive work and had more responsibility for the children. Not that this responsibility was as onerous as it now is. In those days people had a very different attitude to childhood; children were expected to be independent and contribute to family production at a very early age — from around the age of seven.

Another example of an economic change that affected family patterns was the need for labour during and after a war. At these times, women were welcomed into the labour force, which resulted in changes in patterns of child care and an increase in the dependency of parents on their kinship networks (the extended family). Other more recent changes in family patterns can also be related to economic and social circumstances. For example, the increase in single-parent families, it could be argued, is associated with greater affluence and changes in legal, welfare, and housing policies. Changes in family patterns might also be related to changes in resources within the community — for example, increased child-care facilities increasing the possibility of both parents being employed; women's refuges increasing the likelihood of women leaving a difficult family situation and establishing an alternative family form. And, as will become evident in later chapters, the emergence of the shared-caregiving family described here is also related to economic and employment factors.

Far from there being a natural, necessary, universal, or stable form of the family, a more accurate picture is:

1. There is considerable variety in current family forms, both within highly industrialized urban society and in non-

industrialized societies. There is also evidence that suggests the traditional nuclear family with father employed and mother at home caring for children is not the dominant family pattern in Western industrialized countries today.

2. Community responsibility for child care and extended family networks are significant features of family patterns in several cultures. Furthermore, children being raised primarily in isolated nuclear families by their biological mother is, in terms of the history of the family, a relatively recent phenomenon (cf. Shorter 1975).

3. Marked divisions of labour for child care and raising children, with women having the major or sole responsibility, while being the prevalent pattern, is by no means a universal characteristic of societies. Societies have been identified in which fathers are equal participants in child care.

4. Family patterns are constantly changing. The family is best thought of as a dynamic institution which is responsive to social and economic changes.

Fathers and the Family: A New Direction for Change?

While some people view possible changes in the family as being a potential threat to society, there is yet another group who argue that the family is not changing rapidly enough. This group, represented in part by the feminist movement, argues that there is a need to abolish the family or at least completely restructure it. It is seen as the *source* of many of the ills of our society, and as a repressive institution, especially for women. These two apparently extreme viewpoints – that (a) the family is under threat and (b) the family should be abolished – meet at three levels: (1) both see the family as a very powerful force – the family is at the heart of socialization, and most significant human relationships are defined by the family; (2) both present arguments that are heavily based on traditional notions of the nuclear family – the feminist movement seems not to take account of the variety in family forms either; and (3) both emphasize the role of the mother in the family – the role of the father is almost completely ignored. Moreover, relatively little attention has been given to family roles and child care, and if child care has been prominent in debates about the family, it has usually been associated with a call for the provision of more child-care facilities by governments — "the child-care problem" as it has become to be known. In Anne Summers's book on women in Australia (Summers 1975), for example, there is little mention of child care and the role that fathers *might* play in this. There is some indication of a change in orientiation, however. Betty Friedan, a founder of the recent feminist movement in the United States, points to this void in a recent article (cited in *Sydney Morning Herald*, 12 January 1980) and proposes that the family and divisions of labour for child care represent the *new frontier* for the feminist movement in the 1980s.

The major focus of feminist movements in Western industrialized countries, rather, has been on equality of employment opportunities for women (cf. Newland 1980). Furthermore, a degree of success has been experienced, indicated by policy changes (e.g., anti-discrimination legislation in Australia) and work force participation statistics. The evidence shows quite clearly that compared with twenty years ago, women in general, married women, and particularly mothers with young children are now much more likely to be in the paid work force, (see, e.g., Australian Bureau of Statistics 1977; International Labour Office 1980). Beyond this rather gross indication of change, however, we know very little about the current roles of women and the extent to which other changes are occurring (e.g., changes in the *nature* of jobs held by women). Moreover, we know very little about what impact the change in women's paid work role has had on family work or divisions of labour *within* the home, or what impact it has had on men (cf. Newland 1980; Pleck 1980).

Despite the lack of emphasis on family work, an argument that has begun to emerge with increasing regularity in recent years is that unless men take on an equal share of this unpaid work, then equality in paid work cannot be expected to be achieved (Levine 1977; Newland 1980; Pleck 1980). This argument is particularly relevant in the context of equality for power and status in the paid work force. For while women are still both perceived to have, and in reality do have, the major responsibility for family work, they are not likely to be given equal access to promotion positions; nor will they be able to invest the necessary time and commitment to ensure their promotion. The aspect of family work that is of more particular importance in this context is child care. Unlike housework, child care and the needs of children create constant demands which cannot be put off to accommodate employment demands (cf. Newland 1980).

Questions of the role of the father and of men in general, then, are particularly important for any proposal to change or strengthen the family. Indeed, it seems that the aims neither of those who want to "save the family" nor of those who want to "abolish the family" will be achieved without a radical change in the roles of fathers and men. In particular, if fathers were to take *equal* responsibility for child care, then there could result at the one time both a strengthening of the family (e.g., by men placing more value on family life) and a radical change in the place of women in society (e.g., women would have more time to invest in paid work). Furthermore, it is apparent that permanent changes in sex roles will not result simply from the provision of more child-care facilities (the failure of the Israeli kibbutz system to radically change the role of women is evidence of this). It is the argument of this book that a new role for *fathers*, or a return to an earlier role, will probably be the most important change in the family in the immediate future. What is more, there is strong evidence that suggests this change is occurring already. This contrasts markedly with a traditional view that fathers are, by and large, neglectful of their responsibilities as parents. It may be, however, that part of the explanation of this father-as-neglectful image comes from *fathers being neglected* by researchers and professionals alike; they were not seen as important and therefore were not given any status, either in their day-to-day role as a father, in theories of child development, or in studies of the family (see Rapoport, Rapoport and Strelitz 1977).

One of the major reasons why assumptions about the father role have rarely been questioned (cf. Josselyn 1956), which helps to explain why fathers have been neglectful and/or neglected, is that there is a bias in both sociological and psychological family research. Safilios-Rothchild (1969), for example, has described American family sociology as "wives' " family sociology; while, as Bryson (1975) points out, Australian family sociology is predominantly the sociology of wives and children (e.g., Adler 1966; Herbst 1954). Recent family studies in Australia (e.g., Australian Family Survey 1973, 1975, 1976), in the United States (e.g., General Mills 1977), and in the United Kingdom (e.g., Oakley 1974) have done little to rectify this situation with their emphasis on mothers. Few researchers have adopted an interactive approach by surveying or interviewing *both* mothers and fathers (cf. Fallding 1957; Richards 1978). However, even in the recent Australian studies by Richards (1978) and Harper and Richards (1979), mothers and fathers were not given equal status either in the data collection or data interpretation stages. Apart from two joint family interviews, Richards (1978) reports that mothers were interviewed in the absence of fathers, and that *several* fathers were interviewed while the mother was present. Furthermore, the book reporting the findings, which is heavily based on direct quotations from mothers and fathers, contains nearly twice as many quotations from mothers as from fathers, and a sub-section titled "What is a good father?" is included at the end of a chapter titled "What is a good mother?"

A mother bias is also evident in psychological research. The overwhelming majority of studies on family influences have focused almost exclusively on mothers and their relations with, and effects on, their children. Until recently the only information that was available about fathers was that provided by mothers, whether the fathers were living with their families (e.g., Schaffer and Emerson 1964), or more commonly, were either temporarily or permanently absent from their families (e.g., Biller 1974). Clearly, such studies can contribute very little to our understanding of the role or influence of the father.

There are several possible explanations for this bias in psychological research into the family. First, this research paradigm is a reflection of theoretical frameworks which have had the significant influence on both psychology and cultural beliefs (e.g., Bowlby 1951, 1969; and Freud). These assume that there is a biological tie or attachment between mother and infant which is both unique and necessary. Bowlby also contends that the mother is biologically prepared for child care. Despite the many arguments against Bowlby's theoretical framework and particularly his research evidence (e.g., Rutter 1972, 1979), his views are still widely accepted. Bowlby himself also appears not to have been persuaded by the arguments. In a recent interview he stated that "if mothers don't look after babies then babies are not going to prosper" (Tucker 1976, p. 41).

A second level at which an explanation might be found is in the psychology – or, more generally, the research – of convenience. Psychological research has tended to be based on data collected from the most accessible subjects: first-year psychology students and white Norwegian rats. Family research can be seen as an extension of this; mothers, because they are more likely to be at home during the day, are much more accessible than fathers; and children, because many of them are in institutions, are even more accessible. It is inconvenient to investigate fathers, because they are most likely to be available at night or on the weekend. This approach to research, it may be noted, also results in there being an over-emphasis on the study of traditional nuclear families.

A third explanation for the bias could be that most researchers are male, and it is in their interests to study mothers and reinforce their child-care role in order to keep them at home and out of the work force and from competing with males.

There has been little research within Western culture on male nurturance, father-child interaction, father-child attachment, or the influence fathers have on child development. Studies on these topics, however, have increased markedly in the past five years (see, for example, Lamb 1981 and Parke 1979 for reviews), and findings severely question the assumptions outlined above and refute many of the myths about mother and father roles that have been promulgated under the guise of scientific evidence. There has also been a recent upsurge of writing and research on the male role and masculinity, with much of this also questioning traditional attitudes and values (e.g., Farrell 1975, Tolson 1978, Pleck 1981a; see also Levine 1979).

Most recent studies on fathers, however, have been about fathers in traditional nuclear families. Few researchers have either described or attempted to explain the diversity of father-involvement or the likely impact *high father involvement* might have on fathers, mothers, and children. Moreover, while studies continue to focus on traditional fathers, the findings might serve only to reinforce even further the current patterns of the distribution of family work (and pleasure!). Information is especially needed, therefore, from families in which fathers are not traditional and who are highly participant in child care. Not only is the study of these families important for our understanding of current family patterns and the changes that might be occurring; it is also extremely important for theoretical explanations of family patterns. Findings that fathers are just as competent and sensitive in the caregiving role as mothers are, and that they also develop strong relationships with their children, of course would severely question theoretical explanations that have emphasized biological differences between mothers and fathers. The present book takes account of this inadequacy inherent in previous studies by focusing both on two-parent families in which fathers adopt traditional roles and on non-traditional families in which fathers are highly participant in child care. The emphasis then is both on *modal* patterns of participation and on the *range* of paternal participation. The next chapter presents a description of how information was collected about these families and provides a description of the characteristics of the families studied.

2

The Study: Descriptions of Method and Samples

In line with a general aim to focus on the *range* of paternal participation, emphasis has been placed on two markedly different types of two-parent families. First, the more traditional family in which fathers are employed full-time and mothers assume the major responsibility for the day-to-day care of children. Second, families in which fathers either share equally or have the major responsibility for day-to-day child care. While the emphasis, therefore, is unmistakenly on fathers, every attempt was made throughout the study to give mothers and fathers *equal status*. This was certainly the case for the interviews carried out, a point that is elaborated on below. Other distinctive features of the approach include: a focus on both parental *behaviour* (e.g., day-to-day parent-child interactions) and parental *beliefs* about their roles and about the nature of child development; and the method of sampling – the majority of families were recruited in a quasi-random manner from shopping centres. Another feature of the approach is the emphasis on families with young children, and it is the argument for this emphasis that is presented first. More specific details of the method and sample are then presented.

Emphasis on Young Families

Although the aim was to recruit a sample with diverse family characteristics, there was one major restriction: *ages of children*. The samples of both traditional and shared-caregiving families were selected such that they had at least one child under ten years of age. The argument here was that the young-child stage is when: (a) divisions of labour between mothers and fathers are likely to be at their most extreme; (b) the physical, emotional, and economic pressures on families are high (e.g., the physical demands of having one or more pre-school-aged children; the economic pressures brought on by the loss of one income and the added expense of children); (c) psychological and physical investments in career establishments are likely to be high – the demands of employment, especially for the traditional male, are therefore likely to be high; (d) mothers are more likely to be feeling the effects of withdrawing from the work force and the probable loss in career establishment (which would undoubtedly have long-term effects on their employment prospects); and (e) a basis is likely to be being set for the establishment of longer-term relationships both within the family (parent-child relationships), and outside the family (e.g., employment-oriented vs. neighbourhood relationships).

The young-child stage is thus *the* critical time for examining and questioning current family patterns and parental roles. And it is people who are in the process of experiencing this life stage who are more likely to be sensitive to the issues and arguments. It was with all of this in mind, then, that the decision was made to focus on families with young children. Indeed, nearly 70% of families included in this study had a pre-school-aged child.

Method

Sample Recruitment

Given that this study focuses on two very different types of families, two very different methods of sampling were adopted, neither of which bears must resemblance to traditional university research sampling methods. The most usual methods of recruiting samples for university research projects are to require first-year university students to participate, to place advertisements in papers and magazines, and to send letters out through institutions such as schools. They all conform to the overriding principle of convenience to the researcher, and it is this principle alone that guides many of the research strategies adopted. The methods of sampling adopted here were radically different. All of the *traditional families* were recruited by approaching people in shopping centres. In all, nine different shopping centres were used, seven Sydney suburban centres and two in small country towns. Shopping centres were chosen to increase the possibility of obtaining a diverse sample on traditional social class variables. Approximately 50% of the people approached agreed to participate in the study. The only criteria for inclusion in the sample were that they had a child under ten and that they lived in the area surrounding the shopping centre. While it could be argued that sampling in this way will not ensure a random or representative sample of the population of families with young children, this was not the aim. Rather the aim was to recruit a sample which included a *range* of families, a range of education and occupational levels, and above all, a range of fathers with different styles of parenting and different beliefs. As will become clear in a moment, this range in the sample was achieved in a very striking manner. More complete details of the sampling procedure are described in appendix 1.

The original aim in sampling was to also recruit shared-caregiving families from shopping centres; however, in nearly 600 approaches, only 10 such families were found. As a consequence, additional methods were employed, and in the final event, 51 (out of 71) of these families were recruited either after they had responded to notices placed on university and community notice boards or when they were approached at pre-schools or play groups. Only three potential shared-caregiving families who were approached refused to participate. The criteria adopted for this sample were that fathers should either share or have the major responsibility for child care during the child's waking hours, and that the time spent taking sole responsibility for his children should be 15 or more hours per week.

The Interviews

Information on family lifestyles and beliefs were obtained from interviews. Parents were interviewed in their own homes at a time convenient to them. Most interviews were carried out during the evenings, and all were conducted when both the mother and father were at home. Forty-five per cent of the interviews were conducted by men and fifty-five per cent by women. The interviewer's ages ranged from twenty-two to forty-two. There were two parts to the interview. The first part was conducted jointly with mothers and fathers and the second part separately.

Part 1. This consisted of a series of structured questions covering background information, such as age, residence, occupation, marital status; work and leisure patterns for parents and children; child-care patterns; children's attendance at school, pre-school, playgroups; children's sleep patterns; divisions of labour for child-care tasks; parent-child interaction and family activities; father's attendance at birth. Questions were asked in the same order as they are given above.

The primary aim of the first part of interview was to obtain as accurate information as was possible about what parents actually do. The procedure adopted for specific questions on divisions of labour is described in detail in appendix 2. In brief, each parent was asked separately (but in the presence of the spouse) how often or how much time each week he or she spent doing the following for or with the children: feeding, dressing, changing nappies, bathing, attending to during the night, reading stories to, helping with school work, and playing or interacting with. Play and other interaction was defined liberally to include both child- and parent-oriented activities such as cleaning and gardening.

Part 2. Mothers and fathers were interviewed separately in the second part of the interview. Here, questions were both structured (e.g., parental ratings of child-rearing values) and unstructured (e.g., questions on beliefs about parental roles and responsibilities). The questions covered beliefs, perceptions, and values about parental roles, and about the nature of child development. A full list of questions is contained in appendix 2. At the end of the interview, parents completed the Bem Sex Role Inventory (see appendix 2).

There are two features of the methodology adopted that are integral to the overall philosophy of the study, and therefore require additional explanation.

1. *The strategy of interviewing parents together and separately.* As has already been pointed out, most of the previous data on divisions of labour in families have come from mothers and sometimes children. In a very few studies both parents have been questioned, but separately and sometimes using different methods; for example, Harper and Richards (1979) interviewed mothers, but sent fathers a questionnaire. The present approach involved parents being interviewed together and separately. The aim in the first part of the interview, when parents were together, was to construct a social situation in which the interviewer had some information about the family (e.g., questions on work and leisure patterns and children's sleep patterns were asked early in the interview), and *both* parents had some information about each other's interactions with their children. This, it was postulated, would provide a more accurate account of family lifestyles and parent-child interactions than would have been obtained had data been collected from both parents separately. Indeed, a pilot study of twenty families showed that when mothers and fathers were interviewed separately there

were significant discrepancies in responses in nearly 50% of the families.

In approximately 15% of the interviews at least one of the responses on divisions of labour was modified by information provided by the other parent. It was more common, however, for mothers to disagree with fathers' responses. When parents were unable to agree (and this did not happen very often), the interviewer reviewed their activities of the previous week. To illustrate, in one family the father estimated he changed nine to ten nappies a week, while the mother thought it was closer to two to three (quite a significant difference for this variable!). The father was asked whether he had changed a nappy today ("no"), yesterday ("no"), and the day before ("no"), the day before that ("I don't think so"), and finally, when was the last time he'd changed a nappy that he or the mother could remember? This turned out to be a week before the interview when the mother had gone shopping. Under these circumstances, the mother's estimate was the one accepted.

The same strategy of interviewing mothers and fathers together, however, was not appropriate for questions about parental beliefs. Rather, it seemed necessary to ensure that these data were collected *independently*. The need to adopt this strategy was emphasized very early in my research when, in a pilot interview, I asked questions on beliefs with both parents present. When I inquired about discipline, the mother very curtly replied: "Don't ask me, ask the boss." While this response provided some useful insights into the mother's perceptions, and experiences of power relationships within the family, little knowledge was gained about her beliefs about discipline. Without such information being collected separately from each parent, we are unlikely to be able to understand differences between mothers and fathers and how these differences might influence parent-child relationships. As a further way of ensuring the independence of the responses from mothers and fathers, both parents were interviewed during the same interview session, and therefore it was not possible for them to talk with one another about the questions or their responses until after both had been interviewed.

2. *An emphasis on behaviour and beliefs.* The emphasis on both behaviour (part 1 of interview) and beliefs (part 2 of interview) represents an important difference between this study and others; it is extremely rare for both perspectives to be included in family studies. Psychological studies, by and large, have em-

phasized behaviour, and sociological studies have emphasized beliefs. The incorporation of both aspects here is based on a new perspective for understanding family relationships that has emerged recently within psychology. This is a *cognitive mediational* perspective, the major proponents of which (e.g., Parke 1978) argue that parents' knowledge, beliefs, attitudes, stereotypes, and perceptions *influence* their child-rearing practices, their relations with their children, and their day-to-day family lifestyles. Although there may be some question about whether beliefs influence behaviour or vice versa, the basic proposition that an understanding of parental roles depends on knowledge of *both* behaviour and beliefs, perceptions, etc., can hardly be disputed. This argument is elaborated on further in subsequent chapters.

A Critical Note on the Method

One of the most difficult parts of the study was finding people to interview − to get them to agree to be interviewed after an approach in a shopping centre. The interviewing itself, in contrast, was considerably easier, and certainly more pleasant. There was little problem with people not wanting to talk, and it was sometimes difficult to get out of homes! Indeed, more often than not, people actually thanked *us* for talking with them. Despite the problems with the recruitment method, it did have its benefits. It resulted, for example, in the sharpening of our awareness of the purpose and limitations of research, and gave us an appreciation of the knowledge and insights that people have about research and "the experts". We were continually confronted with people who questioned our value and, on the odd occasion, our very existence (see below).

Among other things, we were mistaken for market researchers, booksellers (especially children's books), potential housebreakers, and rude, suspicious people who continually accost shoppers (when all they want to do is get the shopping in the car and get the kids home). Examples of people's initial reactions included:

"Who are you again?" (a very definite, often threatening question).

"Are you sure you're not selling something? We've had experience with people like you before, who turn up at our house selling books or something."

"I don't really think you would want to talk to me. I'm just an ordinary person."

"Why do you want to talk to *me*?"

"Why are you doing it? Will anyone ever benefit from it, or will it be like all the other university research?"

"I'm too busy looking after the kids to have time to talk to you."

"What will you do with the information? Are you sure you're not working for the government?"

Another positive feature of the recruitment method was that it provided information about why people did not agree to be interviewed. One of the major drawbacks of most research projects is that very little knowledge is ever available about how many people are exposed to research and who conceivably could participate but for some reason don't. How many first-year university students, for example, read a notice board advertising an experiment but then don't volunteer for it? The present approach, therefore, provides information on how many people don't participate and gives some insight into why they don't. The main reasons given for not participating are noted in appendix 1. One of the reasons given by women was: "My husband wouldn't agree." Although it is difficult to know exactly how authentic this reason was, some credibility is given to it from the reactions encountered in one family which was followed up even though the mother expressed some doubt about whether her husband would be interviewed. This experience is related below.

Mrs Williams agreed to participate when she was approached in a shopping centre. She was phoned about a week later to advise her that there would be a delay; she seemed quite happy about being interviewed at a later time. Three weeks later, on a Friday morning, she was phoned to arrange a time. Mrs Williams now wanted more details about "the research" so that she could tell her husband. She wanted to make sure he would agree to be interviewed too, although she wasn't certain that he would. On Monday we phoned to confirm a time for Tuesday night, but Mrs Williams still had not spoken to her husband. She asked more questions about the research; she said she wanted to make sure we weren't selling encyclopaedias. And she again told us that she wasn't certain that her husband would agree to talk. "He is a bit different," she said; "he's a bit funny about things, especially the kids. He has funny ideas about kids – that they should be seen and not heard – he doesn't take much interest in them." Mrs Williams also said that she was keen for us to interview them as she thought she might find out more about her husband's ideas; he might tell us things that he wouldn't tell her. At this stage we became a little hesitant about proceeding any further. However, there was the possibility that this family might be very different from any of the others we had spoken to, that there might be a more extreme group of fathers we had not encountered. We agreed to phone again on Tuesday morning after she had spoken to her husband.

When we phoned again, Mrs Williams told us that her husband was not entirely happy about the idea. He thought we were putting something over her — that we really were selling something. She said that he wanted to make sure that it was legitimate, and felt that if we could satisfy him on this, he would talk to us.

It was with some trepidation, therefore, that the twenty-mile trip was made to their home for an eight o'clock interview. Just beyond the line of trees which formed the front fence, the interviewer heard, coming from the house, in a raucous, rather aggressive voice: "Is this this bloody prick from the university?"

A pause, and then again in a louder voice: "Is this this bloody prick from the university?"

Mother's voice: "What?"

"Walking up the bloody path, is that the bastard from the university?"

By this time the interviewer was at the front door and was greeted by Mrs Williams.

"Oh, you're here." (Surprise, surprise.) "I've just arrived home. We've been out swimming. Come in. I'm not sure whether my husband will talk to you. He's in here."

She showed the interviewer into the lounge room, where the television was on, but all that was left of Mr Williams was the shape of his backside in the lounge chair.

"Jim! Where are you? Wait here, I'll go and see if I can find him." Mrs Williams went out the back door. The interviewer didn't like to sit down but moved back towards the front door. A very heated interchange between Mrs and Mr Williams was then heard, the essence of which was:

"I'm not going to talk to the bloody prick. I'm not going to talk to him at eight o'clock at night." (Bang, bang — a hammer?) "Tell him to piss off. If he doesn't, I'll punch his bloody head in."

By the time Mrs Williams returned, the interviewer was back on the front porch. She said her husband wouldn't talk, but that she would. The interviewer gratefully declined her invitation. Mrs Williams again said that her husband suspected we were selling encyclopaedias.

The final word came from her nine-year-old son. As the interviewer was leaving, he quite innocently inquired: "But mum, what's wrong with encyclopaedia salesmen?"

Mum didn't answer.

In all, nine mothers were interviewed after they had first refused an interview on the grounds that either their husband would not agree to it, or their husbands would not even be at home and available. It was found that these families did represent an extreme group in which the fathers were heavily involved in paid work and were *very rarely* at home when the children were awake, and in three cases the fathers were reported to display a fair degree of hostility towards the children. Unfortunately, none of these fathers was able to be interviewed, and therefore they have not been included in the following analyses. There does appear to be another, more extreme group of very low-participant fathers, therefore, who are not well represented in the present sample.

Sample Characteristics

The present book is based on findings from a total of 309 two-parent families, the majority of whom were either born in Australia or had emigrated from English-speaking countries. This included: 145 families in which only the father was employed full-time in the paid work force and mothers provided the day-to-day care of their children – here termed *traditional families*; 47 families in which the father was employed full-time and the mother was employed part-time (average of 13 hours a week) but still retained the major responsibility for child care; 46 families in which both parents were employed full-time in the paid work force, and in which the children were either at school or were cared for by other people during the parents' hours of employment; and 71 families in which fathers either shared or had the major responsibility for the day-to-day care of their children, with the time of this responsibility being 15 or more hours each week – here termed *shared-caregiving* families. The bulk of the book, however, concentrates on the description and comparision of the 71 *shared-caregiving* families and the 145 *traditional* families, and therefore it is the characteristics of these two groups that are described below. Chapter 4 presents analyses that include families in which mothers are employed either full- or part-time, and the characteristics of those families are described there.

Diversity of the Traditional Sample

There was a considerable range in the sample of traditional families in terms of social class variables, status rankings of suburb of residence, occupational status rankings, and education levels of each of the parents (see appendix 1 for complete details). Fifteen per cent of families lived in suburbs rated 1 (highest) on Congalton's (1969) Sydney suburbs' status-ranking scale, and fifteen per cent lived in suburbs rated 7 (lowest) on the status-ranking scale; the remaining seventy per cent of the sample was spread fairly evenly among the other five points of the status scale. The mean occupational status (Congalton 1969) of fathers was 3.9 and of mothers was 4.7. (Mothers' *previous* main occupation was used for this rating.) More importantly, however, 25% of fathers were classified in the two highest-status occupational groups (e.g., manager of a large company; medical practitioner, university lecturer), and 21% were in the lowest two groups of semi-skilled and unskilled workers (e.g., labourer, fork-lift driver; process worker). The percentages of parents who had (a) completed high school were: fathers 48%, mothers 33%; (b) completed at least ten years of schooling: fathers 36%, mothers 47%; and (c) completed less than ten years of schooling: fathers 16%, mothers 20%. University degrees had been completed by 14% of mothers and 27% of fathers.

As was expected, this was a sample of relatively young families with young children. The mean age of fathers was 33 years and mothers 31 years. Ninety-five per cent of couples were married and had been married for an average of eight years. The mean age of the youngest child was 2.3 years, and of the eldest child, 5.7 years. Family sizes were: 22%, one child; 38%, two children; 28%, three children; and 12%, four or more children.

Comparison between Traditional and Shared-Caregiving Families

The samples of traditional and shared-caregiving families were very similar for the ages of parents and the number of years they had been married. There were significant differences, however, on traditional social-class variables. The shared-caregiving parents tended to be more highly educated; for example, 28% of fathers and 44% of mothers in the non-traditional family group had completed a university degree or college diploma, compared with only 27% of fathers and 14% of mothers in traditional families. Also, shared-caregiving mothers had higher-status occupations (mean 3.8) than traditional mothers (mean 4.7). But while there were these average differences between the samples, the shared-caregiving families were *not simply* an educated middle class. A striking feature of this sample was the diversity of the fathers' present and previous occupations: for example, lawer, milkman, timber worker, labourer, shopkeeper, fireman, policeman, university professor, schoolteacher, actor, writer, taxi-driver, farmer, minister of religion, family day-care father, builder. Moreover, 30% of these non-traditional fathers had occupations that could be classified as either semi-skilled or unskilled (Congalton 1969).

In comparison with traditional families, shared-caregiving families tended to have fewer children (average number 1.7, compared with 2.3) and older children (mean age of youngest 2.9 years, compared with 2.3 years). Thus, the demands of child care might be expected to be less in these families. And as will be discussed later, having a lower level of demand for child care appears to be a major contributing factor to the establishment of a shared-caregiving family pattern.

Summary

This book is based primarily on an interview study of 309 two-parent families recruited mainly from shopping centres using a quasi-random method of sampling. The following chapters particularly emphasize the differences and similarities between two more extreme types of families as far as paternal participation is concerned: traditional families and shared-caregiving families.

The two major types of families as studied here were found to differ significantly on several social class variables and family characteristics: shared-caregiving parents, overall, were more highly educated and mothers had higher-status occupations than their traditional counterparts; and shared-caregiving families tended to have fewer and older children. Nevertheless, *diversity* was found to be a feature of both samples. In particular, fathers in shared-caregiving families, unlike mothers, were found to be very diverse in the types of occupations they either currently had or previously had; they were not simply an educated professional group of fathers. Diversity was also a strong characteristic of the traditional families studied here, with a wide range of social classes and family types being represented, as would be expected given that the sample was drawn from a range of shopping centres in a large city and two country towns.

Information about families was obtained from interviews which focused both on parental behaviour − parents' reports of their day-to-day interactions with their children and divisions of labour for child care − and on parental perceptions, beliefs, and values concerning their roles and the nature of child development. Chapters that follow examine parents' responses to questions in these two major areas of interest in an attempt to (a) explore the range, as well as describe the modal patterns, of parental participation in child rearing and, more particularly, fathers' participation; (b) explore the antecedents of high levels of paternal participation both within the more traditional family and in shared-caregiving families; and (c) examine the possible consequences of fathers being highly participant — consequences not only for fathers, mothers, children, and the family but also, more generally, for society.

3

Traditional and Non-Traditional Fathers

In a pilot study conducted before the project proper started, a group of twenty parents were asked what they thought were the generally accepted, societal expectations of fathers and mothers. The parents questioned had little difficulty in providing an answer, and there was remarkable agreement among them. Both fathers and mothers said that fathers were expected to be the breadwinner, head of the house, the disciplinarian – (especially in more serious matters), to present a masculine model, to be more involved with their sons than their daughters, and to participate in male-type activities with sons (e.g., football). The responses of three of these fathers were:

"The male is expected to be the disciplinarian, to work and be the backbone of the family. He does physical work around the house and plays football and cricket with his son."

"To work and do odd chores. Go to the pub on the way home with his mates. Drink and watch T.V. while waiting for dinner to be ready."

"Work and provide, to be an authority figure. He is someone to look up to for leadership. Dad is usually at the top of the family pyramid."

Parents' stereotypes of mothers were in complete contrast to their stereotypes of fathers. It was agreed that mothers were expected to stay at home and care for their children, to be there when they were needed (either by husbands or children), and to satisfy their families' physical and emotional needs. Again, some of the responses given help to illustrate these parents' perceptions of the roles and responsibilities of mothers:

"A mother is expected to be the person who looks after the house, cooks and irons. She is expected to be there when her husband comes home. She looks after the children and teaches the girls to be ladies." (Father)

"A mother is the one who physically looks after everyone,

washes and changes the nappies. She looks after and attends to the children. A mother is also expected to know everything." (Mother)

"A mother is expected to be a perfect person who is always there, just being wonderful, completely happy and able to care for everyone." (Father)

Although there was little disagreement among parents about what they perceived the expected roles of fathers and mothers to be (and, indeed, it would not be difficult to identify the above descriptions with individual fathers and mothers we know), it is obvious that *all* mothers and *all* fathers do not conform to these expectations. The aim of this chapter is to examine the current roles of fathers and mothers, in terms of parents' perceptions (i.e., their *personal* constructions of their roles) and also their actual family behaviour. As was pointed out earlier, this analysis is based primarily on data obtained from two very different types of families: traditional and shared-caregiving. Given the emphasis parents appear to place on the employment role for fathers and the child-care role for mothers, this analysis will begin by contrasting the two family types on these two factors. An understanding of the fundamental differences in day-to-day lifestyles between the two families should facilitate the interpretation of data presented below on role-perceptions and divisions of labour for child care.

Traditional and Non-Traditional Child-Care and Employment Patterns

Child Care

As expected, the two family types differed significantly for the distribution of responsibilities for the day-to-day care of children. In traditional families, all mothers were the primary caregivers (or primary caretakers), and spent an average of 40 hours each week as the *sole* caregiver. Traditional fathers, on the other hand, spent an average of only 1 hour each week as the primary caregivers for their children. In shared-caregiving families, however, the distribution of responsibilities was very different. Fathers in these families spent an average of 26 hours as primary caregivers, whereas mothers spent an average of 16 hours each week in this way. (It will be recalled that these latter families were recruited *because* the fathers either shared or had the major responsibility for day-to-day child care.)

Employment Patterns

Traditional families. All fathers in traditional families were employed full-time in the paid work force, and all mothers were not employed. Fathers were outside the home for employment purposes for an average of 51 hours a week, somewhat more than the normally accepted 35-40 hours a week. Overtime, time spent on second jobs, and time spent travelling to and from work account for this apparently higher than expected figure.

Shared-caregiving families. All mothers in these families were employed in the paid work force: 86% full-time and 14% part-time. Mothers, on average, were outside the home for employment purposes for 35 hours a week. Only 48% of fathers were employed full-time, with 30% being employed part-time, and 22% were not employed at all. The average number of hours spent by fathers on paid employment was 34. There were four major types of family employment patterns represented in the shared-caregiving sample:

1. *Both parents employed full-time* (32%): e.g., mother employed as a schoolteacher, and father employed at night as a process worker and caring for their two-year-old daughter during the day; mother employed as a nurse's aide on a late afternoon–evening shift, and father employed as a labourer during the day, coming home at four o'clock to care for their two school-aged children.

2. *Mother employed full-time/father employed part-time* (30%): e.g., mother employed as a schoolteacher, and father conducting a part-time business from home while caring for their four-month-old son; mother employed as a social worker, and father, who was a retrenched engineer, employed as a part-time child-carer, as well as caring for their own three children.

3. *Mother employed full-time/father unemployed (22%):* e.g., mother employed as a clerk full-time and as a receptionist part-time on the weekends, and the father an unemployed lawyer who cared for their three-year-old son; mother employed as a nurse, and the father a retired army captain who cared for their 12-month-old daughter.

4. *Mother employed part-time/father employed full-time* (14%): e.g., mother employed part-time as a car wash attendant, and father employed full-time as a fork-lift driver on a night shift, caring for their four-year-old daughter when the mother was at work; mother employed four afternoons and

nights as a nurse, father employed full-time as a builder, caring for their two daughters when the mother was at work.

There was also one family in this group who shared the same job *and* child care. In this family, both parents were employed as ministers of religion, sharing the parish in a country town.

Thus, in only 14% of the shared-caregiving families was it the case that fathers had the major responsibility for family income – these were families in which fathers were employed full-time and mothers were employed part-time. This is in complete contrast to traditional families; in *all* of these families fathers had the *sole* responsibility for family income. It might be expected, therefore, that shared-caregiving fathers and mothers will have views about their roles and responsibilities that are very different from those of traditional parents, and that the two family types will differ considerably in regard to divisions of labour for child care.

It is also possible that roles will vary *within* the shared-caregiving group according to whether or not the father is employed full-time. As was pointed out earlier, however, the primary interest here is in fathers who are highly participant in caregiving, and therefore differences within the shared-caregiving group are not examined in this chapter. They are examined, however, in chapter 5 and subsequent chapters.

Perceptions of Parental Roles and Responsibilities

At the beginning of the unstructured part of the interview, parents were asked what they saw as being their role and responsibilities as a parent. Most people found little or no difficulty in answering this question, and many responded at considerable length. All parents were given every opportunity to respond in as much detail as they wanted. Responses to this question were content analysed and classified into one of twenty-four different categories (see appendix 3 for details of this procedure).

The focus here then is simply on parents' *descriptions* of their roles. This is, of course, only one aspect of the complex combination of parental beliefs about their roles that may influence, or be related to, the actual role adopted. Subsequent chapters examine additional components of parental beliefs, such as their *explanations* of *why* mothers and fathers differ so much in their responsibilities for child care (see chapters 4, 5, and 6).

Parents' role descriptions, in general, were expressed in two different ways: some responded in terms of their day-to-day roles or behaviour (e.g., "the breadwinner", "giving love and affection"), and some responded in terms of child-rearing goals (e.g., "making sure they know right from wrong", "giving them a good education"). A complete list of response categories and the percentages of each type of response for the two family types is given in table 26. What I want to do here is concentrate on the most commonly occurring responses, and those responses that clearly fit with the previously mentioned descriptions of the stereotyped mother and father roles.

The Father Role

The responses given most often by fathers in traditional families were: being the breadwinner (mentioned by 59% of fathers); general socialization – teaching and setting an example (43%); looking after the day-to-day needs of their children (23%); ensuring their children are well-mannered and know right from wrong (22%); play (20%); giving love and affection (18%); ensuring their children have "good" morals and values (18%), and are happy (14%); providing discipline (14%); assisting in their children's education (13%); being the head of the house (12%). In comparison with the stereotype, then, fathers' individual descriptions of their roles and responsibilities are somewhat different. While it was the case, in agreement with the stereotype, that 59% of traditional fathers included breadwinning in their role description, only 14% mentioned being the disciplinarian, and only 12% appeared to place any importance on being the decision-maker or head of the house. In apparent contradiction to the stereotype, there was a highly significant "socialization" response, and "day-to-day care" and "providing love and affection" occurred quite frequently! These are all aspects of parental roles that had previously been clearly associated with mothers. It appears, therefore, that a good many fathers do not perceive their roles as being as restrictive as the stereotype might lead us to expect.

How different are traditional and shared-caregiving fathers? As would be expected, shared-caregiving fathers were much less likely to include "the breadwinner responsibility" (28% vs. 59%) and "head of the house" (2.8% vs. 12%) in their descriptions, and much more likely to include the "day-to-day care of their children" (41% vs. 23%) and "being there when they are needed" (13% vs. 3%). Nevertheless, it should be noted that although these latter two response-types occurred more frequently in the answers given by shared-caregiving fathers, they still occurred more frequently in the answers given by shared-caregiving mothers. Perhaps, surprisingly, shared-caregiving fathers were *not* more likely than traditional fathers to include "providing love and affection" and "ensuring the children's emotional stability" in their role descriptions. Yet, these were responses given very frequently by mothers in both family types.

Thus, while shared-caregiving fathers appear less likely to describe their role in stereotypic terms (e.g., breadwinner, head of the house), apart from seeing themselves more as the day-to-day caregivers of their children, they do not appear to incorporate other aspects of parental roles more clearly identified with mothers (e.g., providing love and affection). Nevertheless, there seemed other differences between traditional and shared-caregiving fathers that were not well represented in the categorical analysis discussed above. In particular there was a significant qualitative difference between the two family types, with more extreme, highly *stereotyped* responses being given by traditional fathers. Some examples help to illustrate this point:

Responses from Traditional Fathers

"To bring up a happy family and provide for them. Make sure the kids grow up to be solid, morally reliable citizens."

"To govern the house and set the standards. I give the orders, my wife executes them."

"I am the head of the house, every major decision should be mine – after all, I am a product of the British Empire."

"To teach my daugher, when she is a teenager, how to best use her powers of influence over others (especially men)."

"To try to train my son to become someone of high standing."

"There's no discipline here unless I'm around. I get the straps out."

"To fulfil the role that the children expect of me. It is more of a reactive role. I try not to dominate, but to mould my role according to the situation."

"Being a father is a sacred responsibility. One of the things I have to do is train my wife."

"It is different from being a mother. The mother is the heart of the home. It is the most wonderful thing a woman can do."

Responses from Shared-Caregiving Fathers

"Taking care of the children. Developing their skills and co-ordination, showing them things around the place, naming things, developing their vocabulary and sense of awareness."

"Being sure children are safe and secure, emotionally and financially."

"To provide intellectual and emotional guidance — to give them a financial base, also intellectually and culturally. But, let them grow up in their own way, to be their own people."

"To give them every chance to end up well-adjusted and happy. To be the guiding principle for their long-term welfare."

"Bring up the children as we both think best. Give them as much time as possible, and give them the best education possible."

"To provide authority and leadership within the family unit. To provide the male influence so that the child has an equal serving of masculine and feminine ideas."

"Being there when I'm needed. That covers everything — the need to be clothed, fed, play, to be seen and to relate."

"To do the best I can for her; to provide for her physically, emotionally, right across the spectrum. To encourage her, help her to develop as an individual. To create an example (this applies whether I have a job or not; I have the same responsibilities). Being a father is a hell of a responsibility all the way around."

The Mother Role

The most commonly occurring responses for mothers in traditional families were: providing the day-to-day care for their children (a response given by 59% of mothers); socializing — teaching and setting an example (43%); providing love and affection (33%); ensuring their children are well mannered and know right from wrong (31%) and that they are healthy (28%); being there when they are needed (23%); ensuring their children are happy (19%), have "good" morals and values (17%), and are emotionally stable (16%); and providing discipline (13%). Apart from the last category of providing discipline, mothers' individual descriptions of their roles conformed very closely to the stereotyped mother role described earlier. Moreover, this summary of mothers' perceptions of their roles and responsibilities is entirely consistent with their having the major day-to-day responsibility for child care.

How different are traditional and shared-caregiving mothers' role descriptions? Not as different as we might expect. Shared-caregiving mothers were less likely to describe their roles in terms of being there when needed (9% vs. 23%) and ensuring their children are well mannered (20% vs. 31%) and healthy (13% vs. 28%) and have good morals and values (6% vs. 17%). For most other categories, however, there were few differences (e.g., for their perceptions of having responsibility for day-to-day care; providing love and affection), and shared-caregiving mothers were not found to be significantly more likely to incorporate breadwinning into their role descriptions. Moreover, it was difficult to differentiate the two groups of mothers on the qualitative nature of their responses (apart from a very few responses – see below). Some examples of responses given by mothers in the two family-types are as follows:

Responses from Traditional Mothers

"My role is to care for the children and make them happy."
   "To be there when I'm needed. Also, to teach them right from wrong."
   "The complete bringing up of the children. To give them a secure feeling without making them feel ruled."
   "To be home, to listen to them when they feel like chatting."
   "To give them a cuddle when they need it."
   "I tend to their basic needs, their emotional, spiritual, educational and health needs. My husband is the leader of the family, the patriarch, the strength. He could not stay at home and look after the children. He would be frustrated in his ambitions. It is his role to work and achieve his ambitions."
   "I have more to do with the day-to-day things. Harold is the big gun."

Responses from Shared-Caregiving Mothers

"To provide a happy and secure environment for my child. To make sure she knows she is loved. To try to bring her up with Christian values."
   "To teach my child attitudes, feelings, and conventions. To be a stable figure of security that they can relate to. To feed, clothe, and look after their physical needs."
   "To guide them, love them, and be availabe when I'm needed. To be patient, but strict at times, and forgiving."
   "Give them lots of love and attention. Also the basic care – the typical mothering tasks (feeding, clothing etc)."

Thus, although all mothers in shared-caregiving families were employed and none of the traditional mothers were, there were few differences between the two groups in the ways in which they perceived their roles and responsibilities as parents. Mothers, in contrast to fathers, therefore, *did not* perceive bread-winning or their contribution to family income as an integral part of their parental role. A finding that shared-caregiving and traditional mothers perceived their roles in similar ways is perhaps not all that surprising when the data to be presented in the next section are considered. There it will be shown that despite an involvement in employment, shared-caregiving mothers, unlike traditional fathers, are still vitally involved in child care.

Divisions of Labour for Child Care

As was mentioned earlier, shared-caregiving and traditional families differed significantly regarding divisions of labour for time spent being the primary caregiver (or caretaker) of the children: Traditional mothers spent an average of 40 hours each week, while traditional fathers spent only 1 hour a week. In contrast, shared-caregiving fathers spent 26 hours a week and shared-caregiving mothers 16 hours. Additionally, in both family types it was the case that *parents* had the major responsibility for child care – none of the children attended child-care centres, nor were they cared for by others for extended periods of time. Given these patterns, we might expect major differences between the two family types in regard to divisions of labour for specific child care tasks, and that fathers would be more highly participant than mothers in shared-caregiving families. What follows is an analysis of divisions of labour for child care in the two family types – emphasizing the *modal* patterns and the *range* of paternal participation (both within traditional families and between family types). The analysis examines mother/father differences in time available to children, time spent and frequency of performing various child-care tasks, and playing with their children, in addition to providing an analysis of mother-father differences in responsibility taken for children. Finally, the findings from this Australian study are compared with recent findings from other cultures.

Time Available to Children

How much time are parents at home and available to their children when they are awake? This was calculated by taking into account (a) time spent out of the home for employment and leisure activities and (b) the sleep, school or pre-school attendance, and leisure patterns of children. In shared-caregiving families, fathers were found to be available to their children for an average of 54 hours a week and mothers for 50 hours a week. The corresponding figures in traditional families were: fathers, 33 hours; mothers, 76 hours. Furthermore, 16% of traditional fathers were available to their children for less than 20 hours and only 11% were available for more than 50 hours a week. Despite these major family differences in the distribution of time that mothers and fathers were available, the *total time* for which both parents were available to their children (i.e., the total time for potential adult contact) was comparable in both family types: in shared-caregiving families it was 104 hours and in traditional families 109 hours a week. This is not surprising when it is considered that in neither family type were children cared for for any major portion of their waking hours each week by other people or child-care or pre-school institutions.

Performance of Specific Child-Care Tasks

Who changes the nappies, feeds the children, and gets up in the middle of the night if children wake? These are the nitty-gritty aspects of caring for young children, and it is the performance of these tasks that is to be discussed here. Estimates of the amount of time spent by each parent each week performing a range of specific child-care tasks are presented in table 1. As can be seen from the figures presented there, it is traditional mothers who spend far and away the most time on these activities, and it is traditional fathers who spend the least time. Nevertheless, there was a considerable range in the involvement of traditional fathers. To illustrate: 35% of fathers did not feed, dress, or bath their children each week; 50% of those with infants did not regularly change nappies; whereas 3% of fathers shared equally in all of these tasks with mothers, and two fathers took over completely when they were both at home.

In comparison with traditional parents, shared-caregiving fathers were significantly more involved and shared-caregiving mothers significantly less involved in child-care tasks. Although there is an obvious trend for shared-caregiving mothers to spend

Table 1. Divisions of labour for child-care tasks and play (all figures in hours per week)

	Shared-Caregiving		Traditional	
	Mother	Father	Mother	Father
Availability	50[d]	54[c]	70[b]	33
Sole responsibility	16[ad]	26[c]	40[b]	1
Feed	5.6[d]	4.5[c]	11.4[b]	1.1
Dress	2.0[ad]	1.2[c]	3.5[b]	0.5
Change nappies	1.0[d]	0.75[c]	2.1[b]	0.2
Bath	1.75[d]	1.3[c]	2.2[b]	0.5
Attend to at night	0.6	0.4[c]	0.7[b]	0.2
Read stories to	1.7	1.6[c]	1.7[b]	0.85
Help school work	0.38	0.35	0.45	0.32
Play	20.0	21.5[c]	20.5[b]	9.0

[a]Difference between mothers and fathers in shared-caregiving families, $p < .05$
[b]Difference between mothers and fathers in traditional families, $p < .05$
[c]Difference between shared-caregiving and traditional fathers, $p < .05$
[d]Difference between shared-caregiving and traditional mothers, $p < .05$

more time on these tasks than their husbands, the only category for which this difference is statistically significant is dressing children. This, it appears is an activity that is more clearly seen as the mother's domain.

As a way of providing a more comprehensive picture of divisions of labour for time spent in child-care tasks, time estimates for feeding, dressing, changing nappies, bathing, and attending to children during the night were combined into one summary figure: *time spent on all day-to-day caregiving activities* (DC). For traditional fathers this figure was 2 hours a week (or 9%), and for traditional mothers, 20 hours a week (91%). Again, there was considerable variability in this figure for traditional fathers; 20% of fathers did not spend any time at all on DC tasks, and 14% spent 7 or more hours each week.

Divisions of labour in shared-caregiving families were again quite different. Shared-caregiving fathers spent an average of 9 hours a week on DC tasks (45%) and mothers 11 hours a week (55%), a somewhat more balanced distribution than in traditional families. Nevertheless, although shared-caregiving fathers spent more time as the primary caregivers and were available more to their children, they did not spend more time than mothers on child-care tasks; mothers still did slightly more. Moreover, it was only in 35% of shared-caregiving families in which fathers did more, and only 3% in which more than 15 hours a week were spent by fathers on child-care tasks.

The data presented here for both traditional and shared-caregiving families suggest very strongly that the performance of child-care tasks is not just a matter of time. When the amount of time traditional fathers are at home is taken into account, it would be expected that they would perform 35% of child-care tasks *if* they shared these equally with mothers during their time at home. The actual figure, as noted above, was 9%. In the same way, if we take into account the time that shared-caregiving mothers are at home, it would be expected that they would perform 43% of child-care tasks if they shared these equally with fathers when they are both at home. The actual figure was *above* this — 55%. Indeed, it was only in 20% of shared-caregiving families in which mothers did 43% or less of the child-care tasks. Child care, therefore, appears to be seen as more in the mothers' domain irrespective of which parent is at home and available to the children.

Play and Other Activities

Time Estimates

Parents were asked to estimate how much time they spent each week playing with their children, reading stories to them, and helping them with homework. It was often difficult for parents to give an estimate of how much time they spent in play, and so to assist in this the activities of the day on which the interview was conducted were reviewed to provide a basis for estimation. Play was defined rather more liberally than in other studies. The major criterion was that it be a joint activity — either parent- or child-oriented. Thus, a young child helping to vacuum the home, to garden, or to wash the car were included. The argument here is that these tasks often provide the context for significant interactions similar to those that might occur in traditional play. A summary of the average amounts of time spent by parents on these three activities is given in table 1. As can be seen from that table, traditional mothers spent significantly more time on story reading and play than traditional fathers, and slightly more time on helping with homework (although this was not statistically significant). Variability was again a feature of fathers' participation: 45% of fathers compared with 20% of mothers did not regularly each week read a story to their children, whereas 9% of fathers compared with 23% of mothers did this every day; 53% of fathers with school-aged children regularly helped with school work, compared with 74% of mothers; finally, 40% of fathers compared with 10% of mothers spent less than one hour each day playing with their children, while 6% of fathers spent 3 or more hours a day, compared with 30% of mothers.

The only significant differences between traditional and shared-caregiving families emerged for fathers' involvement in story reading and play: shared-caregiving fathers spent significantly more time on both of these activities. Although shared-caregiving mothers were significantly less available to their children than traditional mothers, this does not appear to have had an effect on the amount of time spent on story reading, helping with school work, and play – they spent as much time on these activities as traditional mothers did.

Types of Play Activities

Previous observational (Lamb 1976) and interview (Russell 1979b) analyses have shown that in traditional families mothers are more likely to be involved in indoor, conventional, cognitive, and toy-oriented play, while fathers are more likely to be involved in outdoor and physical and rough-and-tumble play, differences that conform by and large to traditional stereotypes of mothers and fathers.

Differences in the specific types of play activities engaged in by parents were examined here in two ways. A comparision was made (1) between indoor (e.g., singing) and outdoor (e.g., playing on swings) activities, and (2) between activities that were defined as cognitive and creative (e.g., painting) and those that were more physical, fun, and amusement oriented (e.g., ball games).

In agreement with previous findings, fathers in traditional families were found to be more likely to be involved in outdoor than indoor play (64% of play activities were outdoor, 36% indoor), and for mothers it was the reverse (34% outdoor, 66% indoor). Differences between mothers and fathers in shared-caregiving families, however, were considerably reduced: fathers 55% outdoor, 45% indoor; mothers 43% outdoor, 57% indoor. This pattern of mother-father differences was also evident in comparisons between cognitive/creative and amusement-type play. The figures for traditional families were: fathers 35% cognitive/creative, 65% amusement; mothers 55% cognitive/creative, 45% amusement. The figures for shared-caregiving families were: fathers 44% cognitive/creative, 56% amusement; mothers 45% cognitive/creative, 55% amusement.

Thus, while differences between mothers' and fathers' play interactions were still evident in shared-caregiving families, they were nevertheless not as marked; shared-caregiving fathers were more likely to be involved in indoor, creative, and toy-oriented play. Such a change is entirely consistent with the increased time spent by fathers within the home caring for children. This analysis, therefore, confirms previous analyses in showing fewer differences between mothers and fathers in shared-caregiving than traditional families. In traditional families the differences are very marked and conform closely to the stereotyped roles described earlier.

Responsibility for Child Care

While it may be the case that some fathers, and especially those in shared-caregiving families, perform many of the day-to-day child-care tasks, it may also be that they do not assume overall responsibility for these tasks. Mothers might retain their traditional responsibility in these domains. Thus, while a father might dress his children every morning, the mother could buy the clothes and decide what the children will wear each day. Precise information on the distribution of responsibilities for specific child-care tasks, unfortunately, were not collected in this study. Questions were asked, however, about the amount of time each parent spent taking sole responsibility for their children and what their perceptions were of the distribution of overall responsibility for child care. In addition, several shared-caregiving parents, during the course of the interview, commented on the nature of family responsibilities for child care.

Sole Responsibility

Sole responsibility was defined as the time when one parent was alone with their children, the children were awake, and the other parent was not at home or could not be called upon. A father taking his children to the park while the mother was at home was not included, as the father could take the child home if a problem arose. A father caring for his children at home while the mother was out shopping was included, however. It has already been mentioned that shared-caregiving fathers had this type of responsibility for 26 hours a week, whereas fathers in traditional families spent an average of only 1 hour a week taking sole responsibility. Moreover, 80% of traditional fathers did not regularly each week take sole responsibility, and 60% of fathers had *never* had this type of contact with their children.

The major activities traditional mothers were engaged in while fathers were taking the responsibility for the children were shopping (in over 50% of families) and social and recreational activities. In shared-caregiving families, of course, the major activity of mothers was their employment.

Taking sole responsibility for child care, and the type of significant/intimate parent-child contact it often involves, is likely to have consequences for parent-child relationships and the degree of responsibility assumed for specific aspects of child rearing. Fathers and mothers in shared-caregiving families expressed the view that this type of contact was an invaluable part of their establishing a close relationship with their children (see chapter 7), that it provided the first step to developing skills and confidence in the child-care role and in assuming responsibility for the day-to-day needs of their children. Yet very few traditional parents felt it important for fathers to spend time *alone* with their children. In one such family, for example, the mother inquired about the importance of several questions, one of which was this sole responsibility question. After the likely significance of the question was explained she argued very strongly that it was unimportant, and besides, her husband would not want to spend time alone with his children — *he* preferred to have everyone at home all the time.

The most common reaction by traditional mothers and fathers to this question about time spent taking sole responsibility was that fathers were not capable. "What would he do if a nappy had to be changed?" Some mothers said they would not trust their husband, and one in particular was adamant that she would not allow it under any circumstances! She said she had tried it once, but the father had forgotten to feed the children!

It is difficult to know exactly why so few fathers spend time alone with their children. It is most likely a mixture of: fathers not having the necessary skills (not enough practice); fathers not having the confidence; mothers not wanting them to (think it is not a father's job, or reluctant to give up part of their domain); fathers not wanting to (expect it to be difficult and involve a lot of problems); and there not being a situational demand for this type of involvement by fathers (e.g., if mother is not employed or has no active interests outside the home). This issue of explaining fathers' non-involvement will be returned to in later chapters.

Parental Perceptions of Relative Responsibilities

Parents were also asked a general question about who they thought had the major responsibility for the care of the children. Again, the differences between the two family types were striking. Mothers were seen as having the major responsibility in 99% of traditional families, but in only 35% of shared-caregiving families was this the case. Fathers were not seen as having the major responsibility in *any* traditional families, but they were in 18% of shared-caregiving families. Shared responsibility was reported in 1% of traditional and in 47% of shared-caregiving families.

Thus, although the distribution of responsibilities for child rearing is more evenly distributed in shared-caregiving families, there is still a significant subgroup (35%) in which mothers are perceived to have the major responsibility. Additional support for this pattern of responsibilities was given by the comments many parents made throughout the interviews. For example:

"We split the physical care fifty-fifty, but I am still the psychological parent. I still observe a little more closely than Alan." (Mother)

"I suppose when the kids get sick they look for mother, and she usually takes them to the doctor. That is something, the comfort and love, I think women have that more than men." (Father)

Clearly, the present analysis needs to be taken one step further in future studies, to examine in detail divisions of labour for both task performance and task responsibility, to obtain a more accurate account of the nature of divisions of labour for child-care in different types of families. This issue is taken up again in the final chapter.

How Do Australian Fathers Compare with Fathers from Other Cultures?

Although there has been an increased emphasis on the study of fathers in recent years, little attention has been given either to divisions of labour for day-to-day child care or to the range of father participation. Rather, most of the work has been on the observation of father-infant interaction under highly structured conditions. From the few studies that have been reported, however, it appears that Australian fathers are comparable to those from other Western industrialized societies.

Studies of Traditional Families

Availability

Studies of middle class American fathers with young infants report that fathers are at home and available to their children when they are awake for approximately 25 hours each week (Kotelchuck 1976; Pedersen and Robson 1969), compared with a figure of 33 hours reported here. This difference is most likely due to the different ages of children in the various studies. Both the American studies involved families with very young infants, whereas the present study included many families with older children who are of course more likely to be awake during the evenings when fathers are more likely to be at home.

Time Spent on Child Care

Despite differences in methods employed, findings for the number of hours spent each week by fathers on basic child-care tasks (e.g., feeding, changing nappies) are remarkably consistent across several studies. Estimates for American fathers have been reported to be 2.1 (Robinson 1977; Walker and Woods 1976), 1.7 (Pleck and Rustad 1980), and 2.8 (Kotelchuck 1976). And a time-budget study which was conducted in thirteen countries (mainly European, both East and West), estimated the figure to be 1.6 hours a week (Newland 1980). All these figures are very close to that reported here of 2 hours a week. Differences between mothers and fathers have also been reported to be quite marked, again in agreement with the present study. For example, time spent by unemployed mothers on child care was estimated to be 9 hours a week (representing 85% of the total time spent by both mothers and fathers performing child-care tasks) in the thirteen-nation study (Newland 1980). In the present study, mothers were found to perform 91% of child-care tasks. Unfortunately, few studies provide a breakdown of fathers' participation in specific child-care tasks. Two other studies, however, do provide such data.

In his American study, Kotelchuck (1976) found that fathers spent an average of 0.26 hours a week on feeding their children, and 0.3 hours on cleaning them. The respective figures reported here were 0.27 and 0.21 (the sum of changing nappies and bathing), again highly comparable. Also 43% of fathers were reported by Kotelchuck (1976) to have never changed a nappy. In the present study, 50% of fathers interviewed had never changed a nappy. A comparison can also be made with Oakley's (1974) British data on father-participation in nappy changing (this information was provided by mothers). Oakley reported that only 25% of fathers regularly changed dirty nappies. In the present study the equivalent figure was 21%. So on the basis of available data it seems levels of paternal participation in specific child-care tasks are roughly equivalent across three cultures.

Other studies have attempted to estimate levels of father-child interaction. Pedersen and Robson (1969), also using maternal reports, found that time spent by fathers interacting with their young infants varied from 45 minutes to 26 hours a week. Rebelsky and Hanks (1971), on the other hand, using microphones placed on fathers, found that fathers verbalized to their young infants for an average of only 37.7 seconds a day. While this might be seen as a surprisingly low level of interaction, it can be argued that time spent in verbalizations is not likely to be a good indicator of time spent in child care. Furthermore, the sample size in this study was very small – ten.

Time Spent in Play

Fathers have consistently been found to be more likely to spend time playing with their children than performing child-care tasks. This pattern has been found in the United States both in a home observation study of father-infant interaction (Lamb 1976) and in interview studies (e.g., Kotelchuck 1976). Kotelchuck also reported that fathers spent approximately 9 hours a week playing with their children, the same as that reported here. In further agreement with this Australian study, Kotelchuck also found that even though fathers spend more time on play than on performing child-care tasks, they still spent less time on play than mothers did; he estimated mothers spent 14 hours a week playing with their children. This compares with 20 hours a week reported here. Again, differences in ages of children in the two studies might account for this difference.

Mother-father differences have also been found for *types of play* activities. Lamb in his observational study found that fathers were more likely to be involved in physical, rough-and-tumble, and idiosyncratic play, and mothers were more likely to be involved in conventional, toy-oriented, and creative-type play. Also, a recent study in the United Kingdom found that mothers were much more likely to read stories to their children (Jackson 1980). Both of these findings are entirely consistent with the present study.

Degree of Responsibility Taken for Children

Few studies have inquired about the degree of responsibility taken either for the day-to-day care of children or for specific child-care tasks; most have focused instead on time spent with children, or on the relative frequency of carrying out various tasks. Only one other recent study has reported data on differences in responsibility taken by mothers and fathers. In his American study, Kotelchuck found that only 7.5% of fathers shared child-care responsibilities equally with their wives, and 75% did not take *any* responsibility at all for the day-to-day care of their children. Again, this finding can be interpreted as supporting the current finding for fathers in traditional Australian families, who were also found to take very little responsibility for the day-to-day care of their children.

Non-Traditional Families

Several recent publications have reported on families in which fathers were *highly* participant in day-to-day child care. In many of these families fathers had equal or major responsibility for child care, and in most, the breadwinning responsibilities were shared or were the sole responsibility of the mother (such families have been variously described as shared or reversed-role). This family pattern has been noted in Norway (Gronseth 1978), Sweden (Lamb et al. 1981, 1982), the United States (DeFrain 1979; Field 1978; Levine 1977; Radin 1980), and Israel (Sagi 1981).

Comparative analyses of these studies on highly participant fathers are difficult, as sample characteristics and methodologies have been quite varied. Nevertheless, one point is abundantly clear from all studies: the fathers described are indeed highly participant in comparison with modal patterns. In Radin's American study, samples of fathers were reported to perform between 41% and 54% of child-care tasks, while in DeFrain's study fathers were reported to perform 46% of tasks. Although Sagi does not provide specific data on levels of father-participation in his Israeli study, he does state that in fifteen families it was agreed that the father was more involved than the mother was, and there were twenty families in which mothers and fathers agreed they had equal responsibility for child-rearing. In this Australian study, it will be recalled that fathers were reported to spend an average of 26 hours a week taking sole responsibility for their children (compared with 16 hours a week for mothers), and they performed 45% of child-care tasks (spending an average of 9 hours a week doing them).

Although comparisons between studies are difficult, it seems that time spent in caregiving, and therefore fathers' commitment to this role, might be higher in the present sample than in others. The present sample also had families with younger children than any other — a factor likely to increase the absolute amount of child care that has to be done. Other samples were also more likely to include families in which there were school-aged children or children who were attending pre-schools or child-care centres. In Radin's sample, for example, children were spending an average of 17 hours a week in pre-schools, compared with an average in the present study of only 6 hours a week. Also, Radin's sample of father–prime caregivers included only one father who was not employed in some way, whereas the present sample included seventeen such fathers.

There is no indication how prevalent these types of families are within each of the cultures studied. If the sample drawn from shopping centres in this study is any guide, it might be estimated that they constitute 1–2% of families in which there are young children. It will be recalled that ten shared-caregiving families were obtained using the quasi-random sampling method of recruitment at shopping centres. This is ten out of three hundred who *agreed* to participate, but only ten out of six hundred who were approached. And, given that the agreement rate overall for these types of families was of the order of 95%, it might be expected that there were in fact only ten such families encountered. Irrespective of the accuracy of this estimate, it is clear that this type of family is indeed a minority, but one that appears to be on the increase if the recent interest in them by researchers in several cultures is any indication (as was pointed out earlier, researchers are usually lazy, only studying the most commonly occurring and convenient aspects of behaviour).

Conclusions: Four Types of Fathers?

The modal pattern of paternal participation in traditional families appears to be one of fathers being much less likely than mothers to be available to, or to interact with, their children, a pattern that holds true even when time spent at home is taken into account. Of the time mothers were reported to be available to their children (76 hours a week), 57% of it was spent interacting with their children, either in caregiving or play, whereas fathers only interacted with their children in these ways for 38% of the 33 hours a week they were available. Thus, no matter which way the figures are examined, the modal participation levels of fathers in physical care and play are considerably lower than those of mothers. Moreover, this appears to be a consistent finding reported in several cultures. Another consistent pattern reported is that, overall, fathers' participation is much more play-oriented, and they engage in types of play activities different from those engaged in by mothers. Furthermore, 80% of traditional fathers' interactions were associated with play, compared with only 53% of mothers' interactions. Finally, fathers were found to be significantly less likely than mothers to take responsibility for the day-to-day care of their children, and it was found that the majority of fathers had *never* taken the sole responsibility for their children without the mother being at home or available.

Patterns in shared-caregiving families were entirely different from those in traditional families. Fathers in these families spent an average of 26 hours a week as the person solely responsible for their children, and spent an average of 9 hours a week performing basic child-care tasks and 20 hours playing with their children. Furthermore, divisions of labour for specific child-care tasks approached equality, although, on average, mothers still performed more of them (55%) despite being available for slightly less time than fathers. It was also found that, overall, mothers in these families still tended to have more *responsibility* for being aware of their children's needs. Despite this, it was abundantly clear that fathers in shared-caregiving families were, in comparison to traditional fathers, extremely highly participant in child care, and that their definition as such is completely justified.

What conclusions then can we draw about the patterns, and especially the range, of paternal participation? The picture that emerged from the data already presented, together with other analyses (to be presented later), is that there are perhaps four distinct groups of fathers, three of which are more clearly associated with traditional families, and one with non-traditional families:

1. *The uninterested and unavailable father.* Fathers in this category are those who rarely, if ever, either perform or take any responsibility for the day-to-day care of their children. They are the fathers who have never changed a nappy, have never got up

in the middle of the night to one of their children, who rarely play with their children or read them a story, and who, because of what they see as the demands of either their jobs or their leisure, are very rarely at home and available to participate in other activities. They are also fathers who are more likely to define their roles as the breadwinner, head of the house, and the aloof disciplinarian.

2. *The traditional father.* Traditional fathers do have strong but nevertheless traditional commitments to their families. While still seeing his role primarily as the breadwinner, the traditional father also defines his role in terms of his *participation* with and responsibility towards his children. His participation is usually manifested in his availability and involvement in play. Although he will somewhat reluctantly "help out" with child-care tasks (e.g., bathing, dressing an older child) when there is pressure to do so, he sees child care as being the primary responsibility of mothers (who he feels are biologically equipped for such tasks).

3. *The "good" father.* It sometimes occurred during the course of an interview that a mother described her spouse as a "good father; he's not your traditional dad". These were fathers who, like the traditional father described above, had a strong commitment to their family and were highly available but, unlike the traditional father, did not restrict their participation to traditional domains. These were fathers who regularly took sole responsibility for their children and who were happily involved in all aspects of child care – nappy changing, feeding, getting up in the middle of the night, etc. Despite their high levels of participation, however, these fathers were still seen as being "good to help the mothers out". Rarely did they see themselves as having equal status, responsibility, or ability with mothers for child care.

4. *The non-traditional, highly participant father.* Fathers in this group are those described in the shared-caregiving families who have taken their participation one step further, to publicly reject traditional notions of fatherhood by assuming a major responsibility for the day-to-day care of their children – a task usually carried out by mothers or by other women (in their homes or in child-care centres or pre-schools). These fathers were also much more likely to argue that mothers and fathers should have equal responsibility and that they are both as capable of caring for their children. (This latter issue about mother/father differences in abilities to care for children is discussed in detail in subsequent chapters.)

The picture presented above of four different types of fathers is probably an oversimplification of the nature of paternal participation, and all fathers would not fit easily into one of the categories. A father who shared child care, but who is reluctant to do so and who holds traditional views about child-care responsibilities (a type found in the present study, which is discussed in chapter 5), is one exception. The classificiation system is, however, given considerable support from an analysis of the interview responses and appears to be consistent with recent analyses presented of fathers in the United States and Britain.

R.A. Fein, in his analysis of American fathers (Fein 1978), discusses three types: (1) *traditional*, the aloof and distant father whose main concern is his breadwinning role; (2) *modern*, emhasizing the idea that fathers are capable of influencing their children, especially in the areas of sex-role identity, academic achievement, and moral development, and that it is *contact* between father and child that facilitates these developmental outcomes (participation, therefore, is integral to this category of father); and (3) *emergent* − the emphasis here is on fathers being capable of participating in all aspects of child care and child-rearing, that men can be effective nurturers of their children. Clearly, these three types of fathers or ideas about fatherhood closely resemble the analysis presented above except that the present analysis differentiates two types of emergent fathers − those from traditional and non-traditional families.

In a recent study of twelve thousand British fathers who had a child of five years of age, Jackson (1980) also argues that there are three distinct groups of fathers. As he describes them, one group "cannot or does not play much of a close personal role in rearing a five year old or in keeping the day-to-day household running. They may be away at work, unlikely to help with shopping, housekeeping, taking the child to school. They are not there at story time or bedtime; and do not back up if the mother goes out to work."

At the other extreme, Jackson reports a group which "has all the cluster of opposite features. They *are* getting home by bedtime, they *are* playing a substantial part in running the home as well as hunting in the economic jungle; and they are probably society's major care service if the mother goes out to work." Jackson reports that there is a third group of fathers who occupy a "misty region" in between these two extremes. Again there is a resemblance between the three groups of traditional fathers presented here and Jackson's groups.

Even though there might be some doubt about the validity of classifiying fathers into four groups, it can hardly be disputed from the data presented here and by others that there is a considerable range in paternal participation. The question arises, then, whether there is an explanation for this range. Why is it that some fathers are highly participant and others are not? Why do some families adopt radically different patterns of child care and others do not? These questions are examined in the next two chapters. Chapter 4 examines explanations for father-participation in traditional families, while chapter 5 focuses on an analysis of the possible antecedents for the adoption of a shared-caregiving lifestyle.

4

Explanations for Father Participation: The Case of the Traditional Family

Data presented in the previous chapter indicated that there was a considerable range in the degree of participation by fathers. This was shown to be the case within traditional families as well as when comparisons were made between traditional and shared-caregiving families. The primary aim of this chapter is to examine possible explanations for the range of paternal participation within the framework of traditional families. An understanding of the factors associated with high father participation in traditional families, while contributing to the explanation of the observed variability in this type of family, might provide additional insights into why some fathers take the more radical step of having the major or equal responsibility for the day-to-day care of their children. It is possible, for example, that high participation in a traditional family *preceeds* the adoption of a shared-caregiving lifestyle.

An objection could be raised at this point, however, about the present emphasis on traditional families as a way of investigating explanations of the variability in paternal participation. As was noted in the introductory chapter, families in which fathers are employed in the paid workforce and mothers are not employed and are at home caring for children represent only *one* type of family pattern. Indeed, in nearly 30% of the three hundred families recruited from shopping centres for this study, mothers were employed for some part of the week. It may be that this significant structural change in employment patterns and the associated change in women's roles and expectations has of itself had an impact on father participation. Because of the higher demands on time, fathers in families in which mothers are employed might be more likely to participate than those in which mothers are not employed. This chapter begins, therefore, with an examination of this possibility, by comparing levels of paternal participation in families in which mothers are not employed, and in which they are employed either part- or full-time. The latter part of the chapter returns to the more general examination of factors that might influence the extent to which fathers participate in child care and play.

Maternal Employment: Its Impact on Father Participation

Although the focus of feminist movements has been on women's participation in the paid work force, and little attention has been given to changes in the distribution of family work, this is not to say that changes in women's roles have not had an impact on men. It may very well be that the movement of women into the paid work force has of itself created a change in the distribution of labour within the home. Several recent studies in Australia, the United States, and the United Kingdom have examined the impact of maternal employment on husbands' contributions to family work. However, these studies have varied considerably in the methodologies they have employed, in terms of (a) who supplied the data (husband/father, wife/mother, or both parents) and how data were collected (e.g., interview, time-use diary, structured questionnaire), and (b) the form in which data were collected and reported (e.g., on the basis of the relative amount of involvement of each spouse or as separate absolute *time estimates* for each parent). It is this latter methodological difference that has received most attention in the literature (e.g., Ericksen, Yancey, and Ericksen 1979; Pleck and Rustad 1980).

Studies that have reported figures in *relative* terms are consistent in their findings that, when wives are employed, husbands are more involved in family work. Furthermore, this pattern has been found in studies conducted in three countries: Australia (Russell 1979a; Harper and Richards 1979), United Kingdom (Young and Willmott 1973), and the United States (Blood and Wolfe 1960; Ericksen, Yancey, and Ericksen 1979). Another finding has been that this relative increase is greater for general household tasks than for child-care tasks (Harper and Richards 1979; Ericksen, Yancey, and Ericksen 1979).

As has been pointed out elsewhere (e.g., Pleck 1980), however, the expression of family work participation in relative terms — that is as the proportion or relative frequency of work done by husbands and wives — could provide a misleading picture. It could be that husbands whose wives are employed are not spending more time on family work than other husbands, but employed wives are spending *less* time than unemployed wives. Clearly, the presentation of figures for relative involvement can only provide a very crude indication of the impact maternal employment has on the distribution of family work.

The pattern of findings from recent studies from the United States that have employed estimates of *actual time spent* by husbands and wives on both paid and family work are somewhat different from those that have been based on *relative scores*. Studies using extensive time-use diaries completed by both husbands and wives (e.g., Robinson 1977; Pleck and Rustad 1980; Vanek 1973; Walker and Woods 1976) are all in agreement in reporting that husbands' involvement in family work only shows a small and non-significant increase when their wives are employed, and indeed, wives who are employed do less family work than those who are not employed. Pleck (1981b), using a different methodology, in contrast reported that fathers' family work increased with maternal employment, especially for child-care tasks. This study used parents' summary estimates of their time spent in family work rather than detailed diaries. In attempting to reconcile these conflicting findings, Pleck and Rustad (1980) argue that data based on parents' summary estimates are generally inflated over estimates from time-use diaries. It is difficult to know, however, why parents' summary estimates should produce differentially inflated figures for families in which mothers are employed.

A major limitation of all studies conducted to date is the lack of emphasis on child care and associated tasks; most studies have focused on general household tasks. Ericksen, Yancey, and Ericksen (1979), for example, employed only one question as an index of involvement in child care: whether or not the father looked after the children without the mother being present, at least once a week. It is child care, however, that is probably the most demanding and constant of family work tasks, and it is the divisions of labour for child care and associated beliefs about parental roles that form the basis of sexual divisions in other domains (cf. Russell 1980).

The present analysis aims to take account of the lack of emphasis on child care in previous studies by examining the effects of maternal employment on divisions of labour for several aspects of child care and parent-child interaction. This presentation, however, is not simply limited to an analysis of the amount of time spent carrying out specific child-care tasks. It is possible that while fathers may not have increased the amount of time spent on child care, they may have increased the *degree of responsibility* they take for their children. A first test of this hypothesis is attempted here by examining the effects of maternal employment on the amount of time fathers spend taking sole responsibility for their children and the degree to which fathers are perceived to share in the overall responsibility for the care of their children.

Another important aspect of the present analysis is the investigation of the influences that differences in family characteristics might have on findings for the effects of maternal employment. A consistent finding of maternal employment studies (e.g., Hoffman and Nye 1974; Ericksen, Yancey, and Ericksen 1979) has been that families in which mothers are employed tend to have fewer and older children. Thus it would be expected that child-care demands, in absolute terms, would be much less in these families, and it could be that this family difference in child-care demands has confounded previous findings. Compared with families with similar aged and number of children, therefore, fathers whose spouses are employed might in fact be doing more.

One recent American study (Pleck and Rustad 1980) has made a fairly crude study of the impact of family characteristics. These researchers examined time spent by fathers in family work as a function of maternal employment status, separately for families in which there was a child under five and in which there was a child six to seventeen years old. No effects were reported for maternal employment status in either group. Data were not presented on the mean ages of the youngest child, and so it still could be that the maternal employment groups had older children (e.g., those with children under five might have had more four-to-five-year-olds), and no account was taken of the number of children. The present investigation extends the analysis of Pleck and Rustad by examining both age-of-child and number-of-children variables.

The sample. The sample reported on here included the 145 traditional families described previously, together with 47 families in which mothers were employed part-time, defined as being less than 25 hours a week (the average was 15 hours a week), and 46 in which the mother was employed full-time (the average was 38 hours a week). Fathers were employed in all families. All families were recruited and interviewed in the manner outlined earlier for traditional families. Families in which mothers were employed full-time had (a) mothers with higher-status occupations (mean status ranking according to Congalton 1969: full-time, 4.3; part-time, 5.1; not employed, 4.7), (b) mothers who were more highly educated (percentage completed university: full-time, 21%; part-time, 11%; not employed, 14%), and (c) fathers who were not as highly educated (percentage completed university: mother employed full-time, 8%; mother employed part-time, 6%; mother not employed, 27%).

Maternal Employment and Family Work

Table 2 presents findings for the amount of time spent by each parent, expressed in hours per week, for specific child-care tasks, play, reading stories, and helping with homework. Two

Table 2. Time estimates for family work and parent-child interactions (in hours per week)

	Maternal Employment Status		
	Unemployed	Part-Time	Full-Time
1. Child-care tasks			
Feeding			
Fathers	1.1	1.4	1.1
Mothers	11.5	9.5	7.0
Dressing			
Fathers	0.5	0.45	0.93
Mothers	3.5	2.9	1.7
Changing nappies			
Fathers	0.2	0.2	0.3
Mothers	2.1	1.25	0.5
Bathing			
Fathers	0.5	0.75	0.65
Mothers	2.2	2.3	1.8
Attending to at night			
Fathers	0.2	0.2	0.2
Mothers	0.7	0.6	0.6
2. Parent-child interaction			
Play			
Fathers	9.0	9.5	9.0
Mothers	20.0	18.0	12.0
Story reading			
Fathers	0.9	0.6	0.8
Mothers	1.7	1.7	1.3
Help with school work			
Fathers	0.32	0.31	0.21
Mothers	0.44	0.65	0.42

trends are evident in this table. First, it is clear that employed mothers do spend less time on child care and play than mothers who are not employed. Second, maternal employment appears to have little impact on the amount of time spent by fathers on specific child-care tasks, play, or other interactions. The only hint of an effect was for the amount of time spent by fathers in dressing their children (0.9 hours a week when mother was employed full-time compared with 0.5 hours a week when mother was not employed). In order to investigate the overall impact of maternal employment, the data presented in table 2 were combined into two scores as defined earlier: (a) *day-to-day care* (DC), the sum of the time-weighted scores for feeding, dressing, changing nappies, bathing, and attending at night; (b) *play and other interaction* (PI), the sum of the time-weighted estimates for play, story reading, and helping with schoolwork.

As a first step in assessing the effects of maternal employment status, the following variables were included in a multivariate analysis of variance (see appendix 3): DC and PI scores for both mothers and fathers; time spent by fathers taking sole responsibility for their children; time spent by fathers in paid work (N.B.: this included travel time, overtime, and other work-associated activities); number of children; age-of-youngest child; age-of-oldest child. Means for each of these variables for the three maternal employment groups are presented in table 3. A multivariate analysis of variance yielded a significant effect for maternal employment status. Analyses of individual variables using univariate F-tests indicated that when mothers were employed (a) mothers spent less time on child care and play; (b) fathers spent more time taking sole responsibility for their children; and (c) there tended to be fewer and older children in the family. Significant effects were not found for the time spent by fathers on child care or play or for the amount of time fathers spent on paid work.

This analysis of combined scores, therefore, confirms the data presented in table 2 and the findings from previous studies. Fathers do not appear to become more involved in either child care or play when mothers are employed either full- or part-time. Maternal employment status does, however, appear to have an effect on time spent by fathers taking the sole responsibility for their children. This effect will be discussed further below.

The present findings also support those from previous studies in showing that families in which mothers are employed tend to

Table 3. Differences between maternal employment groups for (a) total time spent in child care and play and (b) family characteristics

	Maternal Employment Status[1]				
	Un-employed	Part-Time	Full-Time	Uni-variate F value (2,235)	p
Day-to day care (DC)	(hrs/wk)	(hrs/wk)	(hrs/wk)		
Fathers	2.5	3.0	3.1	<1	NS
Mothers	21.0	16.6	11.3	16.69	.001
Play and other interactions (PI)					
Fathers	10.0	10.0	9.0	<1	NS
Mothers	23.0	20.0	14.0	5.43	.005
Fathers − sole responsibility	1.0	4.0	4.7	15.96	.001
Fathers − paid work	51	51	57	1.21	NS
Number of children	2.4	2.2	1.6	4.41	.01
Mean age − youngest child	2.3	3.1	3.9	5.56	.005
Mean age − oldest child	5.7	6.8	6.1	1.13	NS

[1]Multivariate F(34,394) = 4.13, p < .001

have fewer and older children. As was pointed out earlier, this difference in family characteristics might have an important bearing on the conclusions drawn from previous studies. Two further analyses were therefore carried out to ascertain if the failure to find a significant difference between maternal employment groups for fathers' involvement in child care might be explained by differences in family characteristics.

The first analysis explored the possible effect of the age-of-the-child variable. To do this, a 3 (three maternal employment groups) by 2 (youngest child under three; youngest child three or over) multivariate analysis of variance was conducted. A moderately significant interaction between family-type and age-of-youngest child was found. The two variables that contributed most to this interaction were time spent on child care by mothers and, to a lesser extent, time spent on child care by fathers. While this latter effect was not highly significant, there is an indication of a trend here in support of the hypothesis. An inspection of the means summarized in table 4 illustrates this more clearly. As can be seen from that table, when the youngest child in a family is *over* three, there is very little difference between maternal employment groups, but when the youngest child is *under* three, fathers spend more time on child care tasks when the mother is

Table 4. Time spent by fathers on child-care tasks as a function of maternal employment status and family characteristics (in hours per week)

	Maternal Employment Status[1]	
	Unemployed	Full-Time
Age of youngest child		
Less than three years	3.15	4.4
Three years or over	1.96	1.83
Total number of children		
One child	2.74	3.17
Two children	3.31	2.96
Three or more children	2.27	3.06

[1]Interaction between family-type and age-of-youngest child: multivariate $F(7,230) = 2.14$, $p < .04$; univariate analysis for time spent by fathers on child care: $F(1,236) = 3.28$, $p < .07$

employed (4.4 hours a week), than when she is not employed (3.15 hours a week).

A second multivariate analysis of variance was conducted with total number-of-children included as a variable. Three groups of families were defined as having one child, two children, and three or more children. The interaction between maternal employment status and number-of-children was not found to be significant. Thus, it seems that family-type differences in number of children cannot explain the absence of a finding of a difference between maternal employment groups for fathers' involvement in child care.

A Significant Trend? Changes in Parental Responsibilities

Data presented above show quite clearly that the major impact maternal employment has on father-involvement concerns the amount of time fathers spend taking sole responsibility for their children. As can be seen from table 3, when mothers are employed full-time, fathers spend an average of 4.7 hours a week having sole responsibility for their children, compared with only 1 hour a week when the mother is not employed. A further indication of a shift in responsibilities comes from responses to a general question asked during the interview about who has the major responsibility for child care. When mothers were not employed, 99% of the families said the mother had the major responsibility and 1% said it was shared; when mothers were employed part-time, the figures were 95% and 5%; however, when mothers were employed full-time, the figures were 82% and 18%.

Conclusion: Maternal Employment — a Minor Impact?

Findings from the present analysis provide qualified support for previous time-use studies of the impact that maternal employment has on fathers' involvement in family work. In agreement with Robinson (1977), Pleck and Rustad (1980), Vanek (1973), and Walker and Woods (1976), when a simple analysis is conducted comparing maternal employment groups, no significant differences were found in the time spent by fathers in either child care, play, or other interactions. Additional analyses of these data, however, taking into account family characteristics, and considering other data relating to responsibility taken for children, indicate that the situation is not as clear-cut as these analyses might first imply. These latter analyses tend to support more the findings of Pleck (1981b) in showing that maternal employment has a small but nevertheless significant impact on father-involvement.

Data reported here indicate that age-of-children is an important variable to be taken into account in the analysis of the effects of maternal employment. There was a trend evident in the data showing that in families in which child-care demands were at their highest (i.e., when there was a child under three), fathers did spend more time on child-care tasks when mothers were employed than when they were not employed. While this difference was not highly significant, the trend is of a sufficiently substantial nature to warrant that it be investigated in a more systematic manner in further studies.

By far the most significant finding to emerge from the current analysis was that maternal employment had a highly significant effect on the time spent by fathers taking the sole responsibility for their children. When mothers were employed, fathers were spending much more time in this type of situation with their children. That fathers do take more responsibility for child care was also supported by parents' responses to the general question about overall child-care responsibilities; fathers whose spouses were employed full-time were much more likely to be perceived as having equal responsibility. Further research is needed on this question, however, before firm conclusions can be drawn. The question of parental divisions for child-care responsibilities needs to be examined in relation to more specific child-care tasks (e.g., responsibility for clothes and dressing the children; responsibility for checking homework; responsibility for children's health).

Thus it is clear that the movement of mothers into the paid

work force has not been paralleled by a movement of fathers into the unpaid family work force. Maternal employment, therefore, appears to have had the greatest impact on women: it has increased markedly the absolute amount of work they do, or as it has been indicated in the literature for quite some time now, they have dual roles. Further support for the conclusion that maternal employment primarily affects mothers comes from additional data collected here on time spent on personal leisure and on paid work. Employed mothers were significantly less likely to spend time on personal leisure than employed mothers (1.3 vs. 2.8 hours a week), whereas the difference between fathers in these two types of families was relatively minor (4.2 vs. 4.7 hours a week). Thus it seems that mothers adjusted their lifestyles to accommodate the extra pressure and demands of having both parents employed. Mothers were also more likely to accommodate employment demands to family demands. Mothers who were employed, compared with fathers who were employed, spent significantly less time outside the home in association with their jobs (38 vs. 57 hours a week). This difference was mainly accountable for by mothers' being more likely to have a job close to home and not spend time at work beyond normal hours, either doing overtime or in socializing.

Thus, nearly every aspect of family or employment activities examined here point to the conclusion that maternal employment has little impact on fathers' participation in child care and play. It may be, however, that there are other variables which, when combined with maternal employment, do result in an increase in father participation. This possibility is examined in the next section, where a multivariate analysis of father-participation is presented.

Effects of Family, Parental, and Lifestyle Characteristics on Father Participation

The present study permitted the investigation of the possible influence of several variables on the degree of father participation. These included family (e.g., number of children) and personal characteristics (e.g., age and education levels of parents), work and lifestyle variables (e.g., the number of hours fathers spent on paid work), psychological variables (e.g., parental sex-role orientiations), and the previous experiences of parents (e.g., whether they attended childbirth education classes). While there are many ways of assessing the possible influences of these variables (e.g., by simply correlating time spent by fathers on child care with each of the variables of interest), the method chosen here was to establish three criterion groups (high, medium, and low father involvement) for each of the two summary child-interaction variables: the amount of time spent on day-to-day *care* tasks, and the amount of time spent on *play* and other interactions. The three groups defined for time spent on *child-care* tasks were: high − above 4 hours a week (28% of the sample); medium − between 1.2 and 3.9 hours a week (44%); and low − below 1.1 hours a week (28%). The three groups defined for time spent on *play activities* were: high − above 13 hours a week (28%); medium − between 6 and 12.9 hours a week (44%); and low − below 6 hours a week (28%). Tables 5 and 6 show the means for each of the various family, personal, and lifestyle variables for the three father-involvement groups for child care and play respectively. This analysis included the families in which mothers were employed either full- or part-time, as well as those from the original traditional sample.

Multivariate analyses of variance were employed to examine the differences between the three father-involvement groups on each of the two measures. Significant multivariate F values were obtained for both child care and play, indicating that there are differences between the father-involvement groups on some of the variables chosen for analysis. Results for each of the individual variables thought to possibly influence father participation are considered below.

Family Characteristics

A consistent finding from family observational studies (see Parke 1979 and Lamb 1981 for reviews) is that fathers display a preference for interacting with sons. Although this preference is apparent in father-newborn interactions, it is much more pronounced when children are around the age of two years. While all studies to date on sex-of-child effects have been with pre-school-aged children, there is no reason to expect that the pattern should be any different for older children. Indeed, it may be as Belsky (1979) and Block (1979) have suggested, that sex-of-child effects will be even more pronounced for older children; this is the time when fathers are probably more likely to become involved. This is especially likely given that the accepted "expert" and "lay" view is that father-child relationships are not very important during the infancy period; rather it has been seen

Table 5. Father participation in child-care tasks[1]

	Low	Medium	High	Age of Child Not Accounted for		Age of Child Accounted for	
				$F_{(2,235)}$	P	F	P
Family characteristics							
Age of youngest child	3.9	2.2	1.9	15.1	.001	1.16	NS
Age of oldest child	8.1	4.9	4.7	14.2	.001	0.99	NS
Number of children	2.5	2.0	2.2	4.4	.02	3.8	.02
Parental characteristics							
Father's age	35.4	32.5	31.2	7.6	.001	1.16	NS
Mother's age	33.1	30.0	29.2	8.8	.001	0.99	NS
Father's years education	12.4	12.5	13.1	< 1	NS	< 1	NS
Mother's years education	11.2	11.7	13.0	3.6	.03	3.24	.04
Father's occupational status	4.0	4.3	3.9	1.2	NS	< 1	NS
Mother's occupational status	4.9	4.8	4.5	1.9	NS	1.4	NS
Suburb status ranking	4.8	4.8	4.6	< 1	NS	< 1	NS
Years married	10.7	7.1	6.7	17.9	.001	3.8	.03
Work and lifestyle variables (hours/week)							
Father's work time	53.0	51.7	50.0	< 1	NS	1.03	NS
Mother's work time	17.8	17.6	24.9	< 1	NS	1.3	NS
Father's leisure time	4.9	4.1	4.0	< 1	NS	< 1	NS
Mother's leisure time	2.7	2.4	1.9	< 1	NS	< 1	NS
Father's availability	31.2	33.1	35.1	1.9	NS	6.04	.001
Mother's availability	69.2	70.3	73.4	1.0	NS	< 1	NS
Sex-role scores							
Father's masculinity	5.1	5.2	5.1	< 1	NS	< 1	NS
Mother's masculinity	4.1	4.2	4.4	1.1	NS	< 1	NS
Father's femininity	4.5	4.7	4.8	1.1	NS	< 1	NS
Mother's femininity	4.9	5.1	5.0	1	NS	< 1	NS

[1]Multivariate $F_{(46,412)}$ = 1.86, p < .002

Table 6. Father participation in play activities[1]

	Low	Medium	High	Age of Child Not Accounted for		Age of Child Accounted for	
				F(2,235)	P	F	P
Family characteristics							
Age of youngest child	2.7	2.9	2.2	1.8	NS		
Age of oldest child	6.1	6.1	5.3	< 1	NS		
Number of children	2.2	2.3	2.2	< 1	NS	< 1	NS
Parental characteristics							
Father's age	33.9	33.8	31.2	3.8	.03	2.3	.10
Mother's age	31.2	31.7	29.0	4.3	.02	2.7	.07
Father's years education	12.1	13.2	12.2	1.4	NS	1.5	NS
Mother's years education	12.2	12.1	12.9	1.5	NS	3.9	.02
Father's occupational status	4.1	4.0	4.1	< 1	NS	< 1	NS
Mother's occupational status	4.8	4.7	4.6	< 1	NS	< 1	NS
Suburb status ranking	4.7	4.7	4.8	< 1	NS	< 1	NS
Years married	8.1	8.9	7.2	2.8	.07	1.5	NS
Work and lifestyle variables (hours/week)							
Father's work time	54.8	52.5	48.9	3.3	.04	4.1	.02
Mother's work time	22.8	20.7	21.0	< 1	NS	< 1	NS
Father's leisure time	3.6	5.0	4.3	< 1	NS	1.4	NS
Mother's leisure time	2.6	2.8	1.9	1.5	NS	1.7	NS
Father's availability	30.4	32.0	38.1	8.9	.001	13.7	.001
Mother's availability	72.3	69.2	72.3	< 1	NS	< 1	NS
Sex-role scores							
Father's masculinity	5.2	5.2	5.0	< 1	NS	< 1	NS
Mother's masculinity	4.1	4.2	4.5	< 1	NS	< 1	NS
Father's femininity	4.6	4.7	4.8	1	NS	< 1	NS
Mother's femininity	4.9	5.0	5.0	< 1	NS	< 1	NS

[1] Multivariate $F(46,412) = 1.77$, , $< .003$

as their job to provide economic and emotional support for mothers during the early years. Furthermore, only 15% of fathers interviewed for the present study believed the early years were important for fathers; the majority felt their role was more important during middle childhood and adolescence.

A third family characteristic that might be critical is the *number of children*. As the number of children increases in a family, child-care demands will also increase, and, therefore, it might be expected that there would be more pressure on fathers to participate (cf. Lamb 1978*a*). While Robinson (1977) failed to support this hypothesis in a study of American families, sufficient account was not taken of the ages of children in that study. It may be that an effect will be found when there are two or more pre-school-aged children, but not when there is a pre-school and a school-aged child (who, of course, would be more independent and might even take over some of the responsibility for the care of younger brothers and sisters).

The analyses revealed that *family characteristics* were important for participation in child-care tasks, but not in play activities. Father participation in child care was significantly higher when there were fewer, *not more*, children and when there were younger children in the family. No significant effects were found for play activities. The analysis for sex-of-child was not included in the multivariate analysis because of the difficulty of taking into account that some families had children of only one sex. Instead, separate one-way analyses of variance were employed to examine differences in levels of child care and play participation for fathers as a function of sex-of-child. Mean levels of participation are shown in table 7. None of the analyses

Table 7. Mean scores for father participation in child care and play activities as a function of sexes of children

	Child Care	Play
Sexes of children		
All female	2.0	10.1
One male	2.2	10.2
Two male	2.2	10.2
Three or more male	1.8	9.1
Sexes of children		
All male	1.9	10.4
One female	2.3	10.5
Two female	2.0	8.6
Three or more female	1.6	9.9

revealed any significant sex-of-child effects (all F values were less than 1.5). Furthermore, a significant interaction was not found between sex-of-child and age-of-child; that is, fathers *were not* more likely to interact with older boys.

Contrary to the predictions made earlier, then, fathers are not more likely to participate in either child-care tasks or play and other activities when they have male, older, or more children. This absence of a sex-of-child effect is contrary to the very strong findings from observational studies (see Parke 1979). The current analysis, however, emphasized the *amount of involvement*, and not the content of parent-child interactions. It may be, for example, that there are sex-of-child effects for the type of play activities a father engages in, a factor that has not been taken into account here.

Findings for father involvement in child-care tasks, and age-of-child and number-of-children variables, are in fact in the oppostie direction from what had been predicted. That is, the more highly involved father tends to have younger and fewer children. Child-care task demands are likely to be greater when there are younger children, and therefore a finding of the nature of the one reported here is not all that surprising. The finding that fathers with fewer children are more involved is contrary to the "family pressure" argument put forward earlier and is not as easy to explain. It may be that there is a novelty effect for the first child that wears off by the time a second or third child arrives. This finding for the number-of-children variable, therefore, supports the previous finding in an American sample reported by Robinson (1977) and is contrary to the arguments put forward here and by Lamb (1978).

A finding that involvement in day-to-day care tasks is higher when there are younger and fewer children raises the very important question about the nature of this measure of father participation. In families with older children, of course, it is not necessary for parents to carry out tasks such as feeding, dressing, bathing, etc., and so it would be expected that this measure would be biased towards families with younger children and, therefore, younger families. Analyses for further variables therefore took this factor into account. This was done by including the age of the youngest children as a covariate. The results of these analyses, together with results when the age of the youngest child is not taken in account, are presented in tables 5 and 6.

Before proceeding with the discussion of the effects of other variables, it should be noted from tables 5 and 6 that taking account of the age-of-child variable did not affect findings for the number of children; high father participation in child care was still found to be associated with *fewer* children.

Background Characteristics of Parents

Predictions for parental characteristics are more difficult to formulate than those for family characteristics. In terms of the traditional cultural transmission theory, it might be predicted that it is the more highly educated fathers and fathers with higher-status occupations who are more likely to have been exposed to any recent shift in emphasis towards fathers, and therefore it is these fathers who will be more likely to participate. Research findings, however, do not offer clear-cut support for this hypothesis. While recent studies in the United Kingdom (Oakley 1974; Newson and Newson 1965) and in Australia (Harper and Richards 1979) report that middle-class fathers are the most highly participant, recent studies in the United States as reviewed by Pleck (1983) reveal a much less consistent pattern. For example, of the studies of the effects of fathers' education reviewed which used absolute estimates of father participation (i.e., estimates of actual time spent by fathers), one reported that more highly educated fathers participate more, two that they participate less, and two did not report an effect.

It may be, however, as Ericksen, Yancey, and Ericksen (1979) have argued (and indeed found), the characteristics of mothers are more important, and fathers might be more likely to participate when *mothers* are more highly educated. Ericksen, Yancey, and Ericksen point out that it is perhaps the more highly educated woman who is likely to have greater power within the family and therefore will be in a better bargaining position with her husband with regard to the distribution of child-care tasks. Perhaps it is also the more highly educated woman who has been exposed to recent shifts in emphases towards fathers. In support of this hypothesis, mothers in the present study were found to be more likely to have read books or magazine articles on children and related issues than fathers (70% vs. 40%), and it was the more highly educated mother in particular who was even more likely to have done so (88% of mothers who had completed high school, as against only 50% of mothers who had not completed high school, had read books on the subject). It is more likely, then, that it is educated *mothers* who have been exposed to the recent shift in interest towards fathers. The analysis of the effects of background variables (age, education, previous experience, occupation) in the present study therefore included data for *both* mothers and fathers.

Other characteristics of parents that may be important are age and the number of years a couple has been married. If the current academic interest in fathers has had any impact on attitudes and behaviour, then it might be expected that this impact would be greatest for younger fathers, especially those married more recently, and, therefore, couples who have had their *first* child more recently.

As can be seen from tables 5 and 6, high father participation was not associated either with the father's or the mother's occupational status, the father's education level, or the status ranking of the family's suburb of residence. In agreement with the predictions made earlier, and with the recent findings of Ericksen, Yancey, and Ericksen, however, fathers were more likely to be highly participant when the mother's level of education was higher. Whether this is because it is these mothers who are more likely to have been influenced by recent trends in professional views about fathers' involvement in child-rearing, or whether it is more an indication of power relationships within the family, as has been argued by Ericksen, Yancey, and Ericksen, it is difficult to say. The former explanation, however, is weakened somewhat by the findings (discussed below) which show that it is fathers' and not mothers' beliefs about parental roles that are related to father participation.

A second trend to emerge here was for high father participation in child care to be associated with younger families — families in which the couple had been married for fewer years. This was significant even when the ages of children had been taken into account. Perhaps this is an indication of a trend towards greater participation by fathers that is associated with a general cultural shift in which more emphasis is placed on the father's role (e.g., the recent practice of encouraging fathers to be present at births).

Work and Lifestyle Variables

The analysis presented earlier in this chapter suggested that the amount of time mothers spend on paid work has little effect on father participation in either child care or play. It may be, however, that it is *fathers'* involvement in paid work that is the more critical variable here. The demands of a father's job might place constraints on his available time, and, therefore, fathers who spend less time in paid work might be expected to be more involved in child care and play. Pleck (1983) in his recent review of findings in the United States reports the weight of evidence is in support of this hypothesis: there is a small but nevertheless significant negative correlation between time spent in paid work and time spent in child care. The present study, while presenting analyses for time spent on paid work as previous studies have, includes two additional variables: (1) time fathers are at home and available to their children and (2) time spent by fathers on personal leisure activities. The inclusion of the first variable takes account of the possibility that while two fathers might spend the same time at work, one might be at work while his children are asleep and the other while they are awake. Involvement in personal leisure, of course, places another time constraint on fathers that might limit their participation in child care and play.

While the amount of time a father spent on paid work was related to the amount of time he spent playing with his children, it was the amount of time a father was at home and available to his children that was far and away the most critical work or lifestyle variable. Fathers who were at home more often were significantly more likely to spend time on both child-care tasks and play. So it seems that time spent at home does matter, although it still could be that it is the more highly committed father who chooses to spend time at home in the first place. That is, these fathers place more value on their family participation and have adjusted their expectations and demands in the employment domain to take account of their family involvement.

In agreement with data presented earlier in this chapter, and other recent studies of the effects of maternal employment (e.g., Pleck and Rustad 1980; Walker and Woods 1976), the amount of time mothers spent on paid employment was not found to be related to father participation. And neither was time spent by fathers or mothers on personal leisure found to be associated with higher levels of father participation.

Sex-Role Variables

Very little research has been carried out on the psychological characteristics of fathers who are highly participant. Of the small number of studies that have been reported, two variables have dominated: beliefs and attitudes towards sex roles (sex-role ideology), and the sex-role orientations of parents. Both groups of studies are based on the one general hypothesis: that it is the less stereotyped masculine father who is more likely to become involved in the very rigidly defined female role of child care. Previous findings are generally consistent with this hypothesis, but the relationship between sex-role attitudes and male involvement in family work is small in absolute terms (Pleck 1983). It may be, however, that the analysis of general attitudes about sex roles which have been the focus of most of the previous studies is not the most appropriate analysis. Perhaps it is specific beliefs about *parental roles* that are more critical in this context. Questions of this nature were asked here. They tapped beliefs about the existence of a maternal instinct, fathers' ability to care for children, and whether or not a mother's place is in the home.

Support for the general sex-role hypothesis for fathers' participation also comes from recent sex-role studies. Several studies have been reported which show that men who score higher on the traditional femininity scale on the Bem Sex-Role Inventory (BSRI) (Bem 1974) are more likely to perform what might be considered to be cross-sex behaviour (e.g., interact with a baby). This relationship has been found both in laboratory studies (Bem and Lenney 1976; Bem, Martyna, and Watson 1976) and in an interview study of fathers' involvement in child care (Russell 1978). The present multivariate study also included scores for both mothers and fathers on the BSRI (see appendix 2 for details).

The variables derived from the BSRI, masculinity and femininity, were included in the multivariate analysis of variance; beliefs about parental roles were analysed separately using chi-square tests of significance. Although there was a trend for high father-involvement in child care to be associated with higher levels of masculinity in mothers (high = 4.4; medium = 4.2; low = 4.1) and higher levels of femininity in fathers (high = 4.8; medium = 4.7; low = 4.5), they were not significant (p > .05). It seems, therefore, that sex-role personality variables as measured by the Bem Sex-Role Inventory are not strongly related to father participation.

Analyses of beliefs about parental roles, however, did support the sex-roles hypothesis. Summaries of the beliefs of both mothers and fathers, as a function of high, medium, and low father-participation groups for child-care measures, are shown in tables 8, 9, and 10. Fathers who were more highly participant in child-care tasks were found to be more likely to reject the notion of a maternal instinct (X^2_2 = 5.65, p < .05) and slightly more likely to say that a father has the ability to care for children (but this was not statistically significant). There was also a non-significant trend for these fathers to be less likely to say a woman's place is in the home (p > .05). No significant trends were evident either for child-care participation and mothers' beliefs, or for play participation for either parent's beliefs. Analyses taking into account the age of children essentially duplicated these findings. Regardless of whether there were younger (age of youngest less than three) or older children (age of oldest greater than five), fathers who were more highly involved were again found to be less likely to believe that there is a maternal instinct (p < .01 in both analyses) and more likely to believe that fathers have the ability to care for children (p < .05 in both analyses).

Findings for beliefs about parental roles therefore support the sex-roles hypothesis for fathers but not for mothers. Fathers who were more highly involved were found to be less likely to hold stereotyped beliefs about their roles; however, high father participation was not found to be associated with mothers' beliefs. Of special significance was the belief by the more highly involved fathers that they had the ability to take over the caregiving role. It seems, therefore, it is fathers' own beliefs that are important and not necessarily the beliefs of mothers. It is still possible, however, that the beliefs of mothers *are* critical. Data presented in tables 8 and 9 indicate that as a group mothers hold less-stereotypic beliefs than fathers. Also data already presented here and elsewhere (Ericksen, Yancey, and Ericksen 1979) indicate that high father particpation is associated with mothers who are more highly educated. It may be, then, that it is the more highly educated mother who is more likely to have *transmitted* her beliefs to the father. Thus it is still possible that it is *mothers'* beliefs that have influenced the beliefs of fathers.

A word of caution is needed here, however, both for findings on beliefs and for findings on sex-role personality variables. While the present analysis indicated that perhaps it is the less stereotyped masculine father who is more involved, no conclusions can be drawn about whether or not the high level of participation is caused by the less stereotyped views. It may be that the high level of participation preceded the adoption of the

Table 8. Opinion of fathers and mothers on whether there is a maternal instinct

| | Father Participation in Child Care | | |
	Low	Medium	High
Fathers[1]			
Agreed	78%	80%	65%
Disagreed	22%	20%	35%
Mothers[2]			
Agreed	70%	73%	62%
Disagreed	30%	27%	38%

[1] $x_2^2 = 5.65$, $\rho < .05$
[2] NS

Table 9. Opinion of fathers and mothers on whether a father has the same ability as a mother to care for children

| | Father Participation in Child Care | | |
	Low	Medium	High
Fathers[1]			
Agreed	37%	47%	52%
Disagreed	49%	39%	32%
Were uncertain	14%	14%	16%
Mothers[2]			
Agreed	58%	63%	57%
Disagreed	25%	22%	32%
Were Uncertain	17%	16%	11%

[1] $x_4^2 = 4.61$, NS
[2] NS

Table 10. Opinion of fathers and mothers on whether a mother's place is in the home

| | Father Participation in Child Care | | |
	Low	Medium	High
Fathers[1]			
Agreed	85%	73%	71%
Disagreed	15%	27%	29%
Mothers[2]			
Agreed	56%	62%	55%
Disagreed	44%	38%	45%

[1] NS
[2] NS

beliefs. Intervention studies focusing on changing specific beliefs about parental roles and in breaking down stereotyped views about the male role are needed to answer this question of cause and effect. This same problem of cause and effect occurs for the analysis of the effects of previous experience.

Previous Experience

It may be that an important differentiating variable for fathers is the extent of their previous experience. Fathers' participation might be related to their knowledge, skills, and self-confidence in child care. The present study allowed for a preliminary investigation of this hypothesis. Data were collected about the extent to which a father had read or consulted books on child care or related topics. Both of these contacts − books and courses − could be sources of knowledge and skills. Data were also collected on whether fathers had attended the birth or not. As well as being a source of knowledge, this type of intimate contact might also facilitate the development of a father's attachment to his child, and this could be related to higher levels of father particiation.

Table 11 shows the percentages of fathers who had or had not read books, who had attended pre-natal classes, and who had and had not attended the birth of their child, as a function of the three father-involvement groups for child care (no trends were evident for play activities and therefore figures for this measure are not presented). There was a non-significant trend for fathers who

Table 11.   Previous experience of fathers

	Father Participation in Child Care		
	Low	Medium	High
Read child-care books[1]			
Yes	34%	39%	52%
No	66%	61%	48%
Attend pre-natal classes[2]			
Yes	12%	20%	30%
No	88%	80%	70%
Attended birth[3]			
Yes	29%	39%	56%
No	71%	61%	44%

[1] $x_2^2 = 4.9$, $p < .05$
[2] $x_2^2 = 6.6$, $p < .05$
[3] $x_2^2 = 10.2$, $p < 0.1$

were more highly involved to be more likely to have read books on child care and a significant trend for more involved fathers to have attended ante-natal classes and to have attended the birth of their child. Findings for fathers' attendance at birth were particularly strong (see table 11).

Additional analyses revealed that, irrespective of the ages of children in the families, highly participant fathers were found to be more likely to have attended pre-natal classes ($p < .02$), and to have attended the birth of their child ($p < .02$), but it was only the highly involved fathers with younger children who were more likely to have read books on child-rearing or child care ($p < .02$). Despite these findings it may be, however, in line with the argument above, that fathers who attend ante-natal classes and births are more committed to begin with. Again, intervention studies are needed to explore the possible effects of this in more detail. That this type of experience is likely to have some type of effect, however, is clearly supported by the intervention study of Parke, Hymel, Power, and Tinsley (1980). That study showed that intervention at the attitudinal and child-care skills levels was effective in increasing the level of participation by fathers. Given that most hospitals now allow and actively encourage fathers to attend the births of their children (about 70% of fathers are now attending in Australia), effects for birth attendance probably will not emerge as strongly in future studies. More specific data will be required for the actual level of participation before and after their experiences of classes and their early contact with their children. While not being able to show a causal link between participation and fathers' attendance at ante-natal classes and the birth, findings of highly significant positive relationships at least indicate that there is every reason to continue the practice of encouraging fathers to become involved at these levels.

CONCLUSIONS

While it is evident there is considerable variability in fathers' levels of participation in child care and play in traditional families, there seems no obvious, all-encompassing explanation for this. Perhaps it is easier to conclude what father participation is *not* related to. It is clear, for example, that it is not related to the traditionally used social class variables: father's education levels and occupational status, and status ranking of suburb of residence. Father participation in Australia appears to transcend traditional class barriers. For example, consider the following description of a family in which the father was highly participant.

This father was a fitter and turner in a large factory from the outer western suburbs of Sydney (traditionally associated with the working class). He greeted the interviewer at the front door with a "pat on the belly" and the comment: "It looks like you sink a few [beers] too, mate." Inside, the interviewer joined the family (mother, father, mother's father and uncle) in a few beers while they finished their evening meal. The men had been at the "boozer" for a few hours that afternoon, and so they were running late. As well as being a fitter and turner, the father worked as an S.P. bookmaker on Friday nights and Saturday afternoons. To complete this "typical male" image, he owned a young greyhound which he hoped to race and went to the club on Sunday nights to watch the football replays on colour television. The description up to this point is something that has usually been associated with the working class *traditional* Australian male. But, there *was* another side. The father had cooked the evening meal that night, he was totally involved with his children (bathing, feeding, changing nappies), and had taken his holidays to look after his first child when his wife spent a month in hospital before the birth of their second child. What is more, he had attended *every* visit his wife made to the doctor before the birth of both children — the only father in the sample to have done this. To him, the children were as much his responsibility as they were his wife's. He wanted to be involved in all aspects!

While traditional social class variables associated with fathers did not appear critical, the mother's education level was found to be important, as were the number of years married, the amount of time the father was at home and available to his children, the father's beliefs about parental roles, and the previous experiences of the father. It is only the first two of these, however, that can be interpreted clearly as being possibly linked in a causal way to father participation.

Mothers having higher education levels and couples being married for fewer years might be associated with the same underlying effect. It may be that it is evidence of a slow but nevertheless significant shift in father participation resulting from the increased academic (e.g., research on fathers) and professional interest (e.g., fathers being encouraged to attend the birth) in fathers. More highly educated mothers might be both more likely to have been exposed to recent changes in views and perhaps are more likely to have transmitted this new "knowledge" to their husbands. Furthermore, if there is an effect in this regard, it would be consistent that younger couples be even more likely to have been exposed to it.

Another possibility is that mothers with higher education levels are in a much stronger power position with respect to their husbands, and therefore are in a better bargaining position for the distribution of family work. Alternatively, it may be that a mother having a higher level of education is an indicator of her being socialized in a less traditional way. These mothers might be less likely to have been strongly socialized into the maternal role and therefore might not identify as closely with this role, making them less likely either to feel child care is their domain exclusively, or to feel threatened by fathers' participation in this. Future research is needed to explore these possibilities in more depth.

The other variables that have been found to be associated with high father involvement are much more questionable with respect to cause and effect. While it is possible that the fathers have become more involved *because* they are available more, hold less stereotypic views about parental roles, have had more experience with children, and have more knowledge about child care, other interpretations are possible. Some of these are the fathers who were more committed before and as a consequence (1) reduced their non-family activities (e.g., work or leisure) and (2) attended ante-natal classes and the birth. Additionally, it may be that holding less stereotyped views about parental roles is a *consequence* of having become more highly participant. Future research is obviously needed to examine these alternative explanations. The next chapter takes this search for explanations of father participation one step further by examining the characteristics of shared-caregiving families and comparing traditional and shared-caregiving families on the variables covered in the present chapter.

5

Adopting a Shared-Caregiving Lifestyle: Possible Explanations

A family in which the father is the primary child-carer represents a radical departure from accepted cultural beliefs and, as was pointed out earlier, constitutes only 1–2% of the population of families with young children. Furthermore, shared-caregiving parents reported they were continually reminded about how different they were and encountered many negative reactions from friends, relatives, and acquaintances (see chapter 7). That this type of family pattern is either adopted in the first place or continued in the face of constant social criticism therefore suggests that the underlying determining factors must be strong indeed. The aim of this chapter is to attempt to determine the antecedents and to explain why it is that some families take the apparently radical step of having *fathers* care for children.

The present chapter includes an analysis of the same group of variables as those considered in the previous chapter: personal and family characteristics, prior experiences, beliefs about parental roles, and sex-role personality characteristics. Comparisons are made between shared-caregiving and traditional families on each of these. A father taking on a significant day-to-day role in child care, however, is much more substantial and much more *public* than a father "helping out" by changing a nappy or feeding a baby when he is at home from his job during the evenings or weekends. The factors that underlie the decision to adopt a shared-caregiving lifestyle, therefore, might differ from those factors found to be associated with high father participation in traditional families. As such, possible additional explanations are sought by examining (a) parents' *own* interpretations of why they adopted a radical child-care pattern and (b) the characteristics of the jobs held by parents in shared-caregiving families. Parents' own explanations are considered first.

Parents' Explanations

Parents were asked what the main reasons were for their adopting their particular family pattern and whether they thought one parent had been more influential than the other in making the decision to change lifestyles. Although four major types of explanations were clearly distinguishable, there were two other features of the explanations that were salient as well. These were (1) the families' general attitudes to child-care responsibilities and (2) the changing nature of their explanations — for some people, the initial reason why they changed was very different from the reasons why they continued.

General Explanations

1. *Inability of fathers to gain employment* (seven families). Five of the fathers in this group were unable to get a job they were happy with; they could be classified as unemployed and seeking work. For example, one father was a lawyer who had been retrenched and was unable to get a job in this profession. He applied for other jobs but was rejected because he was too highly qualified. It was easier, therefore, for his wife, who had secretarial skills, to obtain employment. Also, in this case the mother *offered* to find a job to support the family. In the other two families in this group, the fathers were in poor health and unable to cope with the demands of their previous employment (one had been in the army and the other a public servant).

2. *Financial benefits* (twenty-four families). Parents in this group agreed that the major reason for their having adopted the lifestyle was to increase family income. They included people who either needed the extra income (because the father's salary was very low) or saw it as necessary to achieve a "desired" standard of living (e.g., to buy a house; to establish a business). Two examples of parents' explanations in this category were:

"It was for economic reasons, we wanted our own home." (Father)

"It was because of Tom's work — he wanted to branch out. But there was potential financial insecurity in that too, so we decided I should go back to work." (Mother)

3. *Career factors* (sixteen families). Most of the families in this category (twelve) were those in which a change in lifestyle was associated with the desire of the mother to pursue a career. The others (four) were families in which the father had taken time off

from his employment to complete some course of study, the completion of which would have benefits for his career in the future. Three examples of responses in this group were:

"Housework gives me the shits. I get a lot of job satisfaction and I wanted to go back to my job." (Mother)

"Anne was always frustrated about never having the opportunity to get on in her job." (Father)

"I wanted to finish my master's degree. Taking a year off work and staying at home, I thought, would enable me to do it." (Father)

4. *Beliefs about parental responsibilities and equality between the sexes* (twenty-four families). Parents in this group said the major reason for their having changed lifestyles was their ideological commitment to shared parenting and equality between the sexes. It was their view that both parents were responsible for their children, and both should be involved in child care. For example, two parents had this to say:

"It was just a gradual development. We both have careers, and both feel fairly strongly about women's issues. Shared child care was just a natural extension of this." (Mother)

"It allows both of us to share and give in the relationship with Timothy, and in our self-fulfilment in our education and careers. It is not a sacrifice for either of us, or for Timothy either. Having both parents caring and nurturing is ideal." (Father)

There was also a small group of fathers in this category who rejected traditional career values and offered this as an additional explanation. As one father said: "I wanted to get out of my job and work for myself. I was cheesed off with my career, the politics, and my boss. Also my general work environment wasn't very good. I looked for a business that allowed me to be at home with the kids during the day. I settled on a milk run."

Finally, there were six families in which the boredom the mother experienced with being at home was offered as an additional explanation to that of shared child care. One mother expressed it this way: "I didn't want to stay at home. I thought I had strong maternal feelings. But I felt isolated, cut-off, lonely. It was hard work. It was hard when I had one. By the time I had the third child I was sick of the routine. It was time for David to share in some of this too."

Parents who offered the first two types of explanations, by and large, saw their change in family patterns as being *necessary* (thirty-one families), while the latter two groups were more inclined to say that the decision to change had been a matter of *family choice* (forty families). Most families who said they had been virtually forced to change also felt this was not the ideal family situation. As is discussed below, however, some of these families changed their views after they had experienced a shared-caregiving lifestyle. As might be expected, there were significant differences between these two broad groups of families on background and lifestyle variables. Those families who were classified as having *chosen* to adopt a non-traditional lifestyle were more likely to have mothers who were highly educated, and mothers and fathers with higher-status occupations. Additionally, fathers in this group performed more child-care tasks, and mothers were employed for longer hours, were available for less time, and played less with their children. Analyses presented in subsequent chapters take account of these differences within the shared-caregiving sample.

Attitudes to Child-Care Responsibilities

When answering the question about why they had adopted their particular lifestyles, eighteen families in which both parents were employed offered an additional explanation to those listed above. This revolved around child care and the responsibilities of parents. For example:

"It was for economic reasons. . . . We also chose our work times so that we could look after Amanda, though. We want to have the influence at this early age which is so critical. We didn't want to have a baby-sitter." (Father)

"If Tom couldn't have looked after them, I wouldn't have agreed to it." (Mother)

"A child needs at least one member of the family at this age — it is very important." (Mother)

"We chose our family organization so that we wouldn't have to use other people to look after our children." (Father)

"I'd rather have my kids come home to their father than to a stranger or a nan or pop." (Mother)

"The children are our responsibility to look after and care for." (Father)

Thus for a significant number of families a non-traditional family pattern was adopted only because they felt that child care was still the responsibility of parents; a child-care institution was not an option that was seriously considered. Instead, they had looked for jobs that allowed them to retain a fairly traditional pattern of child care — that is, one which involved parents as the only caregivers. They were apparently highly successful in this regard too, as the average number of hours each week for which children were cared for by someone else outside the family was only six. Attitudes to child care and the welfare of children, therefore, were instrumental in the decision to adopt an alternative family pattern, especially in those families in which both parents were employed.

Which Parent Was More Influential?

Although there were some minor disagreements between parents on who they thought had been more influential in the decision to change, there was agreement in the overwhelming majority of families. Mothers were perceived to be more influential in 33% of families, fathers in 15%, and in 52% the decision was described as a joint one. Overall, then, mothers were perceived as being more influential than fathers, playing a significant role in 85% of families. Although not statistically significant, when the decision to change was seen as being necessary it was more common for mothers to be reported as having been more influential; and when the decision was more a matter of choice, fathers were reported as having been more influential. Such a finding might be interpreted as being consistent with the previous discussion about the specific reasons people gave for changing. For those who saw the change as being financially necessary, the most significant aspect of the decision (initially at least) was probably the mother being employed – the decision for the father to assume the responsibility for child care, on the other hand, was probably a secondary consideration. It might be expected, therefore, that mothers are more instrumental under such circumstances. In contrast, however, when the change was by choice, fathers' participation in child care probably was more prominent in the decision-making process, and we would expect fathers to be more involved in this decision.

The Changing Nature of Explanations

The impression given up to this point is that the decision to change was a reasonably static process; once the decision was made, that was the end of it. Interview responses, however, indicated otherwise. The actual experience of a shared-caregiving lifestyle resulted in people changing their views, and for many the reasons why they adopted the lifestyle initially were very different from the reasons why they continued. As one father said: "Initially it was to allow Helen to progress with her career. Later it was also important that we were better off financially. Now, it just seems like a better way of life."

There were two reactions to the changed lifestyle that stood out as having an impact on people's reasons why they continued. For mothers, there was the satisfaction they derived from their jobs; for fathers, there was the enjoyment they derived from their improved relationships with their children. Two fathers expressed it like this:

"My wife wasn't very keen on it at the time. She is now, however, as she enjoys her job."

"We started out doing it because of money — we wanted to buy a house. Barbara wanted to stop working, she wanted me to go back to a nine to five job. I didn't want to because that would have meant I wouldn't have seen the kids as much. I felt I had as much right to see the kids as she did. The way we were, meant we both took care of them for about equal time. I want to stay like that."

Thus, for several parents, the experience of a different pattern of divisions of labour for paid and family work had altered their attitudes; they perceived a different value in what they were doing, a value that was not so much economic as concerned with the quality of life and the quality of their children's lives too (e.g., "The children get a better deal too — they have two people to relate to").

Conclusions

In developing an explanatory model, emphasis might need to be placed on (a) the family financial situation; (b) the nature of parental employment, especially the mothers' employment; (c) beliefs about parental roles; and (d) parental satisfactions with their alternative roles — for fathers, satisfactions with their child-care role; for mothers, satisfaction with their jobs. Although the family financial or employment situation was prominent in many parental explanations, there may be several possible alternatives for family change, given these conditions. For example, if a family is in financial difficulty, possible alternatives might be: father takes a second job; both mother and father work, and their children are cared for by another person; both parents work but in jobs that permit them to organize their hours of employment so that they can share the care of their children. The first two alternatives are, of course, the most commonly chosen ones. Why is it, then, that the present families have chosen the alternative of fathers caring for the children? Are there any family or personal characteristics that make it more likely this group of families would make this choice. It seems there are; several factors appear to mediate this change.

Variables That Possibly Mediate Family Change

Family Characteristics

While it was a reasonable hypothesis that in traditional families fathers would be more highly participant when child-care demands were higher, in shared-caregiving families the position is likely to be very different. It could be argued that a non-traditional lifestyle involving a radical change in caregiving patterns is *more likely* to eventuate when the demands of caregiving are reduced. Shared-caregiving families therefore might be more likely to have fewer and older children than traditional families. Data presented in chapter 3 comparing the two family types on family characteristics lend some support to this hypothesis. Shared-caregiving familes were found to have significantly fewer children; 52% had only one child, and only 14% had three or more. Also, shared-caregiving families were slightly more likely to have older children, and few had *very young* children; only *ten* of the seventy-one families had a child under six months of age, and only *two* had a child under two months of age. Having a lower level of child-care demands might therefore be a necessary precondition for a father either to contemplate or to agree to take on full-time caregiving.

A finding that shared-caregiving families have fewer and older children, however, could be associated with another factor. Fathers' being involved in child care in families with these characteristics conflicts less with cultural beliefs about child care, such as the desirability of breastfeeding, the importance of mother-infant bonding, and the very strong belief that young babies need their mothers. The degree of either perceived or actual conflict between the family pattern and accepted cultural views might therefore be important. Subsequent chapters examine this hypothesis in more detail.

Potential for and Type of Employment

A decision for fathers to assume a caregiving role and for mothers to be employed might be more likely when a mother's potential for employment is higher — when her training and background are such that she can gain employment readily and/or she has a higher earning capacity. In support of this hypothesis, mothers in shared-caregiving families were found to be more highly educated and to have occupations of higher status than mothers in traditional families. Higher-status occupations are also likely to be more interesting or career-oriented and thus have the potential to be more rewarding for mothers. Mothers would be less likely to be attracted outside the home to low-status, repetitive, and menial occupations. Support was found here for this argument: only eleven of the mothers in this sample had semi-skilled or unskilled occupations.

Shared child care might also be more likely to eventuate when parents have flexibility in their hours of employment, enabling them to organize their jobs around family needs. Again, present findings support this hypothesis; in all families in this sample *at least one parent* had some flexibility in hours of employment, *or* the hours at the place of employment were fewer than "normal" (i.e., nine to five) hours. This latter employment characteristic was especially common for mothers. Indeed, there were only three mothers in the entire sample who had hours of employment and job demands (e.g., travel, overtime, etc.) comparable to what is commonly found for fathers in traditional families. Nevertheless, in 29% of families some significant accommodation of work to family (Bailyn 1978) had taken place; that is, people had either changed their jobs, had selected work hours to enable them to change caregiving patterns, or had reduced their commitments to their jobs. Moreover, this accommodation of work to family was much more common for fathers. For example, one father changed his shift at a factory from day to night to enable him to care for his child while the mother was employed as a schoolteacher; another changed his teaching commitments and reduced his career investment in his university job to share the care of his two pre-school-aged children. Thus, coupled with the earlier report that, for a few fathers, the prospect of reducing their job commitments and career aspirations was a contributing factor to the decision to change, there appears to be evidence here of a significant group of fathers who have rejected or at least seriously questioned traditional male work and career values.

Prior Experiences

As was argued for traditional families, there might be a link between these fathers' and mothers' adoption of a non-traditional lifestyle and their own family experience and relationships with their own parents (e.g., a father whose father was very involved might be more likely to become involved). Although this type of information was not collected here, both Radin (1980) in her American study and Sagi (1981) in his Israeli study report data which support such a hypothesis. Of particular importance, it seems, is having had a mother who herself was employed (Radin 1980) and a father who was himself highly participant (Sagi 1981). Another possibility, as was outlined before, is that a father's more recent experiences, especially with his own children, might be instrumental in his willingness to adopt the caregiving role. For this hypothesis, as before, it would be expected that fathers who (a) have more knowledge about and are more competent in child care and (b) have had more contact and experience and therefore are more self-confident with their children will be more likely to assume the child-care role. Support was found for this hypothesis when shared-caregiving families were compared with traditional families.

Fathers in shared-caregiving families were more likely to have attended pre-natal classes (53% of shared-caregiving fathers compared with only 28% of traditional fathers) and were more likely to have attended the birth of their children (63% of shared-caregiving fathers had attended, compared with 40% of traditional fathers). Finally, more shared-caregiving fathers had read books on child care or child rearing (65% compared with 46% of traditional fathers). These data, therefore, support the findings reported in the previous chapter for traditional families in showing that a father's previous experiences and knowledge are related to the degree of his current participation. Again, however, it is difficult to know whether these experiences have been instrumental in the process of a father becoming highly participant. It may still be that these fathers were more committed to parenting *before* they had these experiences, and that *earlier* socialization experiences are much more relevant.

Beliefs about Parental Roles

As was pointed out before, there is likely to be a link between parental behaviour and beliefs, and that parental cognitions about child care and their roles are instrumental in the adoption of non-traditional family patterns. In line with this argument, Bem (1979) has suggested that differences in *sex-role* behaviour in particular might be a consequence of differences in beliefs about the two sexes. Thus, parents' decisions to adopt non-traditional *family* sex roles might be linked to their *beliefs* about the underlying bases of differences in parental roles. It was hypothesized, therefore, that parents in shared-caregiving families would be less likely to believe in the existence of a maternal instinct, more likely to believe that mothers and fathers had equal abilities to care for children, and more likely to attribute current sex differences in parental roles to *social* factors.

Maternal Instinct

Responses for the two family types to the question whether or not differences in the role of mothers and fathers can be explained by the existence of a maternal instinct are presented in table 12. As can be seen from that table, a high percentage of parents believed there *is* a fundamental biological difference between mothers and fathers enabling mothers to be better at caring for children. The percentage of parents who believed in a maternal instinct, however, was much higher in traditional families, and this was more particularly the case for fathers. Statistically significant differences were found between fathers and mothers in traditional families, and between traditional and shared-caregiving fathers. No differences were found between mothers and fathers in shared-caregiving families. Of the parents who did not agree that there was a maternal instinct, 60% reported that male-female differences in family roles are attributable to socialization practices or social factors.

Differences between traditional and shared-caregiving parents in their beliefs about the bases of parental roles were quite striking. On the question of a maternal instinct, two shared-caregiving parents had this to say:

"No there isn't a maternal instinct. It's all rubbish. If a person

Table 12. Opinion of fathers and mothers in shared-caregiving and traditional families on whether there is a maternal instinct

	Shared-caregiving		Traditional	
	Mothers	Fathers[1]	Mothers[2]	Fathers
Agree	44	57	66	78
Disagree	56	43	34	22

[1]Family type differences for fathers: $x^2 = 10.3$,   .01

[2]Difference between mothers and fathers in traditional families: $x^2 = 4.24$,   .05

wants to — if a man wants to, a man can do it just as well. Obviously he can't breastfeed, but he can do everything else. If you want to — that is what is important." (Father)

"Yes, there is something like a maternal instinct, but whether it's biological or cultural, I don't know. I don't know whether I loved babies because others told me I should love babies, or whether it is inbuilt. Physically I took to motherhood quite well. I enjoyed breastfeeding. When I gave up work I expected to be happy in the home, that I would be the nucleus of the family, sweet, gentle, loving mother and wife. But I didn't feel that way when I was in the situation. I don't know whether it was that I just wasn't told about the problems." (Mother)

Now contrast this with the beliefs of a traditional couple. A fuller description of the family is given to accentuate the differences in lifestyles and help place the beliefs into the context of a more extreme traditional family. This also provides an excellent example of the way in which a set of beliefs can help to *maintain* a particular family pattern.

In this traditional family there were four boys, ranging in age from fifteen years to six weeks. All four children presented some type of problem to their parents, ranging from poor performance at school and a likely failure in the school certificate to feeding and sleeping problems with the baby. In the words of the mother (Wendy):

"He doesn't sleep at all during the day; he just bellows. I've tried everything, gripe water, infacol, boiled water, rocking him, nursing him. I let him cry until he screams and then I get him up. I can't get anything done. I took him to the clinic sister and she said it was because I was too tense — it was rubbing off on him. He's in pain all day, you can see it in his face — how could I do that to him? I took him to the doctor's last Friday. I had the last appointment at 5.40. I had to wait until then until Ted came home. I didn't get in until 6.30. Barry screamed the whole time. The doctor wouldn't give me anything; he was very short with me. That upset me. Maybe he had a bad day and made him cranky. I think he could have given me something. I'm not sure how much longer I can take this."

Wendy was very negative about all aspects of her role as mother, the constancy of it, the nagging and yelling she had to do all the time to ever get her children to do anything. She also felt that her husband, Ted, could help a lot more. Ted, however, seemed not to be aware of many of Wendy's problems. Ted, a bootmaker by trade, was now in the regular army, where he was a driver. He usually left home at about 6.30 a.m. and returned between 5 and 6 p.m. Every fifth weekend he was required to spend at the army base on guard duty. On Saturdays he played tennis. He very rarely played with his children, and only very occasionally gave the baby a bottle. Some of the contrasting views of Wendy and Ted about their roles as parents were as follows:

Question: What do you see as being your role and responsibilities as a mother/father?

Wendy: "Being a mother is a lot of hard work. You're on the go all the time. Washing, ironing, cooking, looking after them. I don't think I'm looking after them properly.

Ted: "My role as a father is to provide for them, to give guidance to the kids, try to teach them right from wrong. To respect other people's property, to respect elders, to give them a certain amount of discipline."

Question: What about a father's/mother's role (i.e., opposite parent's role)? How do you see that?

Wendy: "It's a man's world, not a woman's world. They have more liberties. I'm tied down with the baby all the time. I can't remember the last time I went out without the children. We don't have anyone to look after them. My parents are both dead, and Ted's mother is too sick, at least that's what she says. We couldn't get other people to look after them unless we paid them. We can't afford that. But no one ever offers; you have to ask them all the time. I don't like doing that. Ted can go out whenever he likes. He goes to tennis every Saturday, and out to the hotel. He should be home helping me more, playing with the kids and helping them with their school work."

Ted: "A father teaches them different things. She nurses them and cares for them. A father handles serious problems, teaches them a goal, something to aim for, something I never had as a kid. A father should have more control over them. I do more than mum, she has enough problems. It is a father's job to teach them discipline."

Question: Do you think that women have a maternal instinct? Do you think that women are more capable than men are at caring for children?

Wendy: "I think so — it's something your mother teaches you, and you just have that instinct. Men are not born with it, but they could do it. They should be able to cook and look after them as good as mother. I think they think that's a woman's job."

Ted: "Yes, a woman is more durable. They have more endurance than men. It's just part of a woman. They go from sun-up to sunset, they don't seem to get sick. A woman is more organized with housework; it just comes natural."

Question: What do you enjoy about being a parent?

Wendy: "Nothing!"

Ted: "I enjoy my kids, playing with them, teaching them things, taking them places."

Question: Are there any things you dislike about being a parent?

Wendy: "The shouting and the nagging. The work, all the washing and ironing for four boys."

Ted: "Nothing. I enjoy fatherhood."

Fathers' Abilities to Be Caregivers

Responses to the question about whether fathers also have the ability to care for children are shown in table 13. As for the previous question, significant mother/father differences were only found for parents from traditional families: fathers in this type of family were significantly less likely to believe that fathers have what it takes to care for children. Also, significant family-type differences were again found for fathers. Fathers in shared-caregiving families were more likely to believe that fathers are capable of performing the caregiving role equally as well as mothers. No differences were found between mothers and fathers in shared-caregiving families. The beliefs of shared-caregiving parents are quite striking. Only 4% of shared-caregiving fathers and 3% of mothers did not think fathers had the ability to care for children. Furthermore, many of these parents admitted they had some doubts *before* they changed lifestyles, but their experiences now led them to believe other-

Table 13. Opinion of fathers and mothers in shared-caregiving and traditional families on whether fathers have the ability to care for children

| | Shared-caregiving | | Traditional | |
	Mothers	Fathers[1]	Mothers[2]	Fathers
Agree	88	88	65	49
Disagree	3	4	22	35
Uncertain	9	8	13	16

[1]Family type differences for fathers: $x_2^2 = 33.5$,   .01
[2]Difference between mothers and fathers in traditional families: $x_2^2 = 15.03$, .01

wise. Some of the ways in which shared-caregiving parents answered this question were:

"Of course fathers have the ability. I do it very day and am perfectly happy doing it." (Father)

"There's no innate abilities a woman has that a man doesn't have. Yes, he can do it." (Father)

"In terms of our own set-up — Phillip is better at child-rearing than I am. He has done more of it and has done it better than I would have done. He has a true empathy with the kids, a naturalness and gentleness." (Mother)

When parents (shared-caregiving and traditional alike) who said that fathers were capable were asked why so few fathers adopted the caregiving role, the majority (62%) explained fathers' reluctance as being associated with concepts of sex-appropriate behaviour. For example:

"The reason why they don't commit themselves to their children is that they're afraid of being knocked by their mates." (Mother)

"A lot of men are dominated by a masculine image. They don't think it is masculine to change nappies and do other things for babies . . . they think they should play with them when they are older and take them to football." (Father)

"They think it's not man's work, that it's women's work." (Father)

Thus, men's roles as fathers were seen by these parents as being restricted by traditional concepts of sex-appropriate behaviour; they thought most men considered it not masculine to be involved in child care and were afraid of being subjected to ridicule from their male peers. The possibility that differences in concepts of sex-appropriate behaviour could provide a more general explanation for shared-caregiving families is examined in more detail in the next section.

Parental Roles and Masculinity, Femininity, and Androgyny

Data presented thus far indicate that personal (e.g., beliefs about parental roles, previous experiences) as well as situational or structural factors (e.g., family characteristics, the nature of parental employment) are potentially critical for an explanation of a shared-caregiving family pattern. Futhermore, findings for personal factors suggest that shared-caregiving parents were different people *before* they began their non-traditional lifestyle. Given that this type of family is not very common, and therefore there is an absence of role models, and that it contradicts accepted cultural beliefs, it is highly plausible that only people with certain characteristics will either contemplate, adopt, or feel comfortable in this non-traditional family pattern. In agreement with this argument, both Radin (1980) and Sagi (1981) point out that non-traditional fathers could be considered to be *role makers* (cf. Aldous 1974) and therefore are likely to be high on self-esteem, independence, and interpersonal sensitivity. Within the context of the recent literature on sex roles, therefore, we might expect caregiving fathers to be more likely to be *androgynous* – that is, that they would score high on both traditional masculinity (e.g., independence, self-confidence, assertiveness), *and* traditional femininity (e.g., interpersonal sensitivity, expressiveness).

In addition, mothers in the shared-caregiving families are all employed and therefore are taking on a traditional *male* role. It might be expected, therefore, that these mothers, in comparison to traditional mothers, will also be more likely to be androgynous, and to score higher on the *masculinity* sex-role scale. The argument here about a relationship between sex-role orientation and family lifestyles, of course, presents the same problems as those encountered in the previous section; that is, it is difficult to ascertain what is causing what – whether the lifestyle is a consequence of sex-role orientation or vice versa (cf. Abrahams, Feldman, and Nash 1978). This issue is discussed further below.

A Comparison between Shared-Caregiving and Traditional Families

Mean masculinity and femininity scores for parents in shared-caregiving and traditional families are shown in table 14. Differences between the two groups of families are greatest for fathers' femininity and mothers' masculinity; both are higher in shared-caregiving families. T tests revealed that the family-type difference in fathers' femininity scores was significant, and the difference between mothers' masculinity approached significance.

Distributions of sex-role classifications (see appendix 2 for a description of this technique) for the two groups of families are presented in table 15. The sex-role classifications: *androgynous*

Table 14. Mean masculinity and femininity scores

	Shared-caregiving		Traditional	
	Mothers	Fathers	Mothers	Fathers
Masculinity	4.54[a]	4.89	4.32	4.99
Femininity	5.01	4.75[b]	4.92	4.46

[a]Difference between family types for mothers' masculinity: $t(281)$ = 1.59, p < .10

[b]Difference between family types for fathers' femininity: $t(281)$ = 3.37, p < .01

(high on masculinity, high on femininity); *feminine* (low on masculinity, high on femininity); *masculine* (high on masculinity, low on femininity); and *undifferentiated* (low on masculinity, low on femininity), were defined using the same medians as those employed in Russell, Antill, and Cunningham (1978). Compared with traditional families, significantly more mothers and fathers in the shared-caregiving group were androgynous, fewer mothers were feminine, and fewer fathers were masculine. Thus, findings for both the mean scores on each of the scales, and for the classification analysis, support the hypothesis outlined above. Furthermore, there were only *two* families in the shared-caregiving group for which there was the traditional pairing of a feminine-mother/masculine-father. Even so, 43% of fathers were *not* high on the femininity scale, and 40% of mothers were *not* high on the masculinity scale, suggesting that further analyses are required.

In an earlier study (Russell 1978) fathers low on femininity married to women high on masculinity were found to participate more in child care than low-femininity fathers married to women low on masculinity, suggesting that the pattern of scores *within* families is important. This relationship between mothers' masculinity and fathers' femininity might also be critical here. It

Table 15. Sex-role classifications

	Shared-caregiving		Traditional	
	Mothers	Fathers	Mothers	Fathers
Androgynous	44%	41%	23%	31%
Feminine	25%	16%	49%	12%
Masculine	16%	21%	9%	37%
Undifferentiated	15%	22%	18%	19%

may be, for example, that if a family has financial difficulties, a sufficient mediational condition for a change in lifestyle might be that *either* parent be a potential role-maker and be high on the opposite-sex sex-role scale. Table 16 shows the within-family relationship between mothers' masculinity scores and fathers' femininity scores (expressed as high and low in relation to the median). A chi-square test was carried out on these figures but did not reach significance. Nevertheless, in 82% of families either the mother was high on masculinity or the father was high on femininity or both were high on the opposite-sex scale. Only in 18% of the families were *neither* parent high on the opposite sex scale. These data obviously show a trend in the direction of there being a relationship between mothers' and fathers' scores, in agreement with the hypothesis; however, further research is needed to clarify the impact this relationship has on the decision to adopt a non-traditional child-care pattern.

Table 16. Family dyad classifications[1]

Mother's masculinity	Father's femininity	
	High	Low
High	42%	18%
Low	22%	18%

[1] $x^2_1 = 1.93$, $p < .10$

Sex-Role Differences within Shared-Caregiving Families

As was noted earlier, explanations given by parents for their changed lifestyles could be grouped according to whether the change was seen as being necessary or as being a matter of choice. Analyses were carried out to examine whether these two groups differed on their sex-role scores. It was predicted that those mothers and fathers who had chosen to change would score higher on the opposite-sex scale than those who had not chosen to change. Although not statistically significant, differences were evident, but not entirely in the predicted direction. Fathers who were caregivers by choice, as expected, scored higher on the femininity scale (4.93 vs. 4.50; t(31) = 1.66 p < .10). The trend for mothers, however, was in the opposite direction from that predicted; when the change was by choice, mothers scored *lower* on the masculinity scale (4.39 vs. 4.74;

$t(31) = 1.4$, $p < .20$). Despite being somewhat at variance with the predictions, these findings are consistent with findings noted earlier: that when the change was perceived as necessary, mothers were more involved in the decision, and when parents said they had chosen their lifestyle, fathers were more involved. Thus, it may be that the critical factor is whether or not the *person* had chosen to become involved in a radically different lifestyle. This possiblity was examined, and the data are presented in table 17. This table shows a breakdown of scores on *opposite-sex* sex-role scales as a function of the person seen as being most influential in the decision to change. As can be seen from the table, a father's femininity is highest when he is the most influential, and a mother's masculinity is highest when she is seen as the most influential. While one-way analyses of variances did not show these differences to be significant (both F values approximately equal to 1.5), a trend is evident which warrants further investigation.

Table 17. The relationship between sex-role scores and perceived influence over the decision to change lifestyles

	Person More Influential in Decision to Change		
	Mother	Father	Joint
Father's femininity	4.53	4.91	4.89
Mother's masculinity	4.77	4.55	4.30

Limitations of Sex-Role Findings and Explanations

Findings presented here are in apparent agreement with the initial hypothesis: mothers and fathers in shared-caregiving families scored higher than traditional parents on the opposite-sex scales of the Bem sex-role inventory; that is, fathers scored higher on femininity and mothers higher on masculinity, and shared-caregiving parents were more likely to be classified as androgynous. Despite this relatively strong support for the hypothesis that sex-role self-concepts mediate the change in family lifestyles, there are several problems with this rather simplistic interpretation.

First, a complex interaction was found between sex-role scores, reasons given for changing lifestyles, and the person seen as having most influence over the decision to change. It is unclear from the present analysis whether one of these variables should be given more status than another. A second, related problem concerns the effect that a shared-caregiving pattern might have on sex-role scores.

The hypothesis put forward at the outset was that sex-role variables are antecedents of the change in lifestyles; that masculinity in mothers and femininity in fathers are instrumental in the decision to change. An alternative hypothesis, of course, is that life experiences *influence* a person's endorsement of personality characteristics (Abrahams, Feldman, and Nash 1978). Differences found here in masculinity and femininity scores between family types, therefore, might simply reflect the different behaviours they perform on a day-to-day basis; that is, fathers are performing a more expressive role and mothers are performing a more instrumental role, and their sex-role self-concepts have changed as a consequence of this experience. Some doubt is cast on this hypothesis by the finding in the present study that the correlation between length of time in this lifestyle and father's femininity is − .20 − a relationship that is in the *opposite* direction from that which would be predicted from the life-experience hypothesis. It may be, however, that this type of analysis is too crude to provide an adequate test. Indeed, it is possible that changes in sex-role scores might be mediated by several factors: length of time of experience, degree of influence the person had in the decision to change, and the person's satisfaction with his or her new role. For example, a father who sees himself as being forced into the change in lifestyle and who is dissatisfied with the caregiving role might react in the opposite direction and overemphasize his "masculinity". Lack of adequate data prevented the exploration of this hypothesis here, but obviously it is one needing further investigation.

Perhaps further caution should be expressed about a simple sex-roles interpretation of a shared-caregiving lifestyle when the present findings are compared with those of Lamb et al. (1981) in Sweden, and DeFrain (1979) and Radin (1980) in the United States. Lamb et al., in their study of highly participant Swedish fathers, failed to find any relationship at all between sex-role scores and levels of participation. DeFrain, also in contrast to the present study, did not find any differences between the sex-role scores of his shared-role and "random" fathers. He did find, however, that shared-role mothers were significantly less feminine than a random sample of mothers. Even so, it is difficult to compare findings, as DeFrain used a sex-role difference score. It is uncertain, therefore, whether his mothers were less feminine because of a lower femininity score or, in agreement with the present study, because their masculinity scores were higher.

Radin, in contrast with both the present study and DeFrain's did not find any differences in mothers' sex-role scores between her three family types — mother prime (caretaker), inter-mediate, father prime. In agreement with the present study, however, she did find differences in fathers' femininity scores. Fathers in traditional families (mother-prime) were found by Radin to score significantly lower on the femininity scale than fathers in her intermediate group in which fathers performed 41% of child-care tasks. Fathers in her primary caregiving group, however, did not score higher on the femininity scale; their scores were very similar to those of fathers in traditional families. Such a pattern of findings is difficult to explain, although it may be that an explanation can be found in the way that Radin had defined her groups. Although her father-prime group was preforming relatively more of the child-care tasks, it may still be that in absolute terms they are doing less than the intermediate group. Moreover, as was pointed out earlier, more precise data from both Radin's and DeFrain's studies about the amount of time fathers spend on caregiving are needed before findings can be compared with any degree of certainty.

Conclusions

It seems there are many paths to the adoption of a family lifestyle in which fathers are caregivers and mothers are employed in the paid work force. Factors found to be important were: family financial situation; the employment potential of parents, but more especially of mothers; flexibility in hours of employment; family characteristics; fathers' prior experiences with their children and knowledge about child care; beliefs about the roles of parents; and the sex-role self-concepts of parents. A complex interaction was also found between sex roles, the reasons why a family changed lifestyle, as well as who the person was who was more influential in the decision to change.

No simple explanation emerged here, and perhaps a simple explanation is not possible given the diversity of the sample. It may be that in some families financial problems override all other factors; for others, financial problems might be a necessary precondition for change, but the change might be mediated by sex-role self-concepts and beliefs; and for still others, beliefs about parental roles might provide the necessary and sufficient conditions for change (even to the extent of being critical in the decision to have only one or two children). Furthermore, the evidence reported here suggests that these variables might combine in different ways *within* families.

If stretched, an economic argument might be used to explain all of the changes in lifestyles. All but ten of the families were better off financially *after* their change. It is difficult to decide, however, just how much emphasis should be placed on this economic gain. Although all two-parent families would realize a substantial gain if both parents were employed, there are, at least in Australia, few families with pre-school-aged children in which both parents are employed full-time continuously and even fewer still in which fathers have taken on a significant caregiving role. To what extent this is due to people not really having a choice because of the structure of society (e.g., rigidity of employment structure) or to personal characteristics of the people involved is difficult to untangle here. Although most of the families in this sample had some flexibility in employment, it was also the case that many had changed their jobs or work hours or modified their career aspirations to accommodate their non-traditional family lifestyle. Nevertheless, it seems obvious that greater availability of job flexibility would at least enable more people to exercise their choice. Whether or not those with job flexibility do choose to share child-care responsibilities, however, is a question that needs to be investigated.

The finding that these families have fewer children, and few had very young children, is consistent with previous studies which have found that families in which mothers are employed are smaller and have older children (Hoffman and Nye 1974). This finding, it was argued, is consistent with the hypotheses that alternative child-care arrangements are more likely to occur when child-care demands are lower and that they are more likely to occur when there is less conflict with cultural beliefs about child care and the needs of children. There is less likely to be a negative reaction to a father caring for one five-year-old than there would be if he were caring for a three-year-old and a baby of two weeks.

Whether or not specific personal characteristics mediate the change in lifestyles is a very open question, as the type of data collected here did not always permit a clear statement of cause and effect to be made. Many of the problems of interpretation, of course, would be solved if it were possible to obtain measures on critical variables *before* people have changed their lifestyles (cf. Lamb et al. 1981) and at various times *after* they have done so. Data of this type would be especially helpful in trying to sort out the importance of beliefs about parental roles and sex-role variables. It was these two variables in particular for which it was impossible to decide whether they were antecedents or consequences. Data collected at various times before and after the change would also help to interpret the complex interaction found here between sex-role variables and explanations parents gave for changing lifestyles, and the person seen as being more influential in the decision to change. Such data are especially needed to help take account of the dynamic nature of this particular lifestyle. Findings presented here indicate that several parents changed their views about shared-caregiving as a result of their experiences. Two particular aspects of the impact of the lifestyle were mentioned: mothers' satisfaction with their employment and fathers' satisfaction with their relationships with their children. Subsequent chapters examine in detail the question of the impact of this lifestyle on parents, children, and family relationships and on their relationships with and the support they obtain from significant others.

Before turning to the impact of the lifestyle, however, I want to discuss the question of paternal competence in the caregiving role. As was stated earlier, the accepted cultural view is that mothers are specially "tuned" to a child's needs and that it is better if mothers care for children, and, as such, a shared-caregiving lifestyle might be seen as a potential threat to the welfare and development of children. The next chapter examines the question of paternal competence and differences between males and females in their sensitivities to children. A later chapter examines the possible impact a shared-caregiving lifestyle might have on child development outcomes.

6

"Fathers are competent too!"

The traditional theoretical, professional, and cultural belief is that mothers are *more competent* at caring for children and therefore they *should* have the major responsibility for child care, especially for very young children. It is commonly assumed that fathers do not have the same capacity for nurturance and are not as sensitive as mothers are to the needs of children, the mother-infant relationship is both unique and necessary, and the father-infant relationship is not very important. Moreover, as was pointed out in the introductory chapter, the assumption is often made that this pattern of mothers caring for children is universal and has an immutable biological base. The development of the mother-child relationship and the sensitivity often attributed to mothers have also been seen as having important consequences for child development — especially a child's social and personality development. These views are well captured in a statement by John Bowlby (Tucker 1976): "Mothers are specially prepared biologically; if mothers don't look after babies, then babies are not going to prosper."

Although a "biological determinist" explanation of parental roles has widespread acceptance, there is surprisingly little research to support this view. Other possible explanations for role differentiation are (a) social expectations and socialization practices and (b) an interaction between biological dispositions, socialization, and experiences. Consider male nurturance, for example. The cultural stereotype of masculinity does not include nurturant, caregiving behaviour, and an integral part of male socialization in Western societies today is the expectation that males will fulfil an instrumental role in the work force rather than an expressive role. Forms of socialization range from: "He can't have dolls, I don't want him to grow up to be a homosexual" and "Don't cry Angus; be a man" to the view that males who take an active part in the home or in child care are either "under the thumb" or "on a promise" (for sexual intercourse). Little study has been made, however, of the extent to which socialization influences males' *display* of nurturant behaviour, and few people have even explored the extent of male nurturance or the biological potential males might have for caregiving. The argument to be put here is that fathers have the potential to be as capable as mothers at child care, in providing nurturance, and in reacting sensitively to children.

Although research on male nurturance is likely to throw additional light on explanations for the widespread gender differences in involvement in child care, it is unlikely to provide an answer to the more fundamental question of whether there *are* biological differences between males and females in their potential for parenting. Biology and culture are likely to interact in complex ways right from a child's birth onwards, making it impossible for us to isolate their relative contributions. Rubin, Provenzano, and Luria (1974) for example, found quite marked differences in parents' perceptions of their children according to the sex of the child, even in the first twenty-four hours after birth. Ethics of research also preclude us from designing studies to systematically vary environmental events.

It may very well be that males and females both have the necessary biological structures for parenting but that they need the *experience* of child care to either trigger or maintain this pattern of behaviour. Data presented in chapter 3 indicate quite clearly that it is women who are more likely to have had this experience. Additionally, parenting behaviour in mothers might be facilitated by biological changes associated with pregnancy and the birth, making it more likely they will respond appropriately when they have contact with their infants. For fathers, however, it might be experience alone that triggers their response. Nevertheless, it would still be highly plausible that males and females are equally competent even though women might have a biological system more disposed to the *initiation* of parenting behaviours.

One way of searching for explanations for current differences in parental roles is to investigate those situations in which modal patterns are not adopted, situations or behaviour patterns that appear to contradict notions about biological determinism. There is now a growing body of literature on such situations both in humans and in non-human primates. Before considering these recent findings, however, the question of parental competence will be considered for the sample of shared-caregiving families studied here.

Competence in Shared-Caregiving Families
— Tentative Statement

Competence is difficult to assess at the best of times, and certainly it is impossible to assess in any definite way using the methods employed in this study. Nevertheless, responses to the question on whether or not fathers have the ability to care for children (which were presented in the previous chapter) might give us some clue to how these parents perceived this issue.

It will be recalled that only 3% of mothers and 4% of fathers in shared-caregiving families said that father *did not* have the ability to care for children. This appears to be overwhelming evidence that both mothers and fathers who have had first-hand experience with fathers in this role perceived them as being competent and as performing the role satisfactorily. It is possible, of course, that there were high social demands for parents to respond positively to this question, perhaps because they did not want to be seen as having "problems". Even so, it is extremely unlikely that social desirability would explain the overwhelming nature of the response. Furthermore, answers given to other questions (see chapter 7) indicated that parents were more than willing to share their problems and doubts with interviewers.

Although both mothers and fathers agreed that fathers were competent, this did not necessarily mean that they also felt mothers and fathers performed the roles in the same way or that fathers always found child care easy. Indeed, although many parents stated that fathers were competent and gave every indication this was consistent with their experience, they also stated that mothers had a maternal instinct and that this made them *more sensitive* to children's needs and signals. As was shown in the last chapter, 44% of mothers and 57% of fathers in shared-caregiving families believed mothers had a maternal instinct. And, for most of these fathers, this implied the mother was the more sensitive of the two. Examples of fathers' remarks were:

"My wife usually gets up in the middle of the night if Jane cries. Women are more sensitive to a cry than men are. It's part of their biological make-up — it's part of a survival type response."

"I am convinced there is a maternal instinct. There is a relationship by nature between mother and child. There is a natural affection and regard between mother and child which a father can't compete with. A child *knows* who his mother is, but has to learn who his father is."

"Oh yes, there is a maternal instinct. For example, last Tuesday, I wanted Lindy to leave him alone when he was misbehaving and crying. But she wanted to go to him — it churns her up inside . . . she gets a gut feeling — it's something physical. When he cries, she wakes up; she hears him much easier than I do. He only has to give a little whimper and she will wake up. I let him go a lot more."

It was also true, however, that many parents believed mothers and fathers were equally sensitive to their children, and in some families the *father* was seen as being the *more sensitive person*. This latter type of response was more likely to be given by mothers (sixteen in total). Some examples were:

"I always thought women were supposed to be the more sensitive ones to children. You should see my husband since he has taken over. He always knows what the problem is."

"No, I don't think there is a maternal instinct. I think there is a parenting instinct. If anything, John is more in tune with the kids than I am."

"David's better with the children than I am; he has a lot more patience than me."

Although many parents still believed, therefore, that there were fundamental differences between mothers and fathers, this view was by no means universal, and some argued *fathers* were more sensitive. And even if parents believed mothers to be more sensitive, they did not feel that this necessarily implied that fathers could not be competent in the caregiving role. The overwhelming response here was that these shared-caregiving fathers were extremely competent, even if they did go through a period of adjustment and doubt (see chapter 7).

Nevertheless, the above conclusions are based on responses from self-report questions, and questions that only inquired about fathers' competences in an indirect way. Also, as has already been suggested, perhaps it is only the *very* sensitive and competent father who becomes involved in this type of family in the first place. Recent data from other studies suggest, however, that the findings from this group of families are by no means an isolated example of male nurturance or competence in child care. Much more variability in male nurturance and participation in child care is evident than was previously believed, and there are now a growing number of highly controlled and very specific studies of males' and females' responses to young children suggesting that gender differences are, at most, minimal. There are an equally impressive number of studies from non-human primates which add weight to this alternative view of male nurturance. Furthermore, there is now a body of research on mother-child and father-child attachments which question the view that there is a unique *biological* tie between mothers and their children. Each of these areas of research will now be considered in turn.

Variability in Male Nurturance

Does this study of Australian families represent an isolated example of highly nurturant males? Certainly not. Several recent studies clearly show that there is considerable variability within cultures; highly participant fathers have been reported, for example, in at least four other industrialized societies, as well as in non-industrialized societies. Furthermore, a major study of adult-child interactions in public places, conducted in ten different industrialized societies, found very few differences between males and females in their display of nurturance towards children. Finally, recent studies of non-human primates also indicate that a *non-nurturant* male is *not* universal throughout the animal kingdom either.

Within-Culture Variations in Paternal Participation in Child Care

As has already been discussed, there are now several current and recently completed studies, in four separate cultures, of families in which fathers are highly participant; Sweden (e.g., Lamb et al. 1981); Norway (Gronseth 1978); Israel (Sagi 1981); and the United States (e.g., Levine 1977; DeFrain 1979; Radin 1980). Each of these projects involves the study of families in which either mothers and fathers share in the care of their children or the father has the major responsibility (variously described as shared-role, androgynous, and reversed-role families). As was pointed out earlier, none of the studies provides detailed information on the exact nature of the distribution of child-care responsibilities; most report this information in relative terms. Despite the absence of these data, though, it can be concluded with confidence that the families studied do include fathers who are highly participant. So these types of families are occurring in sufficient numbers in several different cultures to warrant the attention of researchers.

Father-participation is probably the highest of all in Sweden, where fathers or mothers are able to take six months leave to care for their newborns. According to the most recent reports, about 10% of fathers are taking advantage of this leave for at least some time (the average in 1977 was 42 days). This figure, while not seeming high, is a vast increase from the early years of the programme when only 2% and 6% in the first and second years respectively took advantage of it. Such a finding is an important one, as it illustrates how a change in social policy and, presumably as a consequence, changes in social attitudes can have a significant albeit still small effect on levels of paternal participation. Findings from non-industrialized societies serve to reinforce this point even more.

Between-Culture Variations in Paternal Participation in Child Care

Anthropological studies of non-industralized societies, as was mentioned in the introductory chaper, show that marked divisions of labour are not universal throughout human societies. Two specific examples were mentioned earlier: the Arapesh, who believe that *both* males and females make and *have* babies, and that mothers and fathers should share in child care; and the Trobriand Island society, in which fathers also assume a major responsibility for child care.

West and Konner (1976) have presented a comprehensive review of cross-cultural findings, and they report a wide variation in father-child proximity and styles of fathering across cultures, with *gatherers* showing highest levels of father-proximity and nurturance. Recent data were also presented by these authors which suggested that fathers in one of the gatherer societies, the !Kung San (Bushmen), are more nurturant (defined by the amount of time fathers spent in close proximity to their children) than either American or British fathers.

One of the most comprehensive of the studies on male nurturance and involvement with children is that of W.C. Mackey (1979). He carried out a naturalistic observational study of adult-male-child interactions in ten cultural areas in industrialized socieites: Ireland, Spain, Mexico, the United States, India, Peru, the Ivory Coast, Morocco, Brazil, and Japan. All observations were conducted in public places that males and females had equal access to during daylight hours (e.g., shopping centres, parks). Data were analysed in terms of the extent of association between adults and children – tactile contact (whether they were touching), personal distance (how close they were), visual orientation (whether they were looking at one another). It is these latter measures, which are often associated with adult nurturance towards children, that are especially relevant for the present discussion.

While children were found to be more likely to be observed associating with a female-adult (even when men might be expected to be free to be available to their children, such as on weekends), differences between males and females on the indices of interaction were relatively minor. For example, in one comparison no differences were found between the sexes for tactile contact in seven cultures, and in the other three (Ireland, Ivory Coast, Brazil) men had the *higher* levels of interaction. This same pattern of findings indicating that in the majority of cultures studied there were no sex differences in interaction was also evident in the analyses for personal distance and visual orientation. Moreover, of the 60 comparisons made (3 different indices x 2 different situations x 10 cultures), in 44 there were no significant sex differences; in 7, adult-males were found to exhibit a higher level of interaction; and in 9 it was the adult-female who showed the higher level of interaction.

These findings therefore support the general argument being made here that men are just as capable as women are of nurturance. Nevertheless, by showing that there are few differences between males and females in their display of nurturant behaviour towards children in public places, Mackey's findings might be seen to be in conflict with a hypothesis that social pressures influence the *display* of nurturant behaviour by males. It might have been expected that fathers would be *less* likely to display nurturant behaviour in public places where, presumably, the pressures to conform to societal expectations would be fairly high. Alternatively it could be that it is so public that the men are not conscious of being observed and they behave "naturally". Or, it could be that the measures used by Mackey were too crude to detect differences between the sexes. Investigations using more refined measures of interaction and nurturance under more controlled conditions might reveal entirely different patterns. This possibility is not supported by the laboratory studies to be reported below, which are in basic agreement with Mackey's findings. Before considering these, however, I want to return again to the question of the supposed universality of the absence of nurturant behaviour in males, by briefly discussing recent findings from non-human primates.

Male Nurturance in Non-Human Primates

An often cited argument against having males involved in child care is that it is not natural, and that this naturalness is unquestionably supported by the fact that the division between the sexes for child care is universal throughout the animal kingdom. While it may be true that this division is the most common, we now know that there is considerable variation on this pattern. This variability ranges from male involvement in reproduction (e.g., in the native Australian animal the emu, it is the male, not the female, who sits on the egg for the eight-week incubation period), to male monkeys having the major responsibility for infant care. Indeed, the examples of male involvement in infant care are *too* numerous to be listed here. Attention will be focused rather on the non-human primates, for it is this group that has been studied more closely in recent years.

In one group of studies, W.K. Redican and his co-workers (see Redican 1976) found that when adult male rhesus monkeys were isolated with infant monkeys (not their own offspring), they were capable of "diligent parental care" similar to that displayed by mothers towards their infants. Adult males of this species, when observed in the wild, are normally indifferent, somewhat sensitive to approach and contact, occasionally aggressive, and rarely affiliative towards infants. The infant monkeys were also found to form strong attachments to their male caregivers and did not differ significantly from the mother-reared infants in terms of developmental indices.

These researchers have also noted several differences between male-infant and mother-infant interactions: in the style of interaction – males were more involved in rough-and-tumble play; and in attachment – infants became more attached to their male caregivers over the period of time they were together, whereas the normal pattern with mothers is the reverse. There were, however, two important differences between the male-reared and female-reared *situations* that might explain these differences. First, as has been pointed out by Leibowitz (1978), the females were the biological parents, possibly influencing attachment patterns; and second, the females were nursing the infants, which might affect the nature of parent-child interactions and reduce the possibility that mothers would engage in rough play with their infants.

The studies of Redican illustrate the potential that non-human primates have for behavioural flexibility and suggest that female *and* male rhesus monkeys have the biological capacity for nurturance and for caring for their young. It may be, therefore, that male and female rhesus monkeys have similar nervous systems, but that males need "enabling experience" to get them over the early contact problem which in the normal mother is handled by some mechanism triggered (hormonally?) at parturition. Such a possibility is supported by the findings from the rather more comprehensive studies of rats (see Lamb and Goldberg 1982 for a review). These studies show that (a) while hormones facilitate the emergence of "maternal" behaviour, the continual presence of a pup is necessary to maintain this behaviour; and (b) continuous exposure to pups is sufficient to elicit maternal behaviour in virgin females and adult males. Again, it seems the necessary neural mechanisms are present in both sexes.

Field studies of non-human primates add further weight to these laboratory studies of rhesus monkeys and rats. The most impressive aspect of these field studies, though, is not their showing that male nurturance is universal or even widespread, but in showing that there is considerable variability – that *male non-involvement is definitely not universal.* Male reactions to infants in non-human primates range from the hostility and aggression shown by the rhesus, to regular baby-sitting of young juveniles (e.g., in the Chacma baboon) to having a major responsibility for infant care (e.g., in some species of the New World monkeys). Indeed, Redican reports that in several species of New World monkeys (e.g., the marmosets) fathers have the *primary* responsibility for infant care, and infants spend most of their time with their fathers.

These findings therefore add further weight to the previously mentioned studies of highly participant human fathers to illustrate even further the capacity for nurturance and child care in males and, more generally, the wide extent of behavioural flexibility throughout the animal kingdom. It appears that males do possess the biological propensity to engage in this type of behaviour, but that the emergence of the behaviour is dependent upon environmental conditions, especially exposure to infants.

Laboratory Studies of Human Male Nurturance and Responsiveness to Young Children

There has been a spate of highly controlled laboratory studies concerned with examining whether or not there are gender differences in reactions to and behaviour towards young babies. Some of these studies bear on the question of gender differences in the display of nurturance and some on sex differences in responsiveness to babies and their signals (e.g., baby cries). A consistent pattern has begun to emerge from these studies in showing that the differences between human males and females are much smaller than we might expect.

R.D. Parke and his co-workers (see Parke 1979) have carried out the most extensive study of fathers' nurturant behaviour and sensitivity to infant cues. They observed both mothers and fathers, from a range of social classes interacting with their newborn babies in hospital for ten-minute intervals, at periods of between six and forty-eight hours after birth. Fathers were found to be just as involved with and as nurturant towards their infants (e.g., touching, looking at, kissing, talking to) as mothers were. Also, fathers were just as sensitive as mothers were to infant feeding cues (sucking, burping, coughing), and just as successful at feeding — as measured by the amount of milk consumed. Neither were fathers dependent on the support of mothers for their display of nurturance or their competence in caregiving; they were as nurturant when observed alone as they were when they were observed with the mother present. Similar findings have been reported when fathers have been observed in their homes when the baby was three months old, suggesting that the hospital findings were not simply a function of the demands associated with the cultural expectations of "new" fathers (e.g., that they show a degree of pride). Nevertheless, there were still some differences between mothers and fathers. Mothers tended to smile more to their infants and respond to infant vocalizations with tactile stimulation, whereas fathers tended to vocalize back, indicating that perhaps some aspect of their styles of parenting differ, while still being equally competent and equally sensitive to infant cues.

Thus, it seems, as others also have suggested (e.g., Lamb and Goldberg 1982), sensitivity to newborns does not appear to depend entirely on hormonal changes associated with pregnancy and the birth. An additional point that could be made is that far from there being a general sensitivity-type response (i.e., a fixed pattern of behaviour associated with a maternal instinct) parents have been found to vary markedly in the ways they react to their infants. Most of this work has been with mothers (e.g., Ainsworth et al. 1978). Ainsworth and her co-workers have defined three groups of mothers on the basis of their sensitivity to infants: (1) those who were unempathic and emotionally unexpressive, (2) those who delayed their responses or ignored infant cues, and (3) those who were warm and sensitive. The finding of such a range of maternal responsiveness adds weight to the view that there is not simply a universal biological response to children. It is difficult to say, however, exactly what this variability is dependent upon. It could be the result of individual differences in nervous systems, levels of hormones, child characteristics, or personality and social factors, or a complex interaction between any or all of these factors.

Additional support for an argument that mother-father differences in participation in child care are not based on differences in competence and sensitivity comes from studies that have investigated the physiological and psychological responses of males and females to babies and to their cries and smiles. The view that women are more sensitive than men are to infant signals such as crying has widespread popular support, a view that was encountered often in my interviews with traditional families. Many fathers attributed mothers' greater responsiveness to infant cries to their specially tuned hearing or their innate *biological* reaction to this signal. Available data do not support this view, however.

Physiological Studies

In a series of studies, Frodi, Lamb, and others have investigated sex differences in parents' and eight- and fourteen-year old childrens' *physiological* responses to infants' cries and smiles (Frodi and Lamb 1978; Frodi, Lamb, Leavitt and Donovan 1978; Frodi, Lamb, Leavitt, Donovan, Neff, and Sherry 1978). It should be emphasized here that these investigators were using what might be considered to be more basic or biological indices of responsiveness – changes in skin conductance, heart rate, and systolic and diastolic blood pressure. While they found, like others have, that infant cries produce an increase in physiological indices of arousal, and that cries are reported by listeners to be aversive and irritating, no sex differences were found for any of the physiological indices employed (a finding also supported by Murray 1978). Neither were there any sex differences in responses to infant smiles. Moreover, in a recent comprehensive review of studies of sex differences in responsiveness to infants, Berman (1980) cites eight studies in which physiological reactions to unfamiliar babies were employed, and only one reported that females were more responsive than males. This latter study was a pilot study using pupil dilation, an index which is of doubtful validity in this context. One study cited, however, did report that mothers' changes in heart rate were greater than fathers' in response to the cries of their *own* babies. These were parents from traditional families, and therefore differences in caregiving responsibilities and experience with the baby would most likely explain this difference, as no differences were found in responses to an *unfamiliar* baby. Clearly, what is needed now is a study of fathers who are also highly participant in child care.

Behavioural Studies

Sex differences in responsiveness to babies, however, have been noted more consistently in studies that have employed *behavioural* and *self-report* measures of responsiveness. Frodi and Lamb (1978), for example, reported that their eight- and fourteen-year-old children, while not showing any sex differences on physiological measures, did show sex differences on *behavioural* measures. This finding of sex differences in responsiveness at the behavioural level with eight- and fourteen-year-olds is consistent with other findings showing that sex differences emerge at various stages of the life cycle. In a series of highly controlled laboratory studies, Feldman and Nash (Feldman and Nash 1978, 1979; Nash and Feldman 1980) have found that sex differences in responsiveness to babies (as indicated by such measures as touching or approaching a baby, looking at and smiling, and ignoring) are most marked in samples of teenagers and in couples with a new baby; in both groups, females were found to be more responsive. These researchers argue that the differences they have found across the lifespan are a function of the different socialization pressures exerted on groups of people according to their life situations. Parents with a newborn and teenagers, they argue, are under more pressure to conform to traditional roles. Another finding from this series of studies is that hormonal changes did not seem to affect responsiveness either; pregnant women were no more responsive than single women or married but childless women. It was mothers with infants who, overall, were the most responsive.

Berman (1980) in her review of twenty-seven studies using *behavioural* indices of responsiveness reports that only three studies offer unequivocal support for the sex differences hypothesis. Her conclusion to the review of behavioural studies which included both laboratory and naturalistic observational studies in several different cultures was:

> Mothers, sisters, high school girls left alone with a baby, and even 4½ year old pre-school girls who were assigned to an infant caretaking role were all more responsive to their young relative or charge than were their male counterparts. Sex differences in behaviour towards the young may thus depend on an assigned or assumed role relationship with respect to an infant, with females more willingly or knowledgeably interacting with the young in the role. [Berman 1980, p. 682]

Self-Report Studies

Although Berman (1980) concluded that fourteen out of twenty-nine *self-report* studies of responsiveness (i.e., people rating their own reactions to babies) generally support the sex differences hypothesis, these responses are probably even more open to the influence of social expectations. The studies by Berman and her co-workers (Berman et al. 1975; Berman 1976) demonstrate that the situation a person is in and the pressures of socialization can easily influence the report of nurturant behaviour. In one study, males and females rated the attractiveness of human babies (from pictures) under four conditions: (1) in private; (2) publicly in an all-male group; (3) publicly in an all-female group; and (4) publicly in a mixed-sex group. Males rated the baby more attractive when they did it in private than when they did it in an all-male group, and females rated the baby as less attractive when they did the task in private than when they did it in an all-female group. Also, sex differences were found to be smaller when the ratings were carried out in the mixed-sex group than when they were done in the same-sex groups. Thus, it seems the demands of the situation have an important bearing on the report of nurturant behaviour.

These laboratory studies of the reactions of human males and females, therefore, again support the argument that both males and females have the capacity to respond sensitively to infants and, by inference, to be competent at child care. Lack of experience with infants and social expectations are likely to play a major role in supporting the current pattern of fathers' not being very involved in child care.

Most of the research considered up to this point has been concerned with adults' responsiveness to their young, and little has been said about the relationship that develops between adults and infants. Yet this relationship has also been argued by many to have a biological base. It is this aspect of parenting that is discussed next.

Parent-Child Attachments

One of the most strongly held beliefs about child development is that the mother-infant relationship is both unique and necessary, and that infants are attached exclusively to their mothers; that is, for children the most salient and most important person is their mother. It is often assumed that this "unique" relationship between mother and child is a biological response, is fundamental to the survival of a species, and is associated with mothers' special sensitivity to their infants. Furthermore, this mother-infant attachment bond has been seen to be necessary for both the short-term (e.g., emotional and social development) and long-term (e.g., ability to form deep relationships) development. The majority of attachment studies, however, have been on either lower animals or human mothers and their infants (e.g., Ainsworth and Bell 1970). While it cannot be disputed that these studies show that infants are attached to their mothers, they do *not* show that infants are attached exclusively to their mothers, *nor* that mother-infant attachment is unique or necessary, *nor* that they are not attached to their fathers or other caregiving adults.

Recent comprehensive studies of father-infant attachment have been carried out by M.E. Lamb (see Lamb 1976, 1978b; for a summary see Lamb 1981), and Kotelchuck and his co-workers (see Kotelchuck 1976). Studies have been conducted in highly controlled laboratory conditions and in the more naturalistic home setting. They are all consistent in showing that children from around six months of age display attachment behaviours to their fathers in much the same way as they display them to their mothers.

Kotelchuck (1976) observed the reactions of 6-, 9-, 12-, 18-, and 21-month-olds to brief separations from their mothers, their fathers and strangers in a laboratory situation. He found that infants from twelve months of age protested against the departure of both mothers and fathers, and he therefore concluded that they were *attached* to both parents. In addition, although the majority of infants displayed a preference for mothers (55% of infants displayed a stronger reaction to mothers leaving, whereas this was case with only 25% when fathers left), few infants protested when one parent left *while* the other parent was still present.

Kotelchuck also examined the relationship between parental home caretaking behaviour and attachment. He found a significant positive correlation between proximity to fathers in the laboratory and the extent of fathers' home caretaking. Furthermore, when fathers were active caretakers, the age span of intense separation protest was shortened and their children found the experiment an enjoyable play session and were not distressed when left alone with strangers. The extent of responsibility taken for child care, therefore, appears to influence this attachment response.

It is Lamb (1981) who has conducted the most comprehensive investigation of father-infant attachments. Lamb's work points to some important variations in the display of attachment behaviour as a function of (a) the age and sex of the child and (b) the situation within which attachment is observed. Home observations (in an essentially naturalistic observational setting) of family interaction with 7-, 8-, 12-, and 13-month-olds revealed that infants did not show a preference for either parent in their display of attachment behaviour (here measured by proximity, approach, touch, cry to, and asking to be picked up). Furthermore, laboratory studies of separation protest and greeting did not reveal any differences in mother-infant and father-infant attachments. Two additional findings, however, indicate that the picture is not as simple as it might first appear.

First, in studies of 15-, 18-, 21-, and 24-month-olds, Lamb found that boys displayed a preference for their fathers; however, girls did not appear to differentiate between mothers and fathers. Second, when they were distressed by the presence of a stranger, 12- and 18-month-olds were found to prefer their mothers, indicating that perhaps the mother is the primary attachment figure to whom infants especially turn when they are faced with a stressful situation and need security and reassurance.

This preference for mothers under stressful conditions, however, was not found in studies of 8- and 24-month-olds, suggesting that it is a response that is characteristic of a particular age group. Furthermore, when parents were observed separately with their infants under the same stressful conditions, infants were found to organize their attachment behaviours around fathers, and this attachment behaviour was not found to be qualitatively different from that displayed towards mothers. These findings show, therefore, there are many more similarities than differences between infants' attachment to their mothers and fathers. Although the research has not yet been done, it seems highly likely that the differences that have been observed with regard to children turning preferentially to their mothers under conditions of stress are most likely attributable to the differences between parents in their day-to-day interactions (mothers of course are much more likely to be the primary caregivers).

The studies reviewed here, therefore, show that infants develop strong relationships with *both* mothers and fathers, and that both parents are salient figures to their infants.

The emphasis up to this point has been on the behaviour of infants. However, there is, of course, another important dimension of this relationship – the *parents'* attachment to their infant (or child). Although this is perhaps the least investigated aspect of parent-child relationships, it has been subjected to the same kind of theoretical straitjacket as the study of infants' attachments to parents has. Again, the development of the attachment – or bond, as it has been termed – has been seen to be a biological response, critical for species survival, unique to the mother, and important for the long-term development of the child (Klaus and Kennell 1976). It has also been argued that there is a sensitive period in the first few hours after birth during which mother-infant contact is critical for the development of the bond. Again, however, there has been an imbalance of studies, with most studies investigating mothers' responses.

Despite the inadequacy of research into the topic, mother-infant bonding has quickly become part of the accepted cultural view of parenting and the birth process; it is a rare medical professional or medical student, mother or expectant mother, who is not familiar with the *view* that early contact between a mother and her child is "necessary" for the mother to establish a bond with her child and that the formation of this bond is critical for future relationships and the development of the child. Indeed, it is surprising just how quickly this view has permeated Western cultures, especially given the paucity of evidence to back it up.

Recent evidence casts serious doubts on most of the major tenents of the mother-infant bonding theory as put forward by Klaus and Kennell. Reviews of this evidence (e.g., Lamb and Goldberg 1982) conclude that if bonding does occur it is not simply a biological process associated with mothers but is contributed to much more by social and emotional factors associated with the birth. Weight is given to this conclusion by the following findings. Rodholm and Larsson (1979) observed both mothers and fathers interacting with the newborns for the first time and found they display similar patterns of greeting behaviour. Previous studies of mothers had concluded that the characteristic patterns observed were species-specific *maternal* behaviours elicited by hormonal changes associated with the birth. In addition, several recent studies have failed to replicate previous reports of the effects of early contact between mother and child. In particular, two highly controlled studies have now been reported which have failed to find any differences in mother-infant relationships either thirty-six hours after delivery (Svejda, Campos and Emde 1980) or six weeks after delivery (Carlsson et al. 1979) between mothers who have and who have not had early contact with their infants. As yet there is no reported study that has compared mothers and fathers, or fathers who have and have not had early contact with their infants. Indeed, we know very little about fathers' (or mothers' for that matter) feelings about their children and the way in which they develop attachments to them, or about the effects these attachments might have on fathers over the life span. This issue is returned to again in the next chapter.

Conclusions

The evidence considered here does not lend strong support to the hypothesis of there being significant biologically based gender differences in either responsiveness and sensitivity towards babies and young children or competence in child care. Overall, the evidence favours the argument that responsiveness to infants is a characteristic of the *species* rather than a characteristic of females alone, and that when differences do occur between the sexes they are more likely attributable to a complex interaction between biological factors and differences in experience, social expectations, and socialization. A consistent trend has been noted indicating that it is mothers with young infants who are more likely to be responsive, but more particularly to their own infants. The fact that this enhanced sensitivity does not generalize to other children suggests that experience with the infant is crucial and that fathers who are the primary caregivers might also display this enhanced sensitivity.

Although findings show that mothers and fathers are equally competent and that infants develop strong relationships with *both* mothers and fathers, and therefore both parents are salient figures to their infants, this should not be taken to mean that parents have the same experiences with, and the same influences over, their children. For one thing, as was shown in chapter 3, the day-to-day experiences children have with their parents are very different – mothers are much more likely to engage in caregiving and fathers in play. Moreover, mothers and fathers were found to engage in different types of play. It should not be expected, therefore, that mothers and fathers are essentially redundant in their influences. The differences are far too marked to expect such an outcome. There is still much research to be done in this area, particularly to examine differences in parent-child relationships as a function of different types of family structures. To date, most of the research has been with traditional families, and studies of non-traditional families might reveal an entirely different pattern. This issue is discussed in more detail in chapter 9.

While a finding that fathers have the potential to be competent at child care provides strong evidence to refute the widely accepted belief that mothers *should* care for their children, it does not necessarily imply that all fathers *will* be competent, or that they will find child care easy, or that they will happily adopt this role. Indeed, the evidence to be considered in the following chapters reveals that many of the shared-caregiving fathers experienced considerable difficulty in adjusting to the child-care role, and some did not feel at all comfortable or happy about it.

7

Benefits and Costs of Shared Child Care for Parents

Whenever there is talk about possible changes in family patterns, one of the first questions asked is: "What about the children, what effect will it have on them?" At least this has been my experience whenever I have spoken to parent, community, or academic groups about fathers who have the major responsibility for the day-to-day care of their children. In contrast, an issue which has consistently emerged very low down the list of discussion points is the impact this family pattern might have on fathers themselves. Yet this was an issue that was foremost in the minds of a majority of shared-caregiving parents. A significant number of both fathers and mothers agreed that it was *fathers* who had most to gain from taking on the child-care job. Throughout the interviews, fathers constantly marvelled at and welcomed the changes that had taken place in their relationships with their children; very few had realized just how much of an impact that would have on them. Contrary to the ideas of others, it may very well be that in evaluating alternative family forms, parents will place more importance on the actual or perceived effects on *themselves* (e.g., on their feelings of well-being, or on an improved marital relationship) or on the family unit (e.g., on financial security), rather than on the *possible* effects on children. The aim of this chapter is to investigate the impact that a shared-caregiving lifestyle has on mothers and fathers and also *parents'* evaluations of the benefits and costs.

A shared-caregiving lifestyle of the type described here was associated with significant changes in commitments to both child care and paid employment, for *both* fathers and mothers. Fathers increased their participation in child care and decreased their participation in paid employment, whereas for mothers the reverse was the case. Given the significantly different nature of this lifestyle in the context of (a) family patterns (e.g., an adult male and an adult female are both actively involved in the day-to-day care of children instead of just an adult female), (b) parental roles (e.g., the mother is employed in the paid work force whereas most mothers are at home), and (c) gender roles (e.g., child care is not part of the culturally sanctioned concept of masculinity), the impact of this family pattern on parents is likely to be significant indeed.

Few studies have investigated the effects that alternative family patterns have on parents themselves. One of the more comprehensive of these was that by Rapoport and Rapoport (1976) on dual-career families. Of the costs and benefits these authors identified, several are likely to be relevant here: (1) work overload – this was especially a problem for the women who were employed full-time and still carried out most of the child-care and household tasks when at home; (2) normative dilemmas – stress resulting from the parents' behaviour and personal norms conflicting with social norms (e.g., criticisms from significant others); (3) identity dilemmas – these were dilemmas associated with personal identity (e.g., a mother's doubt about her identity as a female because of her pursuit of a career instead of investing all of her time in child rearing); (4) social network dilemmas – the problems families had in maintaining social contact with friends and relatives, arising mainly because they had less time available for these types of interactions; (5) self-fulfilment – the satisfaction derived from mastering the problems associated with the non-traditional lifestyle; (6) mother's self-realization – satisfaction the mother derived from success in her career; (7) financial gains – the extra income resulting from having two parents employed meant that they enjoyed a more comfortable lifestyle.

A few authors have also discussed the particular problems likely to be experienced by *men* when they become more family-oriented and less work-oriented. Pleck (1979), for example, discusses the possibility that increased family roles will have both positive and negative outcomes for fathers (e.g., there will be conflicts between family and work, and between their behaviour and the attitudes and expectations of peers). Another author, Berger (1979), argues that "individuals in transition experience both institutional constraints on their ability to change, and internal doubts about the rightness of their changing" (p. 639). Institutional constraints for men becoming more family-oriented, he suggests, will include employers' traditional work values and hostility from colleagues. He argues further that problems will arise because of personal doubts and fears (e.g., about their identities as males), and from men being "exposed to new parts of themselves" (e.g., becoming more expressive and vulnerable). Additionally, Berger suggests that men attempting to adopt new roles will need considerable support from significant others, but will be unlikely to receive it from either relatives or friends (e.g., because parents will perceive it as a sign of failure on their part).

The present analysis of the effects of shared-caregiving lifestyles on fathers and mothers is based primarily on responses given to the following questions (asked independently of both parents):

"Have you experienced any problems or difficulties with changing roles?" (asked as a general question and then asked specifically for self, spouse, and children).

"What do you feel have been the major advantages of changing roles?" (again asked specifically for self, spouse, and children).

"How have other people reacted to your changed roles?" (asked as a general question, and then specifically for the reactions of relatives, close friends, neighbours, and workmates).

"Overall, what do you really enjoy or like about your current family organization?"

"What are the things that you really dislike about it?"

An inspection of responses to these questions revealed several major themes, and the chapter is organized around these themes: (1) changes in parent-child relationships (both positive and negative), (2) perceived effects on parents' personal development (e.g., on their self-image, personal satisfaction, career advancement), and (3) the reactions of significant others and the degree of support obtained from them. The final section of the chapter presents an overview of parents' evaluations of a shared-caregiving lifestyle.

Changes in Parent-Child Relationships

In responding to the questions asked them, 63% of fathers and 69% of mothers mentioned a better father-child relationship as a major advantage of a shared-caregiving lifestyle. On the other hand, guilt about leaving the children was mentioned by 23% of mothers as a major difficulty, and a loss of contact between mother and child was mentioned by 33% of mothers as something they really disliked. Although these were the most frequently occurring responses, the changes in parent-child relationships were not as straightforward as this. As the following analysis shows, both positive and negative consequences were evident for both parents.

Fathers and Their Children: A New Experience?

It was pointed out in chapter 6 that there are two sides to parent-child relationships. One of these, which as been studied very little, is the attachment of the *parent* to the child — the feelings of closeness and affection a parent has for a child. Furthermore, more has been written about the mothers' feelings about their children than about fathers' feelings.

One of the few studies of the early development of fathers' relationships with their children was that by Greenberg and Morris (1974). They interviewed fathers about their reactions to their babies within the first three days after birth. Fathers reported they became totally engrossed in the birth and in their babies, had feelings of exhilaration, closeness, and attachment — all feelings that could be interpreted as indicating fathers had developed a bond with their children. These fathers also reported that their early experiences enhanced their self-esteem and that they were surprised by the positive manner in which they had reacted. Beyond this, however, very little is known about the feelings fathers have either for their infants or for their older children.

Findings from the present study of highly participant fathers confirm those of Greenberg and Morris. Fathers studied here, almost without exception, spoke enthusiastically about how their child-care experiences had changed the nature of their relationships with their children. Although there were many facets to this change, the change that was reported most often, and certainly with by far the most enthusiasm, was a change that brought the fathers and children *closer*.

A New Bond?

When asked whether and in what ways the father-child relationship had changed, 62% of fathers stated it had become much closer or that it had improved. Examples of expressions of these feelings included:

"Being with them all the time has helped me cement my relationship with them. Our children now have two people they are close to, too."

"Our relationship has become much closer . . . He shows a lot more affection towards me, and I understand him more."

"I became a lot more involved, I understand her a lot better, and I get on a lot better with her."

"Our relationship has grown so much — there is a stronger bond — we have grown closer."

This new closeness, most fathers reported, gave them immense personal satisfaction and added a new and highly valued dimension to their lives. The following are four examples of fathers' responses:

"I think it increased the amount of pleasure I get from them."

"I'm extremely fortunate in having the contact with my children. I enjoy it. I'm not shy about 'kidding up' to a young baby. I don't have any trouble relating to them."

"We have a better relationship now because they see more of me — this is to our mutual enjoyment."

"I thought I had a good relationship before. I could never have anticipated how much it would change and how much satisfaction I would get from them. I really feel fulfilled in a way I could never have imagined I would."

A positive change in the father-child relationship was not something just noted by fathers. It was reported by 67% of mothers, too (remember that these responses from mothers and fathers were given separately). For example:

"The relationship is closer. They see him as he is — not as a father-figure."

"He is much closer to them than he was before. But he was always as kind and patient with them as he is now."

An improvement in father-child relationships, however, was also a source of conflict and concern for some mothers. Before adopting a shared-caregiving lifestyle, most had been in a traditional family situation, in which mothers presumably had more contact and perhaps greater status as parents (i.e., children were more likely to go to them when they needed something or were hurt, etc.). Thus, fathers being closer to the children would, under many circumstances, have been accompanied by a noticeable shift in mothers' relationships too. The closer father-child relationship was therefore seen as a threat by some mothers. Perhaps this is not without reason when it is considered that it is usually expected that mothers will be closer to their children and that they will be the *primary* parent. This view was well captured in the statement of one mother when she was talking about difficulties she experienced. "I'm carrying too much responsibility," she said. "I'm very tired, very cranky. I have no time to relax. I'm always wound up and busy. I feel guilty about not spending time with the children as soon as I get home. I feel I should spend more time with them. Also, I often feel left out because the children now go to daddy."

Further support for the finding that the *affective* nature of the father-child relationship changes as a consequence of fathers' increased participation comes from responses given to two other questions, both of which were asked *before* the above question. The first, which has already been mentioned, asked parents what they thought were the *major advantages* of their lifestyles. In no way could this be seen as a question loaded in favour of an emphasis on parent-child relationships. Yet, the majority of both mothers (69%) and fathers (64%) agreed that for fathers, the major advantage was the improvement in his relationships with his children. (The next two most common responses were financial gains [39%] and the sharing of child-care tasks [39%]). So even in this very open question the *change in father-child relationships* dominated responses. Given the nature of this response, it appears obvious that both mothers and fathers see the change as a highly significant one.

The other question was one that was asked of both shared-caregiving and traditional parents. This was: "What do you enjoy about being a parent?" Shared-caregiving fathers were more likely than traditional fathers to say they enjoyed the love and affection they shared with their children (33% vs. 14%), the stimulation and fun they experienced (26% vs. 18%), and the satisfaction they derived from watching their children grow and develop (38% vs. 26%). Fathers, therefore, appear to derive considerable satisfaction from the enhanced *expressive* nature of their relationships.

Responses from both mothers and fathers to these three very different questions are consistent in indicating that the father-child relationship had become much closer, that this change was valued by both parents, and that fathers derived considerable satisfaction from the stronger relationships they had. Contrary to the stereotypes of fathers (see chapter 3), when they become involved, fathers appear to enjoy their close physical and affectional relationships.

A question that arises now is: Why does the relationship change? Is it simply a matter of spending more time with children, or is it related more directly to fathers' carrying out specific child-care tasks, to their playing more, or to their having increased responsibilities? Although all of these changes in participation are likely to be important, it was the latter change in responsibility that many fathers and mothers attributed more directly to the change in relationships. Many caregiving fathers reported their relationship changed not simply because of the increased amount of time they spent with their children but because of the *way* in which the time was spent: alone with their children, having the sole responsibility for them. For example: "We are much closer — because I have the total responsibility." To be the person who had the sole responsibility to be the special person who was around at the critical, sensitive times appeared to contribute significantly to the change in their relationship.

Three other recent studies offer support for the present finding of increased participation having a positive effect on the father-child relationship. In an investigation of Australian families in which mothers had returned to study, fathers were found to increase their levels of participation, and, as a consequence, 52% of fathers and 60% of mothers reported the father-child relationship had improved (Kelley 1981). A study of Norwegian shared-role families (shared for both work and child care), also reported that as a consequence of fathers having more time and experience with their children, they had better and more open contact with them (Gronseth 1978). Finally, in an in depth American study of the impact of work scheduling, high participation was reported to be associated with a father's feeling closer to his children (Hood and Golden 1979). These other studies, like the present one too, however, also found other changes in father-child relationships which were not always seen as positive.

Increased Tension and Conflict

In most families it is mothers who have the major responsibility for child care, and therefore it is they who have to deal constantly with the day-to-day problems of bringing up children. Having this type of constant responsibility for children is likely to have consequences for parent-child relationships and for parents' evaluations of their roles and their perceptions of themselves. This is well illustrated by responses from traditional families. When parents were asked how they could change their current behaviour to improve their relationships with their children, 40% of mothers, but only 9% of fathers, said they could be more tolerant or patient with their children; in contrast, the majority of father (50%) felt they could improve their relationships by spending more time with their children. It is mothers, therefore, who appear to be more affected by the pressures of the day-to-day problems and conflicts of children-rearing, and it is *their* perception that their reactions to these problems has an effect on parent-child relationships.

It is not unreasonable to expect, therefore, that if fathers also had to deal constantly with day-to-day child-rearing problems, they would experience the same kinds of reactions as mothers in traditional families. Present findings support this hypothesis: 18% of shared-caregiving fathers (compared with 9% of traditional fathers) reported that their relationships with their children could improve if they were more patient or tolerant. Despite the higher levels of conflict reported, many parents (but more particularly mothers) also considered this as extremely positive. The view was expressed that there was a better balance between mother- and father-child relationships; 31% of mothers reported this. They felt that this had occurred because fathers were now much more involved in the day-to-day problems of child care, rather than simply being the "fun person" who played with the children after a "hard day at work". They rated the father-child relationship as being much more realistic than it was before. Children were now more likely to see another side of their fathers: the irritated, impatient, cranky, nagging side that can come from spending long periods of time alone with children in an isolated urban environment.

Many fathers (24%) were also sensitive to this change in their relationships, and several spoke at length about both the "new closeness" and the adjustment they had to make to the constant hassles and their displays of intolerance and impatience. As one father said, "I used to think of myself as cool, calm and collected – always with plenty of patience. Looking after children all day soon changed that." Some fathers feared that as a result their children might change their images of them. For example, one father said: "It has increased both the amount of pleasure and the amount of pain that I get from my children. I always seem to be nagging them to do something – this was something I never did before. They give you so many day-to-day problems – fighting, falling over and so on . . . I really enjoy the break from them now."

Additionally, several fathers had to adjust to a new self-image, but most thought this had a positive component too – they now felt they had a better understanding of themselves. In the final analysis, *all* concluded that their relationships with their children were now more realistic and not as superficial as before; that is, they were now based on a greater depth of understanding from both sides and, in their words, were "better" or "more healthy".

Mother–Child Relationships

In response to the questions listed earlier 67% of mothers and 59% of fathers reported that the mother-child relationship had not changed in any significant way at all. The next most common response was that mothers were more tolerant towards their children (mentioned by 14% of mothers and 17% of fathers). Parents felt that this resulted because mothers were spending less time with their children and did not have to deal as much with the constant demands of child rearing. As one mother said, "I don't see them as much, but I am more tolerant now and my relationships have improved."

Although responses to the question about whether and in what ways the mother-child relationship had changed indicated the different child-care pattern had had little effect, reponses to other questions suggested that the reduction in contact *was* a concern for many mothers. For example, 13% of mothers and 17% of fathers said the mother-child relationship was more distant, and 33% of mothers said that the thing they disliked most about their lifestyle was the reduction in contact. Furthermore, 23% of mothers and 18% of fathers reported that one of the major problems encountered by mothers was having to cope with the guilt they felt about leaving their children. (Maybe some would think the percentage who reported feeling guilty is surprisingly low, especially given the general cultural reaction to women being employed and leaving their children. One possible explanation for this is that it was fathers who cared for the children; perhaps a higher level of guilt might be found when children are being cared for in institutions or by other people.)

Although most mothers did not perceive their relationships to have suffered to any significant degree, some nevertheless were concerned about *missing out*, and about leaving their children to go to work. This mixture of reactions was expressed in this way by one mother: "He doesn't think I don't love him. The only thing that's suffered is me. I can't wait to get back to him – I can't wait to get back to him full-time. At first it worried me that he would reject me. Not now though; he talks to me about everything he does."

Parents' Personal Development

The traditional view about human development is that the early years are critical and that patterns of behaviour and personalities are set from this period onwards – or at least, they are extremely difficult to change – and that what happens after this period is of little consequence. There is now a growing literature, however, on developmental changes throughout the life span (from birth to death) recognizing that adults too have the potential to change, and to be influenced by their *adult* experiences. Experiences that are likely to influence adult development have been termed *significant life events*; these are, for example, the death of a spouse, the birth of a child, or starting a new job. The salient feature of these events is that they involve a major change in a person's life situation and in relationships with significant others. A father taking on the major or equal responsibility for child care is a good example of such an event. For most of these families this was radically different both from their previous lifestyle and from the modal family pattern. It was thus a significant event for the individuals involved and for others with whom they came into contact. A common response from fathers was that they had changed within themselves, and that their values and attitudes towards family issues had changed too. Many changes were associated with problems experienced in *adjusting* to the child-care role and with their success in resolving these problems. For mothers, the major issues of change revolved around their paid work and the conflict between family and work. Relationships with significant others outside the immediate family also contributed to parents' feelings about the impact of their changed family patterns.

Fathers Adjusting to the Caregiving Role

Few fathers were able to anticipate the difficulties they encountered staying at home caring for their children. Many looked upon the prospect of changing roles with *enthusiasm*, thinking it would give them time to do things they had always wanted to do – read, renovate the house, landscape the garden, or simply relax. It was a rare father, however, who actually achieved all he hoped he would. It was more commonly the case that expectations were completely revised because of the demanding nature of child care, especially in the first few months. When asked what they found difficult about their family pattern, 45% of fathers reported that it was the demands – the constancy, the physical work, and the boredom – associated with child care and housework (58% of mothers also mentioned this as a major problem for fathers). Another 17% of fathers (and 10% of mothers) added that they had difficulty in adjusting to the absence of adult company for long periods during the day.

Some of the comments fathers made were:

"I got exasperated by the mess and the mischief. At the end of the day I was frazzled. I looked forward to her coming home."

"When I first stayed home I found it hard . . . All the nappy changing and just the constancy of it."

"I'm now a lot more sympathetic towards my wife. Housework and looking after children is a full-time job."

"At first, I tended to get into a rut, a woman's rut."

"I got a bit frustrated with it . . . nothing to do . . . I've even resorted to turning the T.V. on. I hate to admit it, but I actually watched Mike Walsh the other day."

"I often feel like throwing it in. It gets very hectic at times and it affects our social life."

However, 11% of fathers reported they had experienced no difficulty with the change in lifestyle. Some examples of these fathers' reactions were:

"It just comes natural to me."

"It comes fairly easily to me."

"No problems, it was totally plain sailing."

It was also the case that several fathers, although experiencing initial difficulties, did adjust successfully and were able to complete *some* of the tasks they set out to do. These fathers described a *process of adjustment* which involved three stages: (1) the initial expectations of achieving a personal goal, and then becoming frustrated when it was realized child care was not a piece of cake, coupled with the resulting conflicts between father and children; (2) abandonment of personal goals, and focusing most, if not all, attention onto the children; (3) some kind of compromise between the demands of the children and the demands and needs of the father. For one father, the second stage meant he spent all of his time observing and interacting with his children. As a result, he discovered that they were most likely to be happy and involved in some activity when he was close by, especially during the early part of the day and just after lunch. In the *compromise* stage, therefore, he organized his activities around these preferred patterns of the children. One consequence of this was that he did not have a traditional housework pattern. Most of the housework was left until late in the morning or late in the afternoon. This, incidentally created some problems if his wife happened to come home early!

Enhanced Self-Esteem and Satisfaction

Although most fathers experienced difficulties in the early stages – difficulties probably not unlike those experienced by women when they first take on this role – it was also a common response that the process of *adjustment* had many *positive* features. For example, there was the straightforward feeling of satisfaction in having achieved something. These fathers had taken on a job males were not normally expected to be capable of performing, had been subjected to a good deal of criticism from others (see below), had experienced difficulties in adjusting, but after all this appeared to be successful. Most of them looked upon themselves as competent caregivers and were seen by others as such too. One mother said, for example: "I now have a lot more respect for my husband. I have to admit I didn't really think he could do it. But he has certainly proved me and others wrong."

For many fathers, therefore, the experience of successfully carrying out the child-care role had increased their self-confidence and self-esteem and was a source of personal satisfaction. This finding confirms those of several other studies that have reported similar outcomes associated with high father participation (e.g., Gronseth 1978; Lein 1979; Sagi 1981). In his study of highly participant Israeli fathers, Sagi found high correlations between measures of paternal participation, but more especially participation in physical child care and nurturance, and fathers' satisfactions with their roles.

Not all fathers, however, viewed their experiences in the child-care role as being generally more positive than negative. Some, in particular, viewed this involvement as being a threat to their identity as a male. It is this issue which is discussed next.

Identity as a Male

Perhaps the most obvious issue for increased paternal participation concerns a father's identity as a male. As was pointed out in the last chapter, cultural stereotypes of masculinity do not usually include nurturant or caregiving behaviour such as changing nappies or wheeling a baby in a pram, and there are decidedly few cultural models of highly participant fathers. It may be, then, that fathers will not feel comfortable being highly participant in child care and will see this as a threat to their identity as a male.

Although highly participant fathers associated the reluctance of *other* fathers to participate in child care with rather narrow views of masculinity and sex-appropriate behaviour, it was not as common for highly participant fathers *themselves* to perceive their behaviour as being inconsistent with their identity as a male. Only five of the fathers studied here, all of whom were both highly participant *and* unemployed, expressed concern about their "failure" to fulfil the accepted male role. Furthermore, part of all these fathers' doubts about their adequateness as a male centred on their not being the breadwinner. For example: "I still don't feel it's a man's job, and I don't feel comfortable doing it. I haven't given up hope yet about getting a job."

This finding that only five out of seventy-one fathers made some overt mention of their concern about being adequate as a male is perhaps surprising, given that fathers encountered negative reactions from their male peer group; only 27% of fathers said their male peer group was generally supportive of their involvement in child care. Perhaps more fathers were actually concerned about this, or at least harboured some doubts or fears, but were unwilling or found it difficult to express these views during the interviews – this was not seen as a *male* thing to do. Alternatively, perhaps it is only those fathers who do not identify strongly with the cultural stereotype of masculinity who become highly participant in the first place. The evidence reported earlier that shared-caregiving fathers are more likely to describe themselves as androgynous, and less likely to describe themselves in a stereotyped masculine way, supports this interpretation. The Norwegian study of Gronseth (1978) gives support to the present finding that few fathers perceive their involvement in child care as a threat to their identity as a male. Gronseth reported that only one of his sixteen shared-role fathers expressed any concern in this regard.

Changes in Attitudes

A common response from fathers and mothers was that fathers' experiences had resulted in a major shift in attitudes (e.g., they placed more value on children and their welfare), child care (e.g., they were more likely to argue for the need for child-care support systems for the family), and the role of women (e.g., they were more likely to be egalitarian in their views about male/female roles and more likely to display an understanding and concern for a person having to care for children full-time). Fathers' changed attitudes in these areas were rated by 24% of fathers and 26% of mothers as being a major *advantage* of the change in roles. Three fathers expressed these changes in this way:

"When I was at home I realized it was a very different thing. It changed me and my attitudes to child rearing. It involved me more in things like when to draw the line in discipline. The day-to-day contact was important. Rebecca taught me a lot of things. I had to take much more responsibility for her – it has made an incredible difference. More fathers should do it. I'm a lot more sympathetic as a person. A lot of men can't understand this."

"It has opened my eyes about the roles of mothers – I realize more than ever now the contribution that they make."

"A lot of men criticize women and what they do when they are at home with children. More men should try it – then they would change their ideas – just like I have."

Identification with the Paid Work Role

For most fathers there was not only an increase in commitment to family work; there was a concomitant *decrease* in commitment to paid work outside the home. The reduction in this area came in two forms: first, there were fathers who had *accommodated* the demands of their employment to the demands of their child-care role (e.g., by changing shifts, or reducing career aspirations). Although this latter change might not seem as drastic as the former, it was perceived by fathers as being highly significant, and therefore is just as likely to have consequences for fathers and families.

A redistribution of work and family commitments is likely to present major difficulties for some fathers, for, as was reported earlier, most fathers define their family role as being the breadwinner. Moreover, it was surprising how often during interviews that shared-caregiving fathers emphasized the point that they were "not just staying at home". If they did not have a paid job or were not studying, then they were "renovating the house", "landscaping the garden", or "catching up on all the little odd jobs". Nevertheless, there are pressures associated with breadwinning responsibilities, and some fathers might welcome a reduction in these pressures and responsibilities; a better balance between time spent on paid work and the family, therefore, could be viewed as a positive change. Too often it is assumed that *all* fathers want and enjoy their jobs and the bread-winner status. Both of these responses — the difficulties experienced adjusting to, and the relief felt from, a reduction in paid work commitments — were found here.

Data presented by Pleck (1980) might lead us to expect that a change in family and paid-work responsibilities would be an easy transition to make. In his review of the American literature on men's psychological involvement in work versus the family, Pleck (1983) reports that despite quite major differences in methodologies, studies are consistent in showing that men are more likely to have a greater commitment and psychological investment in their family than their job. Also, a reduction in job commitment may have ramifications not previously tapped by studies of family versus job satisfaction. A change in social life is one such ramification, and a reduction in political influence and decision-making power at work is another.

The two reduction-in-paid-work situations described above (i.e., no paid work and accommodation of work to family) appeared to present problems of similar magnitude to the fathers involved in each. The significance of this was indicated by the finding that 28% of fathers rated the loss of status associated with paid employment as a major disadvantage of their lifestyle. For example:

"I miss my job and the contact with my peers and friends and workmates."

"I had a lot of difficulty adjusting to the idea of not having a job. I didn't realize how important that was to me."

Fathers who no longer had a work role at all had particular difficulty in adjusting to their loss of identity and status. This loss of status was especially reinforced in their interaction with male peers, many of whom looked upon them as bludgers whereas most shared-caregiving fathers thought that caring for children all day every day was *more* difficult than what they had been doing before, and therefore perhaps they deserved *more* status. They were decidedly unsuccessful in convincing other men of this, however. One father expressed it this way:

"It will be a long, long time before there is a change in Australia. The mateship deal is too strong in Australia. When I first stayed at home, just Mondays, I found it hard . . . all the nappy changing and just the constancy of it . . . all day at home by myself, without a car and no one to talk to. I remember going back to work on Tuesdays, a leisurely 8.30 start, a cup of coffee and a bit of bullshit, working, talking to other people. Lunchtime, down to the pub for a couple of beers, or up to the pool for a swim. I used to tell my mates how easy they had it — I made the point quite a few times, but they just booed and hissed me down. Most of the men I have come across are against my staying at home. One friend, he thinks I'm funny, under the thumb; he can't understand it at all. He doesn't worry me. I know who's got the best end of the stick."

Despite the difficulties experienced by most fathers with their reduction in commitment to paid employment, 20% were extremely happy about it. For these fathers the major advantage of their new lifestyle was the relief both from career pressures and from the strain associated with the breadwinner role. As two fathers said:

"I enjoy the freedom from the routine, pressure, and hassles of work."

"It provided a chance to change, study, think — a break from the ladder of one's profession."

Fathers who maintained some level of employment outside the home but accommodated their work commitments to family needs experienced different kinds of problems from those who were not employed at all. These fathers were more likely to experience day-to-day conflicts between home and work, and it was usually the case that the demands of their family responsibilities impinged upon their employment. As such, these fathers are probably not unlike the single fathers studied by O'Brien (1980). O'Brien reports that single fathers, in comparison with middle-class married traditional fathers, experienced more conflicts between home and work (e.g., child-care demands affecting work attendances) than between work and home (i.e., work impinging on family). Shared-caregiving fathers studied here were less likely to be involved in extras at work (e.g., in committees), to be available before or after work, or to be involved in social gatherings associated with employment (which are often vital for a person's long-term career prospects). They were also more likely to take time off because of the children. Understandably, then, they encountered considerable negative reactions from their workmates and employers — people who usually expect total commitment either to their fellow workers or to the company. As a result, there was increased pressure on fathers at work, their chances of being promoted within the rigid career structures of most types of employment were reduced, and, overall, they experienced a *loss of status* at work. Four fathers found this situation especially frustrating for their long-term career goals. There was a hint of resentment in their reports of others who had passed them on the career ladders.

These difficulties and conflicts experienced by this latter group of shared-caregiving fathers are probably not unlike those experienced by most mothers who are employed and still retain the major responsibility for children. As such, further consideration of this issue might be better placed within the general context of conflict between family and work for *both* mothers and fathers. A further discussion of this issue is presented in the final chapter.

Paid Work: A Mixed Blessing for Mothers

Mothers' reactions to being employed were both strongly positive and strongly negative. When asked what were the major advantages of their lifestyles, 46% of mothers (and 57% of fathers) mentioned the satisfaction they derived from their jobs and success in their careers; 37% mentioned feelings of independence (as did 32% of fathers); 41% (and 39% of fathers) considered the increased mental stimulation to be important; and 16% of both mothers and fathers reported the increase in self-esteem as being a major advantage. Some examples of responses were:

"After going back to work I started to value myself more. . . . I have also become much more tolerant." (Mother)

"I am happier when I work. I need the mental stimulation." (Mother)

"My wife has become a lot more independent, and thank god for that." (Father)

Being employed full-time, however, did have its drawbacks. One of these was that mothers were physically and emotionally exhausted more often than before. Exhaustion as a major problem for mothers was mentioned by 24% of mothers and 17% of fathers, and a lack of time and always feeling rushed was reported by 38% of mothers and 28% of fathers. As was pointed out earlier, however, much of this exhaustion was associated with mothers having *dual* roles. This was a *cost* of the new lifestyle which was expressed with particular strength by those mothers who were married to men who were not totally committed to being at home, and although carrying out the child-care role, did very little of the housework. In one family in which the mother was employed full-time and the father was at home, for example, the mother still did *all* the housework. Indeed, it was common for her to prepare her three-year-old son's lunch before she went to work. As she said: "It's hard doing a dual role, especially when I'm tired. I've found it hard adjusting, it's hard to come home and see things not done and then having to cook tea."

Another mother expressed the increased exhaustion and rush in this way: "Forming friendships with other people suffers. Also, I don't have a great deal of time to myself. Often I think I have so much to do — life is just rushing by — occasionally — children seem to be growing too quickly — seems to be too much of a rush at home. But it doesn't really worry me now. I chose to do it; I want to work. When I think of the alternative of being home all day, it would be much worse. It's just when I'm tired and things get me down every now and then."

As is indicated in the above statement, some mothers also reported that they had been forced to reduce their social contacts, especially those in their immediate neighbourhood. These were contacts that formed the mainstay of their social relationships before their change in lifestyles, but now they had little time for them. The relationships they developed at work did not seem as satisfying as those in the neighbourhood. (Fathers' social contacts evidently suffered too. They missed their relationships with workmates and very rarely developed social networks with mothers in the neighbourhood.) This type of problem may only have emerged in the present study, however, because of the short period of time families had been non-traditional. With further time, it may be that both parents adjust and form satisfying relationships at work and in the neighbourhood.

Although it did not emerge as a major response in the overall analysis of interviews, four mothers reported that by going out to work they actually lost some of their freedom, something that perhaps mothers at home who want to work might find surprising. For example, one mother said: "To a certain extent I've lost my freedom. When I was at home, . . . even though the children were the bosses, when my husband went out the door my day was my own. Thus, I had a little bit more flexibility. I didn't have a 9 to 5 routine. But, I want to see the other side of life. I suppose, though, I've just escaped from one routine to another." So, while the majority of women feel that employment provided them with more independence and personal satisfaction, some were apprehensive about the routine nature of their *new* job, the increased constraints on their time, and their feelings of exhaustion. It seems obvious that these negative aspects of the shared-caregiving lifestyle are likely to have ramifications for family relationships, and especially the marital relationship. This is discussed in the next chapter.

Reactions of Significant Others

Those who adopt a lifestyle that is different from the norm are likely to encounter some type of reaction from people they come into contact with. While many of these reactions will have little impact, the reactions of significant others — relatives, friends, and colleagues at work — are likely to be critical. People who have the support of significant others, for example, might be more likely to feel comfortable and secure in the face of more general societal disapproval. Several questions were asked of parents to gauge the reactions of others and to ascertain the impact these reactions might have.

The first question inquired about other people's *general reactions*. (How have other people reacted to your changed roles?) In reply, 42% of parents reported mainly positive reactions, and 34% reported mainly negative reactions; 30% also mentioned a specific positive response directed towards fathers, such as, "Oh, isn't he marvellous — my husband wouldn't do it", and 18% reported people had difficulty understanding their lifestyle and why they would want to do it (incomprehension and disbelief). There was a considerable range of reactions, both positive and negative, all serving constantly to remind fathers and families just how different they were. Responses ranged from:

"Doing a bit of baby-sitting today?"

"Where's mum — is she off sick today?"

"What's with the kids mate? You must be mad."

"How long are you doing this for? What about your job, won't if affect your career?"

"It's good to see a man take it on — I bet the children find it different."

"Oh, aren't you marvellous, I wish I could con my husband into it."

One father of fifty-five said that some people thought it rather amusing. "Some say that if I'm silly enough to have a kid at this age, then I deserve to have to look after him.'" While the majority of fathers found the comments of others interesting, one father became tired of it all and said: "Other people were sceptical when they first heard about it — it was a point of conversation which ceased to be of interest for me. . . . My relatives also thought I was a bit different and questioned by capability initially."

Parents were also asked about the specific reactions of *relatives*. Mainly negative reactions from relatives were reported by 42% of families, mainly positive reactions by 33%, and the remaining 24% reported both positive and negative reactions (e.g., mothers' relatives were supportive but fathers' were not). Reactions towards fathers mainly related to their reductions in work commitments (e.g., relatives felt it was the responsibility of fathers to ensure their families' financial security), and with the effect it would have on the father's career (most felt it would have a damaging effect). The most commonly expressed negative reactions from relatives, however, concerned mothers. These were mainly of the form that by going out to work they were not "good mothers"; their first responsibility was to their children. There were also reports of initial negative reactions followed by more positive ones. This is what two mothers had to say in this regard:

"I know lots of women who say, 'Aren't you lucky, isn't it great, my husband wouldn't do it.' I think generally speaking there was disapproval from my relatives. They thought it was a big mistake. 'Pat, you are making a big mistake,' they would say."

"My parents were very much against it at first, but they are gradually coming around. I think this contributed to my feelings of guilt, and the reaction of one neighbour I especially remember. She wanted to know how I could leave such adorable children."

A third question inquired about the reactions of *close friends, neighbours, and workmates*. An inspection of these responses revealed that the *sex* of the neighbour or friend was an important factor, and so responses were divided into male and female reactions. Female friends and neighbours were reported to be more supportive than male friends and neighbours; 69% of families said female friends were positive or supportive, whereas only 44% said male friends were positive. The same pattern of gender differences occurred for reports of the reactions of work associates; 64% of families reported that female workmates were positive, whereas only 34% reported that male workmates were. Men especially encountered negative reactions from other men, many of whom described them as being a "bit funny", "a bit of a woman", "under the thumb", and, as was noted earlier, "bludgers". Other men, therefore, reacted in a traditional male way, by alluding to these fathers' possible *inadequacies* as *men*. And, as was mentioned earlier, other men tended to trivialize the job of staying at home and caring for children, not giving these fathers any recognition for it at all. The following are the comments of two fathers in this regard:

"You take my father-in-law. He came up to stay recently and kept saying how hard it must be on his daughter to have a job and do all the housework, etc. He kept telling *her* how marvellous she must be and kept asking *her* what he could do to help. Meanwhile, I was looking after the kids, doing the washing and cleaning, getting his breakfast and running him around here, there, and everywhere, but he didn't seem to recognize that."

"One day the woman next door asked me if I'd look after her two sons after school until her husband came home from work. He turned up very late, after I'd bathed them, fed them, and helped them with their homework. He automatically apologized to Judy, and thanked *her* for looking after them."

Although most fathers were inclined to laugh off these reactions, a few resented them. Not surprisingly, fathers who were most affected by these negative comments from other men were those who were also concerned about their failure to gain employment.

Even though other women were mainly positive about the families' alternative lifestyles, this was not a universal response. Some women thought it was hard on these mothers to have to go out and get a job. A mother in a family in which the father had been retrenched and was not entirely happy about staying at home and in which the mother had volunteered to find a job offered the following comment: "Some people seem to resent the fact that Michael isn't working. A lot of people say: 'You're good to do it for him, to go out to work', and others say: 'I wouldn't do it for him.' No one has said that they think I am lucky to get out and work."

The clear impression that emerges from the above analysis of the reactions of significant others, therefore, is that mothers were given much more support for their change in roles than fathers were. For example, mothers reported positive reactions from 69% of their same-sex friends and 61% of their same-sex workmates, whereas only 27% of fathers' same-sex friends and 34% of their same-sex workmates were positive. Many women envied these shared-caregiving mothers, while decidedly few men genuinely envied the fathers. Maternal participation in the paid work force is much more common than is paternal participation in child care, and therefore these reactions are as might be expected.

Positive Reactions from Women: Another View

The above analyses, taken at face value, indicate that women are much more positive about fathers being caregivers than men are. This is, of course, as one might expect; women appear to have a lot more to gain from this change than men do. For those experiencing the burdens of child care (mainly mothers), the idea of others taking on some of the load must be attractive. Moreover, a proposal that men and women share the care of children, although not a major platform of the women's movement (cf. Newland 1980), is, nevertheless, consistent with the basic aims of equality between the sexes in terms of power and access to resources (Levine 1977; Pleck 1980; Russell 1980).

How deep-seated are these positive reactions of women? A minority of fathers in the present study were sceptical about women's reactions, arguing that behind the initial positive response lurked doubts and fears, not unlike those experienced by men when confronted with women's liberation. It is an often stated view that men have difficulty accepting or understanding women's changed roles and feel threatened by it. For example, the following statement was made in a recent article about careers and families: "However, many husbands feel threatened by their wives' careers. Many men still regard themselves as the breadwinner and may feel insecure, especially if the wife is earning more money than the husband" (Sydney Morning Herald, Home and Family Section, 25 June 1981). The finding that some women feel threatened by men being involved in child care perhaps should be expected, especially when it is considered that for most women, power and competence in the child-care and domestic domains have for a long time been their main sources of status and recognition within the community. It should not be surprising, therefore, if some women find it difficult to relinquish their authority in this domain. The most commonly occurring ways in which fathers described their doubts about women's positive reactions are listed below:

"A good baby-sitter". Five fathers felt that although women appeared to be accepting of them in the child-care role and thought they were competent, they did not see them as being equal to mothers. Rather, they got the impression they were considered to be "mother's little helper". Confirmation of this lesser status was given when they were described as "good baby-sitters" by close relatives.

"Not really trusted". Another group of fathers reported that some women were reluctant to allow their children to be cared for by them. The best example of this was a father whose eldest son attended a pre-school and had a close group of friends there. A mother of one of the other children, who had previously always allowed her child to go to the shared-caregiving home when the mother was there, did not allow this when the father was at home. As the father said, "She would always have some good excuse, but it became obvious after a while."

"Not one of the group". A number of fathers reported that although they experienced a strong positive reaction from other women to begin with, in the longer term they were not fully accepted by women at the social-group level – at play groups, pre-schools, and outside the school gate waiting for the children of an afternoon. In the words of one father: "There haven't been any really adverse reactions except perhaps at school when I collect Rebecca. I'm not really accepted by the mothers. They keep to themselves and essentialy exclude me." A father who took his children to a playgroup found this lack of acceptance uncomfortable and after seven weeks stopped going altogether. It is possible, however, that some fathers may have contributed to this lack of acceptance by their own behaviour and attitudes. This possibility is evident in the following statements from two fathers:

"I feel bored with it, I feel as if I'm stagnating. I talk to the women in the place [block of units], but that is a very limited existence; they always talk about the same things."

"I get along all right with the mothers at the pre-school. But most mothers only want to talk about their children; they have nothing else to talk about. I don't find that very interesting."

"It's good to see a man being hassled by it too". Other fathers who felt they were accepted at the social level in the neighbourhood, and participated in neighbourhood child-care supportive networks, nevertheless said that there was an absence of *mutual psychological support*. That is, their relationships with mothers were not at a level that allowed them to engage in discussions about their doubts and anxieties either as parents or as men. Indeed, one father became somewhat bitter about this as a result of

the reaction he encountered from the mother next-door. He was having difficulty with toilet training his two-year-old, and one morning, feeling a little more exasperated than usual, he felt the need to talk to someone about it. (Incidentally, this was the third child in the family, and the father had actively participated in the toilet training of the other two.) The mother next-door, who seemed highly supportive of his role — they frequently shared child care — happened to walk by. When, in the course of a conversation, he expressed his frustrations with toilet training, the reaction he received was: "It's good to see a man being hassled by it too". This was obviously not what he needed at that time (as he said: "It gave *me* the shits!"), and as such he remains somewhat less than convinced that women are accepting of or are as capable of understanding the changed role of men. He remarked: "What would her reaction have been if I was a woman?"

Some fathers also expressed doubts about their wives' abilities to accept them as child-carers, but these doubts were of an entirely different nature to those expressed in relation to other women. The majority of wives accepted their husbands as being competent child-carers, and many even displayed a degree of pride that they had a husband who could, and indeed *was*, the primary caregiver for their children. What wives had difficulty accepting was *the role* that fathers came to adopt — a role typically ascribed to the nature of women but which it became obvious to most men is much more a function of the caregiver/home-maker situation.

"What have you been doing all day?". It might be expected that women with children would be the group most likely to be able to understand the problems of being at home all day with children. Yet several fathers reported that their wives often came home from work and, seeing some part of the housework incomplete or finding that something needed from the supermarket had not been bought, politely inquired: "What have you been doing all day?" One father who regularly experienced this type of reaction said: "Talk about chauvinistic men — what about my wife! She comes home and wants to know what I've been doing all day. Other times when we might be having a discussion about how hard it is for me to get things done at home, she has said on one or two occasions: 'If I was at home I would get more done than you do; I wouldn't just sit around on my bum all day like you do.' " A few fathers who experienced this type of reception were somewhat jubilant about it! They interpreted it as a sign that they had finally "made it", that they now had full status as a person at home.

Failure of wives to fully acknowledge the problems and doubts of fathers in the caregiving role was also reported. One father said: "I don't think my wife really understands the problems I have. What is more, I don't think she expects me to have problems of the type I have. They are not really problems that men are expected to have. Sometimes I need someone to talk to about it. I can't talk to other men — they would probably make a joke of it. I would have thought my wife would have understood, but it appears she can't."

"It's a con job". Although it was the view of only one father, it is sufficiently significant to warrant being reported here. He believed that having men more involved in child care was a complete confidence trick on the part of women, but more especially on the part of his wife. Both parents in this family *appeared* totally committed to sharing child care, and their decision to change was based mainly on the mother's desire to pursue a career (they agreed the father had had his time in paid employment, and now it was his turn at home). But this father expressed the view that his wife wanted to have her cake and eat it too. He felt she wanted him to be a glorified baby-sitter, being reluctant to give up any of her status and power within the child-care and domestic domains. She apparently tried to dominate and control his performance of the child-care role and his relationships with the children. He felt he was not given the same independence to develop "at home" in the way his wife was "outside the home". The lack of support from significant others and the nature of the demands of the caregiving role all contributed to his feelings of total dissatisfaction and resentment.

Conclusions

A change in commitments to parental and employment roles evidently has a considerable impact on mothers and fathers and on their relationships with significant others. Moreover, the findings reported here are consistent both with the findings reported by Rapoport and Rapoport (1976) for dual-career families and with the predictions outlined by both Pleck (1979) and Berger (1979).

It was a rare father or mother indeed who said the change in lifestyle had had little or no impact. Fathers especially felt the demands of the caregiving role, particularly in the early stages of changing roles; the negative reactions of significant others, particularly their male peers; and the quite marked changes — generally positive — in their self-image and attitudes and in their relationships with their children. Mothers, on the other hand, appeared most affected by the demands of their two roles (family and employment), the reduction in time spent with their children, the negative reaction of relatives, the positive reactions of their female friends, the improvement in their personal well-being, and the satisfaction they derived from their jobs.

At the beginning of this chapter the possibility was mentioned that parents, in evaluating their family lifestyles, might place more emphasis on the perceived effects on *themselves* or on their *family situations* than on the *possible* effects on their children. Some data have already been presented bearing on this question. The aim here is to discuss all of these findings in an attempt to gain an overall perspective. The questions asked that are relevant in this context are those that inquired about difficulties and dislikes (negative aspects) and advantages and likes (positive aspects).

Negative Aspects

The two negative aspects that stood out from the fathers' point of view were (1) problems in adjusting to the caregiver role (mentioned by 45% of sample) and (2) the loss of status associated with their reduction in commitment to paid work (32%). Smaller groups of fathers also placed importance on the lack of adult company (17%), coping with the mothers' tiredness (11%), and strain on the marital relationship (11%). For mothers, the most significant negative aspects were coping with the rush and exhaustion (24%), feelings of guilt about leaving the children (23%), the loss of contact with their children (32%), and the strain on the marital relationship (18%).

Overall, then, mothers and fathers both perceived there to be considerable costs associated with their relative decreases and increases in commitments to family and paid work domains. If the percentages of responses given can be taken as a guide, it seems that fathers had more difficulty in coping with their increased commitment to the family and less difficulty with their decrease in commitment to paid work. For mothers, the reverse was true; mothers reported more difficulty in adjusting to their increased commitment to paid work and less difficulty in their decrease in commitment to their family. Significantly, parents appeared to place much more emphasis on the effects on themselves than their children — there was very little mention at all of the negative effects for children. It was only in 19% of families that children were perceived as having any difficulties, and most of these were reported to be minor problems of adjustment.

Positive Aspects

For fathers, by far and away the most commonly mentioned positive aspect was the improvement in their relationships with their children (63%); for mothers, it was the satisfaction they derived from their jobs (mentioned in some way or another by 60% of families). Two other more family-oriented positive aspects were prominent in the responses: (1) the fact that mothers and fathers shared child-care responsibilities, and that this resulted in a closer family unit (40%); and (2) the financial gains associated with their lifestyle (37%).

Again, changes associated more specifically with children were mentioned far less frequently than those associated either with mothers, fathers, or the family generally. It was only 40% of parents who mentioned a better relationship with the father as an advantage for children, and only 18% of parents mentioned this as something they really liked about their lifestyle.

Thus, the areas in which mothers and fathers reported they experienced most difficulty (fathers with child care; mothers coping with demands of employment) were also the areas that reportedly afforded them the most satisfaction. For most, as has been evident in the quotations from parents presented in this chapter, the benefits far outweighed the costs. At least, this was what was argued at the time of the interview. Just how long the balance remains this way, however, is another question. One way of throwing some light on this question is to go back to these families some time later and explore their feelings on these issues again. This was done in the present study, and these findings are presented in chapter 10. Before discussing these findings, however, the possible impact that a shared-caregiving lifestyle has on the marital relationship and on children will be explored in depth.

8

The Marital Relationship

Apart from concern about the likely effects a non-traditional family pattern will have on children, the next most commonly expressed concern is about the effects it might have on the *marital relationship*. High value is usually placed on marital stability in Western societies; the divorce rate is often used as an indicator of social or moral decay. Although marital stability and marital relationships of higher quality are commonly assumed to be associated with the traditional nuclear family, there are some who argue that this type of family in fact *causes* marital dissatisfaction. A person who has been one of the strongest advocates of this point of view is Jessie Bernard. Bernard (1972) reports that men are usually happier with their marital relationships than women are, and that they stand to gain a lot more from marriage than women do. This discrepancy, Bernard suggests, is due in large part to the nature of the role and responsibilities women have in most families — that is, the child-carer, housewife, and general back-up for the family, always being there! It is having the major responsibility for family life, argues Bernard, rather than marriage itself which is the source of women's marital frustrations and dissatisfactions. A woman's family role has also been linked to what has been termed the *housewife syndrome*, a term that has come to be associated with findings that women at home (and especially those with pre-school children) have poorer mental and emotional health than either women or men who are in the paid work force (Bernard 1972).

Following Bernard's argument, then, mothers in shared-caregiving families who have been relieved of some of the physical and emotional burdens of child care and housework, and who are no longer "stuck at home all day", might be expected to be happier with their marital relationships than mothers in traditional families. Given that fathers in shared-caregiving families have increased significantly their involvment in child care and housework, they might be expected to be less satisfied than traditional fathers. The negative effects on fathers might be expected to be even greater when the father is not employed and has to cope with reduced status in this domain.

Perhaps we should not expect the effects of shared-caregiving to be as simple as this. Very few of the shared-caregiving mothers had completely relinquished their family responsibilities; indeed, many performed *dual* roles. In no sense could they be considered to be equivalent to traditional fathers. Neither could shared-caregiving fathers be considered equivalent to traditional mothers. Few of these fathers spent as much time on child care and housework as traditional mothers, and many were still engaged in paid work. Furthermore, as was evident in data presented in the previous chapter, having dual roles placed physical and emotional demands on mothers which might be expected to increase the level of marital conflict and therefore lead to greater dissatisfaction.

Increased conflict and dissatisfaction might also occur in shared-caregiving families as a consequence of difficulties experienced in adjusting to sharing and exchanging roles. Conflicts are likely to occur in the areas of housework and child-rearing, areas in which mothers traditionally have major control but in which fathers are now also highly participant.

Finally, the effects of a shared-caregiving lifestyle are likely to be moderated by the reasons why this family pattern was adopted in the first place. Marital satisfaction might be expected to be higher in those families in which the decision to change was a matter of choice rather than a financial necessity. Many of the families who chose to change said that a major contributing factor was their egalitarian views about divisions of labour for child care. These families might also hold egalitarian views about marital issues and therefore have relationships characterized by higher quality. When the change has been forced onto the family by financial circumstances, the level of conflict and dissatisfaction might be higher.

The aim of this chapter is to assess the effects of a shared-caregiving lifestyle on marital relationships using two complementary approaches. In the first, marital quality is assessed using a structured questionnaire – the Spanier Dyadic Adjustment Scale (see appendix 2 for complete details). Scores on this scale for mothers and fathers in shared-caregiving families are compared with those of a comparable group of traditional families (a random sample of 31 of the initial group of 145 traditional families). The second approach involves an analysis of the responses of shared-caregiving families to an open-ended interview question. This inquired about their *perceptions* of the impact of their family lifestyle on the marital relationship (i.e., did they think their relationship had changed, and if so, in what ways?). Consistency between these two data sets (e.g., a finding that shared-caregiving mothers both score higher on the scale of marital quality than traditional mothers and report their relationships to have improved since their family pattern had changed), would provide strong evidence for this lifestyle having a significant impact.

Marital Quality in Shared-Caregiving and Traditional Families

The quality of marital relationships in shared-caregiving and traditional families was assessed by Spanier's Dyadic Adjustment Scale (Spanier 1976). This inventory contains 32 items which are grouped into four sub-scales:
1. *Dyadic consensus* (13 items). These items assess the extent to which a couple agree on things such as family finances, leisure activities, and philosophy of life.
2. *Dyadic satisfaction* (10 items). These items are designed to assess the degree of satisfaction people feel about their relationship (e.g. "In general, how often do you think that things between you and your partner are going well?"; "How often do you and your partner quarrel?").
3. *Dyadic cohesion* (5 items). These items inquired about the frequency with which couples engaged in activities together like leisure interests, having a stimulating exchange of ideas, laughing together.
4. *Affectional expression* (4 items). These were items that inquired about agreements and disagreements in sexual relationships and the expression of affection (e.g., "Was being too tired for sex a problem in your relationship during the past few weeks?").

The Spanier scale, therefore, provides scores for each of these four aspects of the marital relationship, as well as a *global* measure of marital quality (the sum of the scores on each of the four sub-scales).

If a shared-caregiving lifestyle has a positive impact on marital relationships, then we might expect differences between the two family types to emerge on the overall score and on all four sub-scales, with perhaps differences being greatest on dyadic consensus (as roles are more egalitarian, agreement is likely to be more common on family and lifestyle issues), and as a consequence, on dyadic satisfaction too. If, on the other hand, shared-caregiving has a negative impact on marital relationships, this might be expected to be more evident on dyadic cohesion and affectional expression, and again, as a consequence, on dyadic satisfaction too. This probability is given strong support from the data presented in the previous chapter on the impact that a shared-caregiving lifestyle had on mothers and fathers. There it was reported that the rush, exhaustion, and lack of time all presented major problems to these parents.

There are, of course, dangers in using a comparison between two groups of families as a basis for examining the impact of the change in lifestyle. It may be that these two groups differed on the quality of marital relationships before the change. Perhaps it is only the very happy and secure couple who even contemplate such a significant change, or maybe couples who are experiencing difficulties with their relationships see the change as a way of solving their problems. This latter possibility is not given strong support from the data presented earlier on parental explanations of their change in lifestyles: difficulty with the marital relationship was not one of the major response categories.

Another danger with comparing the two family types is that they might differ on other variables which influence marital quality. It has already been noted that shared-caregiving families had fewer children, and mothers who were more highly educated. Previous studies (see Rollins and Galligan 1978) generally show that the more children a family has, the poorer the marital relationships tend to be. This finding has also been confirmed in a recent Australian study in which Spanier's scale was employed (Antill 1981). These differences between the two family types are taken into account in the following analyses.

Are Shared-Caregiving Parents Less Satisfied?

The means for the total marital quality scores for mothers and fathers in the two family types are shown in table 18. It is evident from those figures that the major difference that has emerged is between the two family types. Both mothers and

Table 18. Mean scores on Spanier's Dyadic Adjustment Scale

	Shared-caregiving		Traditional	
	Fathers	Mothers	Fathers	Mothers
Total score	111.3	110.6[1]	115.4	116.0
Dyadic concensus	49.1	48.7	49.1	51.4
Dyadic satisfaction	37.9	37.9[2]	41.2	40.0
Dyadic cohesion	15.6	15.3	15.8	15.3
Affectional expression	8.7	8.7	9.3	9.3

[1]Difference between family types significant: $F(1,156) = 5.71$, $< .02$
[2]Difference between family types significant: $F(1,156) = 12.8$, $< .001$

fathers in shared-caregiving families reported their marital relationships to be of *lower quality* than parents in traditional
families. Thus, in apparent contradiction to one of the
hypotheses outlined earlier, shared-caregiving has not had a
positive effect on mothers' satisfactions with their marital relationship. Furthermore, the data presented here also conflict with
previous findings that, overall, mothers are less satisfied with
their marital relationships than fathers are: there were no differences in either shared-caregiving or traditional families.

The possibility that other differences between the two family
types (specifically, differences in the number of children and
mothers' education level) contributed to or enhanced this effect
was also investigated. Both of these variables were included as
covariates in an analysis of variance testing for family-type
effects; however, neither was found to have a significant effect.
Moreover, martial quality scores were not found to be
significantly correlated with either variable in this sample
(*number of children*: mothers, $r = .18$; fathers, $r = .16$; *mother's
education*: mothers, $r = .09$; fathers, $r = .00$), and therefore further
analyses were not conducted on these variables.

An inspection of the means for the four sub-scales, which are
also shown in table 18, reveals that the only scale for which
there is a significant family-type difference is *dyadic satisfaction*;
mothers and fathers in shared-caregiving families both scored
lower on this scale. Contrary to the predictions made earlier
about the possible negative effects of the lifestyle, which were
based on data presented in the previous chapter on the rushed
nature of this lifestyle, shared-caregiving parents do not score
lower on either the *dyadic cohesion* or *affectional expression scales.*

A further analysis was conducted on the ten items which made
up the dyadic satisfaction scale. Staines et al. (1978), in a study of

the effects of maternal employment on marital adjustment, found that mothers who were employed were more likely to report that they wished they had married someone else and that they had contemplated divorce, but did not rate their marriages as any less happy, nor did they report they were less satisfied with their marital relationships. Similar findings might emerge here, as all the mothers in the present sample were employed. Spanier's scale of *dyadic satisfaction* includes ratings of both satisfaction and the frequency with which divorce has been contemplated, and thus, given the finding of Staines et al. (1978), an analysis of individual items appears warranted. This analysis revealed that shared-caregiving parents were more likely than traditional parents to have (a) considered ending their relationship ($p < .001$), (b) left the house after a recent fight ($p < .02$), (c) felt their relationship wasn't going well ($p < .001$), (d) had a quarrel recently ($p < .03$), (e) felt they had got on one another's nerves recently ($p < .01$), (f) rated their relationship as less happy ($p < .02$).

In agreement with Staines et al. (1978), therefore, shared-caregiving parents were more likely to report they had considered ending their relationship; but in apparent disagreement, they also reported they were less happy with and less satisfied with their marital relationship. As well as this, the above analysis indicates that the general level of irritability and tension is higher in shared-caregiving families – they are more likely to report recent quarrels and getting on one another's nerves. This latter finding is consistent with the previously noted increased physical and emotional pressures associated with this lifestyle.

Given the nature of the change in family patterns under consideration here (i.e., fathers becoming more involved in the traditional female domains of child care and housework), responses on two other specific items were also inspected: agreement on housework and child-rearing (an item which was added to Spanier's Dyadic Consensus sub-scale). Surprisingly, shared-caregiving parents reported marginally more agreement on housework than traditional parents, and this was more especially the case for mothers: 62% of shared-caregiving mothers reported they "almost always" or "always agreed about housework", whereas only 46% of traditional mothers reported this level of agreement. For the question on child-rearing, no significant differences were evident between family types, and mothers in both families were slightly less likely to report agreement than fathers were.

At first glance it might appear that responses to these structured questions on agreement about housework and child-rearing indicate that these do not represent problem areas for shared-caregiving parents. The questionnaire asked only about the *frequency* of disagreements, however; it did not ask about the nature of disagreements. Although the two family types might have approximately the same number of disagreements, they could nevertheless be about different things. Traditional parents might have conflicts about whether or not a husband does *any* housework or child care, whereas shared-caregiving parents might have disagreements about the way in which fathers perform these tasks. Interview responses to be discussed below support this interpretation.

Differences within Shared-Caregiving Families

Given the finding that shared-caregiving parents report they have marital relationships of a lower quality, an important question is whether there are any factors associated with this lifestyle that might explain these differences. Three possibilities are considered here: (1) the reasons why a non-traditional family pattern was adopted, (2) the length of time parents had been in this family pattern, and (3) divisions of labour for paid and family work.

Reasons for Changing Lifestyles

The possibility that the reasons for changing lifestyles is an important factor is supported by a recent American study (Bloom-Feshbach 1980). In his study of forty fathers married to employed women, Bloom-Feshbach found that when fathers felt they had little or no choice in whether their wives were employed (because of family financial difficulties) they reported more marital strain and dissatisfaction with carrying out child-care tasks. Also, as was noted earlier, it is plausible that those who have chosen to change are more egalitarian in their attitudes, which results in less conflict and more equality in the marital relationship.

Trends for scores on the scale of marital quality were only evident for fathers. Fathers in families in which the change was by choice had slightly higher total scores than fathers who said the change was necessary (113.6 vs. 108.5), however, this difference was not statistically significant (p = .15). One-way analyses of variance were also conducted to examine whether or not perceived influence over the decision to change was a critical variable. This analysis appeared to confirm Bloom-Feshbach's finding: the fathers who perceived they had more influence than their wives did scored *highest* on marital quality ($\bar{x}$ = 119.0); fathers who felt mothers had the most influence scored lowest ($\bar{x}$ = 104.8); whereas fathers who thought the decision had been a joint one had scores between these two extremes ($\bar{x}$ = 112.0). Again, however, because of the small sample size, this trend was not statistically significant. Similar trends were not evident for mothers' scores for marital quality, however, which indicates that the reasons why the change was made has little effect on their ratings of the marital relationship.

A moderate degree of support has been found, therefore, for the hypothesis that the reasons why a family changed lifestyles are associated with marital quality. Unfortunately, however, the present analysis does not permit us to say whether this is the result of the groups being different to begin with or whether these scores simply reflect differing reactions to the lifestyle according to their satisfaction with it. This question is returned to below when the interview responses are considered.

Time Since Changing Lifestyles

A theme to emerge from the interview responses was that parents experienced more difficulties in the first few months of changing lifestyles. Parents who are in the early stages of their new family pattern, therefore, might have more conflicts and be less satisfied with their marital relationships. This hypothesis was tested by examining correlations between the length of time (in months) people had been shared-caregivers and (*a*) the total Spanier score and (*b*) the scores on the four sub-scales. If the hypothesis is to be supported, we would expect *negative* correlations for the total score and the dyadic satisfaction scale score.

A minor degree of support was found for this hypothesis. Low but non-significant negative correlations were found for fathers' scores: *total score*, $r = -.16$ ($p = .12$); *dyadic satisfaction*, $r = -.12$ ($p = .19$); *expression of affection*, $r = -.16$ ($p = .12$). The other correlations for fathers, and *all* correlations for mothers, were close to 0 (all were between +.06 and -.02). It seems, therefore, that length of time spent in a shared-caregiving lifestyle makes only a minor contribution to the differences in marital quality noted earlier, and this contribution is restricted to fathers. A degree of caution needs to be expressed about this conclusion, however. There were no families in the present sample who were interviewed in the first month after changing lifestyles, and there were only five who had changed six months before the interview. It may yet be that the early stages of changing are critical; the interview responses to be discussed below lend strong support to this proposition.

Divisions of Labour

The rush, the tiredness, and the exhaustion were consistent criticisms given by shared-caregiving parents of their lifestyles, especially when both parents were employed full-time. It was this pressure alone which many felt contributed to their general dissatisfactions, and it may be that it is this which has a negative effect on marital relationships. To test for this possibility, several analyses were carried out to examine relationships between marital quality and time spent by parents on paid work and on performing child-care tasks — here termed *family work*.

In the first set of analyses, fathers' and mothers' marital quality scores were correlated with the time spent on *paid work* by (a) fathers, (b) mothers, and (c) mothers and fathers combined. All correlations were very low, and none were significant. For example, the following were the correlations between the amount of time fathers spent on paid work and the various scores: fathers' total score: -.07; mothers' total score: .07; fathers' dyadic satisfaction: .00; mothers' dyadic satisfaction: -.01. Thus, time spent on paid work alone appears to be of little importance.

The second set of analyses examined correlations between marital quality scores and the time spent by fathers, mothers, and fathers and mothers combined on *family work*. The correlations for fathers' scores were very low and non-significant. A trend was evident for mothers; positive correlations were found between time spent by fathers on family work and mothers' total score ($r = .20$, $p \leqslant .07$), and mother's dyadic satisfaction scores ($r = .18$, $p \leqslant .08$). As a further test of the possible importance of fathers' participation in family work, additional correlations were conducted using the *percentage of family work* carried out by fathers. This score takes account of the absolute amount of family work to be done, and gives a better indication of the *equality* of time spent on family work within each family. It might be whether or not these tasks are shared evenly between mothers and fathers rather than the absolute amount of family work done by each that is important. Again, these scores were found to be positively correlated with mothers' marital quality scores — total score: $4 = .23$, $p \leqslant .05$; dyadic satisfaction: $4 = .22$,

$p < .05$. Thus it seems that, for mothers, the more fathers participate in family work, the happier they are.

A final correlational analysis was conducted to examine whether or not marital quality scores were related more strongly to the *total amount of work* (i.e., the sum of paid and family work) carried out by fathers, mothers, and fathers and mothers combined. All of these correlations were again low, and none approached significance. For example, the correlation between mothers' total score and time spent by fathers in paid and family work was .11. It seems, therefore, that it is fathers' participation in family work – the degree to which he shares in child-care tasks – which is the most important factor for mothers' satisfactions with their marriages.

Limitations of Findings from Spanier Scale

Although shared-caregiving parents scored lower on the scale of marital quality, the scores are obviously not sufficiently low to justify a conclusion that this lifestyle has a drastic effect on marital relationships, and that marital breakdown is imminent in many families. Compared with a group of recently divorced families discussed by Spanier (1976), whose mean total score on this scale was 70.7, the marriages of shared-caregiving parents appear quite healthy. Moreover, differences between shared-caregiving and traditional parents appeared to be limited to only one of the four sub-scales: *dyadic satisfaction*. Shared-caregiving parents were more likely to have recently considered ending their relationships, to have had recent quarrels, to have been irritated by one another, and to have considered that their relationship was not going very well. As was pointed out earlier, these findings are consistent with these parents having reported that this lifestyle increases physical and emotional tension. There are other possible explanations for the differences noted here between shared-caregiving and traditional parents, however.

One possible alternative explanation is that there are only differences between the two groups in their openness or sensitivity to marital conflict and doubts about their relationships. The process of shared-caregiving (working out new roles, increasing communication between parents) might have sensitized these parents to their marital relationships and to the day-to-day conflicts that arise. For this interpretation, therefore, conflicts might not occur more often in shared-caregiving families, but these parents might be more accurate in their assessments of the frequency of their occurrence and more willing to report this.

Another possibility is that shared-caregiving parents had marriages of lower quality *before* they changed lifestyles. The only sure way to determine whether this was the case would be to take measures before the change and at various points after. This was not possible here, and given the nature of this lifestyle and the few families who adopt it, such data will be difficult to come by. Data were collected, however, on parents' *perceptions* of the changes, and it is these perceptions which are considered next.

Shared-Caregiving Parents' Perceptions of Changes in Their Relationships

The second perspective of the impact a shared-caregiving lifestyle has on marital relationships is provided by an analysis of parents' perceptions of whether and in what ways their relationships had changed since they had changed their family pattern. In answer to this open-ended interview question, 32% of fathers and 30% of mothers reported a general improvement because of the increased sensitivity and understanding they each had of their roles and the emotional pressures they each experienced. Greater equality was reported by 11% of fathers and 17% of mothers. More conflict and greater dissatisfaction was reported by 11% of fathers and 15% of mothers, and problems associated with the rushed lifestyle (e.g., tiredness, irritability, and spending less time together) were reported by 24% of fathers and 28% of mothers. Finally, 18% of fathers and 10% of mothers reported that the change in lifestyle had not had any effect at all on their marriages. Changes in the marital relationship were also prominent in the responses to two other questions. In response to the question about what they liked about their lifestyle, 10% of fathers and 13% of mothers said it was that their marital relationship was better. In contrast, 11% of fathers and 17% of mothers said that the increased pressure on the marital relationship was the thing they disliked most about shared child care.

These interview responses suggest that the marital relationship was affected in quite diverse ways. Although approximately 45% of parents perceived the change to be positive, another 40% perceived it to be negative. The degree of consistency between these interview assessments and scores on Spanier's scale of marital quality were also examined. Mothers and fathers who reported the change had been positive scored higher on Spanier's scale (mothers, 112.9; fathers, 112.8) than those who said the change had been negative (mothers, 107; fathers, 109). This difference was only significant for mothers' scores ($t = 1.8$, $p \prec .05$). The trend, however, is quite strong, which gives support to the view that a shared-caregiving lifestyle does have an impact on marital relationships. In addition to these general responses, three significant patterns or themes were evident in parents' descriptions of changes in marital relationships. First, a group of parents described in detail the *process of change*, emphasizing the difficulties they had experienced in the initial stages. Second, some aspects of family life emerged as being more significant than others as *sources of conflict*. Third, another group of families emphasized how changing lifestyles had brought the entire family closer together.

"It's Not Easy to Change Roles — Not When You First Start Out"

Nearly 60% of people interviewed remarked that during the first months of changing roles they experienced some difficulty or another. It was during this period when there was more uncertainty about child-care and housework responsibilities, especially during the time when both parents were at home. Parents also found difficulty adjusting to the different emotional demands they each experienced. One response concerning this initial period of adjustment was: "At first I found it boring at home, and Jill seemed to be always tired from working all day, and then having to come home to a family who expected more out of her in time and effort than she was prepared to give. We both thought that at first it created a strain. I think our experiences and the process of adjustment has helped us to understand one another more, especially in relation to our roles as caregiver and provider, both at the emotional and the financial levels. We have now adjusted to a sharing role which we are happy with. But, it did take some time."

The father from another family said: "We had some problems when we first started. Marilyn wasn't too impressed with my standards of housework, and I tended to put it off, which, as it turned out later, she didn't like. She was also having difficulty leaving things to me; I think she still had the expectation that she must be a good mother and that she should take over when she came home. At times I felt it was her child and I was just looking after it. It took us time to sit down and talk about all of this. We are trying to overcome these problems now."

The mother in the same family had this to say: "I have found it difficult to adjust to being a mother for only half-time. We found it a bit difficult in the first few months. I think it was a communication problem more than anything else. We now try to communicate a lot more often. I used to expect Michael to understand my viewpoint without much explanation, just expect him to know how I felt."

Later in the interview, the following responses were given by this same couple when they were asked what they really disliked about their current family pattern:

"The constant decision-making and how we have to constantly stop and take account of things. The renegotiation of things we take for granted. We have to be more structured in a sense or Marilyn would end up doing a lot more of the housework. Her tolerance and time span are a lot different to mine." (Father)

"The constant negotiation and having to come to an agreement on certain things, like housework." (Mother)

Another family encountered these same problems, but found their own unique way of solving them. This is the way the father described it: "We made a decision not to reverse roles, not for me to take over the housework. My university study is just like going to work. I am not doing the housework. Reversing roles is not good for us. We tried it once and it didn't work. It put too much strain on our relationship. It's not natural. Also, it was a psychological thing; we didn't feel good doing it." This is the father from the family described earlier in which the father did not share the housework and the mother was always tired and found it hard maintaining a dual role. The mother, however, agreed with the father in arguing it was not good for their relationship if they "swapped" roles within the home. Also, their lifestyle was somewhat in contradiction with their religion, which emphasized the authoritative status of men and fathers. Presumably, if the father took on more of a domestic role, this would have been seen as a threat to his position both within the home and within their religious community.

Having increased conflict in the first few months of making such a radical change in lifestyles is as one would expect. This is probably all the more likely if people are *genuinely* trying to share the responsibilities for child care and housework. Attempting to do this in a serious way is likely to sensitize people to the problems and thus produce more conflicts. Whether this is necessarily a negative thing or not is an open question. The distinct impression gained from the interviews was that those couples who had "stuck at it" and attempted to communicate their problems and doubts to one another – to work through their problems – saw it as being a very positive thing. The feeling was that in the long term it had itself provided the basis for a "better relationship".

Sources of Conflict

The major conflict areas mentioned by parents were affectional ties with the children, child-rearing practices, fathers' standards of housework, mothers' dissatisfactions with their roles, mothers' tiredness, and the limited time mothers and fathers had to spend together. Some of these conflicts have already been discussed and therefore will only be covered very briefly here.

Affectional ties led to conflicts because in a significant number of families there was a noticeable shift in the primary attachment of the children from the mother to the father. At times of distress and at the more sensitive moments, children in some families were now more likely than before to go to their fathers, and as has already been mentioned, some mothers found this difficult to cope with and developed some hostility towards their spouses.

Although not common (mentioned by only five families), conflict occurred between parents on *child-rearing practices* because fathers were perceived to be too soft; not coming in as the hard disciplinarian. These five mothers were highly critical of the father letting the children get away with too much, giving the children the run of the house, and creating more housework. Fathers, however, saw this "soft" approach as occurring primarily in the early stages of their change; after a period of adjustment they became firmer with the children and were much more likely to set limits on their activities within the house (fathers soon learned they had to tidy up!).

Mothers' complaints about fathers' lower *standards of housework* have already been mentioned. It is difficult to know just how to interpret these complaints. The common response from fathers was that the mothers were "too fussy" and they expected too much. As one father said: "It's all right for her, she can have dirty dishes in the sink when I come home from being out somewhere, and the kids can have their things all over the floor. But, when she comes home from work, she expects the house to be ready for the queen to come in. I don't feel I should have to keep the house to a higher standard than she does." It may also be that in general fathers' standards and expectations of a "tidy house" are very different from mothers'. Or it could be that this is a subtle ploy on the part of fathers to avoid doing some of this more unpleasant work by demonstrating they are incompetent and having the mother come home and take over. If this was the case, few mothers fell for it, as an equally common response from mothers was: "I have had to adjust my standards of housework and having a clean and tidy house. If I didn't we would be in continual conflict."

Tiredness, irritability, and *a lack of time for one another* have all been mentioned previously. The consensus was that this had important implications for all aspects of marital relationships – from day-to-day communication (just talking to one another and catching up on what had happened) and the frequency of arguments through to the very intimate aspects of the relationship, like the display of affection and sexual relationships. Just how significant these changes were for the overall quality of the relationship is uncertain. The data presented earlier from the scale of marital quality suggest that this aspect of a shared-caregiving lifestyle mainly affects the level of day-to-day quarrels and general dissatisfaction.

Bringing the Family Closer Together

Another theme to emerge was the feeling that a shared-caregiving lifestyle brought families closer together. This happened in two ways. First, mother and father had a new basis for communicating and sharing their experiences – the children. With both parents actively involved with their children, they had a lot more to talk about and share with one another.

A second way in which families were brought closer together was by sharing their leisure time. There were few families in which either parent had a major commitment to work on weekends or outside their normal working hours, and very few reported having worked overtime recently. Furthermore, a common response was that parents had *reduced* their personal leisure activities since changing lifestyles, especially those parents in families in which both parents were employed. Indeed, many of these parents reported that as a consequence they now spent *more* of their free time on family activities than they did before; their rushed lifestyle had made them a lot more sensitive to how they spent their free time.

Two Idiosyncratic Responses

Although not significant in terms of the number of people who gave these responses, there were nevertheless two other responses sufficiently significant with regard to changing lifestyles to warrant their inclusion here.

1. *Now I know how a woman feels when her husband retires.* Women often report how difficult they find it to cope with the changes when their husbands retire. A woman who has essentially had the run of the house, time to herself, and considerable freedom for five days a week suddenly finds all this shattered by the presence of her spouse (e.g., "I know I agreed to marry him for better or for worse, but I didn't know that meant I had to put up with him all day every day from sixty-five onwards."). With the children having left home long ago, the mothers had become accustomed to their easier lifestyle and derived considerable enjoyment from it. Now they found that demands were again present, and they were being forced to change their lifestyles. No doubt this experience is similar to that of many mothers who are suddenly confronted with all of their children during the school holidays, or when their husbands are at home during their holidays.

Although not a major response in terms of numbers, this type of reaction was also reported by a few fathers. These were fathers who had been at home for some time (at least three to four years), and had completely adjusted to their role. They enjoyed their freedom and the run of the house and found it somewhat difficult to adjust to their wife being at home during her holidays. Two of these fathers were married to schoolteachers and were specifically referring to the summer school holidays. As one father said: "I can't wait until Cheryl goes back to work. I'd rather be at home by myself. Also, it has created a few more conflicts because I feel she could take a bit more responsibility for the children if she is going to be here. I suppose I was looking for a bit of a break from the kids too, and that might have contributed to my feelings of resentment about her being at home and my having to change my daily routine. I enjoy getting things done early in the morning and getting on and doing something else. During the holidays, though, it is usually ten o'clock before things get going. Cheryl usually leaves for work at about eight — that's two hours difference."

2. *A lack of romanticism.* Two fathers had a very different complaint to make about their relationship — the mother's lack of romanticism. These were fathers who were not employed and had taken over most of the child care and housework. Also, child-care demands were very high; both had three children, two of whom were pre-school-aged. These fathers pointed out that they occasionally thought it would be pleasant if their wife came home with a bunch of flowers, a bottle of wine, or an invitation out to dinner — things they said they did before but now because of their situation found it difficult to do. Furthermore, they felt it was not their role; it would not mean as much as it did before when their wife was at home full-time. Thus, while some women were *very* sensitive about their husbands not taking over all aspects of the role of the person at home — even to the extent of making the bed in the same way, at least two fathers were just as sensitive about their wives not taking on all the trappings of the breadwinner role — not just trying to get home on time, but occasionally (especially when they were late) to bring home something special.

Conclusions

Findings from both sets of data considered here suggest that a shared-caregiving lifestyle does have an impact on marital relationships. Shared-caregiving couples were found to score significantly lower on Spanier's scale of marital quality than traditional couples, and 40% of the sample reported this lifestyle had had a negative impact on their relationship. Nevertheless this impact is clearly not sufficiently drastic to warrant a conclusion that these families represent a high-risk group for marital breakdown. Moreover, 45% of the sample reported things had improved since changing lifestyles. Two factors appear significant in explaining these positive and negative reactions: whether or not the father was happy about changing roles, and the degree to which fathers participated in family work. Findings reported here show that fathers rated their marital relationship more highly when they were more influential in the decision to change, and mothers rated their relationship more highly when fathers were more highly participant in family work. The number of hours spent by either mothers or fathers in paid work was of little consequence by itself.

Despite there being several different areas of dissatisfaction and conflict mentioned in the interview, many of these did not emerge as significant when responses to Spanier's scale were considered. In particular, conflicts about housework and child-rearing were not found to be more frequent in shared-caregiving families compared with traditional families, and there was even an indication that they were *less* frequent. As was noted before, however, it may be that the nature of the conflicts were different between the two family types, with it still being likely shared-caregiving families have more conflicts about the *ways* in which housework and child-rearing are carried out. Interview responses tended to support this interpretation, but also indicated that their conflicts were more prevalent in the first few months. Consistent with interview responses about the physical and emotional demands of their lifestyles, shared-caregiving families did report significantly higher levels of recent general (but unspecified) conflicts and getting on one another's nerves, and persumably as a consequence, less satisfaction with their marital relationships.

Significant effects on the Spanier scale were not found for the length of time for which families has been in a shared-caregiving pattern. Yet a highly significant response to emerge from the interviews was that people experienced difficulties during the *early stages* of changing lifestyles. Perhaps these two findings are not as contradictory as might be first implied. There were only five families in this sample who when interviewed had been in a shared-caregiving lifestyle for less than six months. It is during this early period when the incidence of conflicts might be expected to be at their highest. Clearly, what is needed now is research that investigates the processes and changes associated with this lifestyle by studying families before and at various points after the change.

Finally, even though a shared-caregiving lifestyle has been found to have an impact, and to present some difficulties for mother-father relationships, this should not necessarily be interpreted as being an entirely negative aspect of the change. For, as was argued earlier, it may very well be that the experiences of these difficulties and their resolution will have a very positive effect on family relationships in *the longer term*. It is important nevertheless to recognize these problems (especially in the early stages of changing lifestyles) and to take them into account in future studies. Also, an awareness of these problems might be helpful for those who either advocate changes of this type or might encounter these issues within a counselling context.

9

"What about the children?"

The patterns of day-to-day parent-child interactions are very different in shared-caregiving and traditional families. In shared-caregiving families, fathers are available to their children more often, children spend more time alone with their fathers and less time alone with their mothers, fathers perform more and mothers less of the child-care tasks, and the styles of play interactions are very different, with shared-caregiving fathers being more likely than traditional fathers to be involved in indoor/creative/conventional play. The question to be considered in this chapter is whether or not these differences in patterns of interactions have any effects on child-rearing practices, parent-child relationships, or child-development outcomes?

Although the proposition that high father participation will be associated with quite significant changes in child development is an attractive one, especially for those who advocate changes in family patterns and sex roles, the effects may not necessarily be very great at all. There are several reasons why this could be so. First, the family is only one source of influence over child development. Consider the case of sex-role development, for example; as well as being influenced by parents, a child is likely to be influenced by models portrayed by other adults and by the media, by the expectations of other adults (e.g., grandparents, schoolteachers) and by the expectations of their own peers.

Second, the quantity and content of parent-child interactions are but two of a multitude of possible contributions to parental child-rearing practices and parental influences over child development. Other potential contributors include the quality of interaction (e.g., the sensitivity and warmth of parents' responses to children), the values and beliefs a parent holds about child development and parental roles, parents' own personalities, their previous individual and group socialization experiences (e.g., males not having child-care experiences during adolescence), and the characteristics of children themselves (e.g., gender, temperament, physical features). This is not to say that quantity and content are not important, or that they do not influence other factors such as quality (e.g., an increase in time spent alone with children might lead to dissatisfaction and therefore to a reduction in the quality of parent-child interactions); rather, the argument is simply that changes in the quantity and content of parent-child interactions should be kept in perspective along with other possible contributors.

There is yet another reason why we should be cautious when examining the likely effects of increased paternal participation on children. This is that it might only be a certain type of father, or a father from a particular type of family, who becomes highly participant in the first place. A father highly involved in child care represents a radical departure from normative parental roles, and therefore it might only be fathers with certain personality characteristics, values, and beliefs who even contemplate this change in lifestyles. Aldous (1974), as was noted before, has argued that people who pave the way for new social roles, like these parents here, are more likely to be high on self-esteem, flexibility, and interpersonal sensitivity, and to have an external locus of control (i.e., they are more likely to believe they have control over their lives). Data presented earlier lend some support to this proposition. Shared-caregiving parents described themselves as being high on both traditionally masculine characteristics – for example, independence, assertiveness, and self-confidence (characteristics that have also been associated with high self-esteem [Antill and Cunningham 1980]) – and on traditionally feminine characteristics – for example, sensitivity, warmth, and sympathy. It is entirely consistent, therefore, that these parents will also share different values and beliefs for child-rearing and child development. On the basis of the arguments of Aldous, we might expect them to be more likely to foster independence and interpersonal sensitivity.

Another possibility is that high paternal participation is associated with fathers being strongly committed to, experienced with, and sensitive towards their children; that is, it is only the sensitive and responsive father who becomes highly participant. Data presented earlier again support this possibility. Highly participant fathers were found to be more likely to have attended childbirth classes and the births of their children and to have read books on child care or child-rearing. These are all indicators of these fathers having been more committed *before* they became highly participant.

A final factor which could mediate the effects of high paternal participation is the reasons why parents changed their lifestyles. A father whose high participation is associated with economic necessity (e.g., he was unable to get a job) might react very differently from a father whose participation in child care was a matter of choice and something the family had planned for.

The possible impact of high paternal participation on children is examined in this chapter by focusing on three different levels of analysis. The first concerns the impact it might have on child-rearing or socialization practices, the goals and expectations parents have for their children, and how these influence the emphasis they place on certain types of child behaviours. The next level of analysis concerns the parent-child relationship − the nature and quality of this relationship. Finally, an analysis is made of the small amount of data currently available on the possible effects on child-development outcomes. Before this, however, a discussion is presented of shared-caregiving parents' own assessments of the consequences of their lifestyles for their children.

Shared-Caregiving Parents' Assessments of the Effects on Their Children

Parents were asked whether their change in lifestyles had presented any problems for their children. In reply, 76% of fathers and 64% of mothers said their children had not experienced any major difficulties at all. A common response was: "That surprised us; we expected some type of reaction." This surprised response came both from parents who were ideologically committed to shared-caregiving and from those who reported they had been forced to change and would prefer a traditional family pattern. Some of those who were ideologically committed to changing sex roles even said they were disconcerted by the absence of effects. As one father said: "I thought it would have some effect. However, you wouldn't be able to pick her from all the other girls in the neighbourhood − she's as sex-typed as the others are."

Nevertheless, 24% of fathers and 20% of mothers reported that their children had experienced some minor difficulties in the initial stages. The most common form of this response was that the children became anxious and cried when mothers left home to go to work. However, only 6% of mothers reported that their children strongly resented their leaving them and that this would have long-term effects on their relationships and would possibly affect their child's personality development. Four fathers also reported that their children took some time to adjust to them and their ways of doing things. "I tended to expect things to be done quicker," one father said. "The children had to adjust to my way of doing everyday things and my organization. Sarah still says sometimes, 'Mum doesn't do that.' "

On the positive side, 44% of fathers and 40% of mothers felt their children had gained considerably from the change in lifestyles because of their improved relationships with their fathers. Furthermore, 34% of fathers and 30% of mothers mentioned the improved relationship with both parents as a major advantage for their children. A common response was that the children now had two parents to relate to and two parents with whom they could develop close bonds. The psychological literature has for a long time subscribed to the view that children are attached to only one parent, and that it is *desirable* for them to have a primary attachment with only one parent or adult. The response of parents here who saw their children as being strongly attached to both parents, however, was that this was "better" from the child's viewpoint. Whether there is a *dual* attachment and whether this has any long-term positive or negative effects on a child's development is something researchers will need to investigate.

Parental Child-Rearing or Socialization Practices

Parental socialization practices refer not only to the types of behaviours and traits parents attempt to encourage in their children but also to the ways and the contexts in which they do this. To illustrate, a parent might value the trait of co-operation and attempt to emphasize this when the child is playing with other children (context) by reacting positively to this behaviour when it occurs (ways/methods). Parents also socialize their children in more indirect ways — for example, parents' interactions with one another and with other adults provide models for the children to identify with and possibly imitate or reject. Although a distinction has been made here between socialization practices, parent-child relationships, and child development outcomes, they are, of course, intimately related to one another in the socialization process. Whether or not a child actually adopts a particular behaviour pattern is likely to be dependent both on socialization practices and parent-child relationships. For example, a child would be more likely to respond to the socialization emphases of a parent with whom the child had a warm and sensitive relationship.

There are two major ways of assessing parental socialization practices. One involves self-report, either by parents or children; the other, observation of parent-child interactions. The most commonly used method for the study of mother-father differences in socialization practices has been the self-report method, and this was the method employed in the present study. What follows is an analysis of differences between shared-caregiving and traditional parents for child-rearing values, beliefs about parental influences, and conflicts between mothers and fathers on child-rearing practices.

Values

The emphasis here on parental socialization values is consistent with the recent interest in cognitive variables as possible mediators of parental behaviour (as discussed earlier). The argument is that parental beliefs and values are linked with parental behaviour, and that parental knowledge and experiences are likely to influence beliefs and values and, as a consequence, influence behaviour too. In support of this argument, parental values and beliefs have been found to be associated with differences in cultural background (Goodnow 1981), socio-economic status (Kohn 1969; McGillicuddy-De Lisi 1981), and maternal employment status (Hock 1980; Hoffman 1977). In the same way, parental beliefs and values might be influenced by the nature and extent of parents' day-to-day interactions with their children. As others also have suggested (Field 1978; Lamb et al. 1982), differences in day-to-day interactions might account for the mother-father differences that have been noted in both observational (see Lamb 1981) and interview studies. It is the interview studies that are more relevant here. These show that fathers, more than mothers, value independence, success, and competitiveness (Block 1979; Russell 1979b; Stolz 1967) and sex-appropriate behaviour (e.g., Block 1979, 1981; see also Hoffman 1977). Mothers, in contrast, have been found to place more emphasis on the expression of affection and nurturance, and interpersonal sensitivity and warmth (e.g., Barnett et al. 1980; Block 1979; Russell 1979b; Russell and Russell 1982). These dif-

ferences, it can be argued, are associated with traditional parental and sex roles; fathers are more likely to be involved in paid
employment and to identify more with achievement and success, and mothers are more likely to be involved in nurturant or
caregiving situations and child-rearing situations that have the
potential to produce interpersonal conflict (cf. Patterson 1980),
all requiring an emphasis on interpersonal relationships,
warmth, and sensitivity. In addition, Block (1981) reviews
several studies which indicate that, overall, men have more
individualistic and instrumental orientations and women are
more interpersonally oriented, suggesting that they might be
more pervasive characteristics of males and females.

A change in parental values may occur when fathers become
more highly participant in child care and have to deal constantly
with the day-to-day problems of child-rearing. As such, these
fathers may be expected to place more value on expressiveness
and interpersonal relations and less emphasis on success and
achievement. They might also place less emphasis on sex-
appropriate behaviour and conformity to social norms of
behaviour because they themselves have adopted lifestyles that
contradict normative family roles.

As a way of examining the possibility of a shared-caregiving
lifestyle being associated with different socialization values,
parents in both shared-caregiving and traditional families were
read a list of twenty-one child characteristics/developmental outcomes (see below) and were asked to rate each on a four-point
scale of importance: *very important* (equated with a score of 1),
fairly important (2), *fairly unimportant* (3), and *not important at all*
(4). The items were based on the most common responses given
by parents to an open-ended question in an earlier study about
their perceptions of desirable child characteristics (Russell
1979b). A factor analysis was then conducted of these responses
and five sub-scales were formed. The scales and the individual
items are listed below:

1. *Interpersonal sensitivity/expressiveness.* Getting on well with
   other children; being co-operative and sharing things; able
   to express love and affection; being sensitive to others'
   needs and feelings.
2. *Independence in thought and action.* Being independent and
   able to stand up for oneself; able to work things out, think,
   and solve problems; having a good imagination and being
   creative; being curious and interested in how and why
   things happen.

3. *Conformity to social norms.* Being honest, having "good" morals; being well behaved and doing what they are told; being well mannered, neat, and tidy; trying hard at things they do; acting like a boy/girl.
4. *Success and achievement.* Having a good and secure job; doing well at school; being good at sport.
5. *Personal well-being.* Having a good sense of humour; being happy; being well-adjusted; being healthy.

Mean ratings for each of the five scales of child-rearing values, for mothers and fathers in the two family types, are shown in table 19. These figures indicate that shared-caregiving parents place less value on "conformity to social norms" and "success and achievement", and more value on "interpersonal sensitivity/expressiveness" and "independence in thought and action". No differences are apparent for "personal well-being". Two other trends are also evident for ratings on "interpersonal sensitivity/expressiveness": mothers in both family types appear to value these characteristics more than fathers; and shared-caregiving fathers appear to place more value on these than do traditional fathers.

Table 19. Ratings of parental child-rearing values

	Shared-caregiving		Traditional	
	Fathers	Mothers	Fathers	Mothers
Sensitivity/expressiveness	1.46	1.37	1.65	1.45
Independence in thought and action	1.48	1.47	1.63	1.66
Conformity to social norms	1.80	1.84	1.58	1.53
Success and achievement	2.42	2.42	2.26	2.17
Personal well-being	1.38	1.44	1.40	1.43

1 = very important; 4 = not important at all

As has already been noted, shared-caregiving and traditional families differed significantly on some personal and family characteristics. The multivariate analysis of variance (MANOVA) conducted to examine family-type and gender-of-parent effects therefore included these variables as covariates. The only covariate which turned out to have a significant effect was mothers' education ($F[5,193] = 4.9$, $p < .001$), and so this was the only one included in the final analysis. Consistent with previous studies (e.g., Kohn 1969), higher levels of education were associated with parents placing more emphasis on independence in thought and action and less emphasis on conformity to social norms. Level of education, however, did not appear to influence values for interpersonal sensitivity/expressiveness. The multivariate analysis of covariance did not reveal a significant family-type by gender-of-parent interaction effect but did reveal a highly significant family-type effect and a moderately significant gender-of-parent effect. The means and F values for the analysis of family-type effects are summarized in table 20. The multivariate effect for family type was highly significant, and this was mainly accountable for by shared-caregiving parents placing less value on "conformity to social norms", and to a lesser extent by their placing greater value on "sensitivity/expressiveness" and "independence in thought and action".

Table 20. Mean ratings of child-rearing values adjusted for occupational and educational covariates

	Shared-Caregiving[a]	Traditional
Sensitivity/expressiveness	1.42[b]	1.54
Independence in thought and action	1.49[c]	1.62
Conformity to social norms	1.79[d]	1.61
Success and achievement	2.36	2.32
Personal well-being	1.41	1.41

[a]Multivariate $F(5,192) = 2.92$ $p < .02$
[b]Univariate $F(1,196) = 3.9$ $p < .05$
[c]Univariate $F(1,196) = 3.9$ $p < .05$
[d]Univariate $F(1,196) = 5.6$ $p < .02$

The multivariate F value for the gender-of-parent effect approached significance ($F[5,192] = 2.12$, $p < .06$). This effect was almost entirely accountable for by differences on only one of the scales — "interpersonal sensitivity/expressiveness" ($F[1,196] = 5.25$, $p < .02$). In agreement with previous research findings, mothers placed more value on these characteristics than fathers did (means = 1.39 vs. 1.52). Thus, gender differences on the values held for interpersonal sensitivity/expressiveness appear to remain, despite fathers' active participation in child care.

Given the consistent finding from previous studies that fathers place more emphasis on sex-appropriate behaviour, a further analysis was conducted to examine family-type and gender-of-parent differences on values for the individual item "acting like a boy/girl". The only significant effect to emerge was a family-type effect, with shared-caregiving parents placing less value on this item (means: 2.65 vs. 2.07; F[1,196] = 14.6, p< .001).

There were many differences within shared-caregiving families which could also influence child-rearing values — reasons why this family pattern was adopted, length of time in this pattern, and time spent by fathers each day performing child care tasks and interacting with their children — and so further analyses were conducted to examine these.

Effects for reasons why this family pattern was adopted (necessity vs. choice) were examined using a multivariate analysis of covariance, with mothers' and fathers' education levels and occupational statuses included as covariates (earlier, it was reported that a change by choice was associated with higher levels on these variables). No significant effects were evident either with or without the covariates included in the analysis (all multivariate F values< 1). Thus, whether or not the change in family patterns was a matter of choice appears to be of little consequence for parental child-rearing values.

The possible effects of within-group differences in levels of participation were examined using correlational analyses. Correlations between parents' ratings on each of the value scales and five measures of participation were all low, and none was significant. For example, the correlations between fathers' ratings on the scale of "interpersonal sensitivity/expressiveness" and the participation variables were: time spent in this family pattern, .04; time available each week, -.02; time spent performing child care tasks, -.05; time spent on play, -.12; time spent taking sole responsibility, .09. The specific level of participation, therefore, appears to have little effect on shared-caregiving parents' ratings of the value of child characteristics.

Although quite significant differences were found in child-rearing values between shared-caregiving and traditional parents, differences that are consistent with their vastly different lifestyles, the analyses do not favour the conclusion that these differences are causally related to differences in the quantity and content of parent-child interactions. Indeed, the value dimension that was expected to be most open to the influence of participation variables — interpersonal sensitivity/expressiveness — still revealed a significant gender-of-parent difference. What is needed now are studies that investigate whether or not these differences in values are reflected in actual socialization practices.

Beliefs about Parental Influences

The roles of parents in shared-caregiving families were much less differentiated than in traditional families — both mothers and fathers were highly involved in child care, and in the majority of families both were employed in the paid work force too. What implications does this have for socialization practices and the influences that parents have? One implication is that the parental and adult models portrayed by mothers and fathers in shared-caregiving families will be very different, and this will have an indirect influence on socialization through identification and imitation processes. Another possible implication is that shared-caregiving parents might be less likely to adopt stereotyped socialization roles (i.e., father emphasizing independence and achievement; mother emphasizing affection) and believe that their influences over their children are much more diverse than traditional parents.

As a way of examining this hypothesis, parents were asked whether they thought each of ten behaviours (listed in table 21) were (a) learnt more easily from fathers, (b) learnt more easily from mothers, (c) learnt equally from mothers and fathers. There were significant family differences, with differences between traditional and non-traditional fathers being more pronounced. In general, shared-caregiving parents' responses were overwhelmingly in the category of the behaviours being equally likely to be influenced by both parents: 84% of their responses were in this category compared with only 53% of traditional parents' responses. Only three items showed any hint of being differentiated by shared-caregiving parents: "coping with rough and tumble and fighting" and "being independent and standing up for themselves", both thought to be learnt more easily from fathers, and "coping with and expressing feelings", thought to be learnt more easily from mothers. Nevertheless, this trend towards parental differentiation was much more marked for traditional parents. As a group, they were significantly more likely to say that the following are learnt more easily from fathers: "coping with rough and tumble and fighting", "being independent and standing up for themselves", "trying hard at things they do", and being "modest about success". Mothers were seen as being more likely to influence "the ability to share and be co-operative", "being affectionate", and "coping with and expressing feelings". These findings suggest that shared-caregiving parents see their areas of potential influence as being less differentiated than do traditional parents. Consistent with the models they portray, shared-

Table 21. Perceptions of role differentiation.[1]

| | Learnt from Father | | | | Learnt from Mother | | | | Learnt from Both Parents | | | |
| | Shared | | Traditional | | Shared | | Traditional | | Shared | | Traditional | |
	Mo	Fa	Mo	Fa	Mo	Fa	Mo	Fa	Mo	Fa	Mo	Fa
Coping with rough and tumble/fighting	33	50	80	100	0	0	0	0	67	50	20	0
Sharing/co-operative	8	8	7	7	8	0	40	40	84	92	53	53
Affection	0	8	0	7	17	8	26	40	83	84	74	53
Honesty	0	0	13	13	8	8	13	13	92	92	74	74
Independence	25	8	20	50	0	0	13	0	75	92	67	50
Coping with/expressing feelings	0	0	13	20	33	17	40	31	67	83	47	49
Accepting failure	16	8	20	31	8	16	29	20	76	76	51	49
Trying hard	8	0	13	50	8	0	0	0	84	100	87	50
Modest about success	0	0	27	13	16	0	27	27	84	100	46	50
Wanting to do well	8	8	7	21	0	0	21	13	92	92	72	66

[1] Figures represent percentages of people who gave each response type.

caregiving parents' roles in socialization therefore are likely to be more diverse too. Observational data on parent-child interactions are again needed to examine whether there is a match between beliefs and behaviour.

Parental Conflicts

Because parents in shared-caregiving families both experience periods when they have total effective control of their children and both are highly participant, this might serve to accentuate differences and lead to an increase in conflicts between parents about child-rearing practices. Alternatively, if conflicts are based on different knowledge, understanding, and expectations about children's behaviour, which are associated with mothers and fathers sharing different day-to-day experiences with their children, then, having both parents actively involved could serve to bring parents' child-rearing practices into closer agreement.

Differences in child-rearing practices were assessed in the present study by asking parents to rate, on a five-point scale, how well each of the statements listed in table 22 described their spouses (the range was from "not at all like" to "very much like").

In disagreement with the possibilities outlined above, a multivariate analysis of variance of responses to these items did not reveal a significant effect for family type. There was, however, a strong effect for sex of parent, and a trend towards an interaction between family type and sex of parent. Overall, fathers in both shared-caregiving and traditional families were perceived to be stricter with the children and to be more likely to take charge of family problems when they arose. This finding that both fathers and mothers report that fathers are stricter with their children is consistent with previous self-report and observational studies (cf. Baumrind 1980).

There were two interesting non-significant trends for family-type by sex-of-parent interactions. First, mothers in shared-caregiving families, compared with mothers in traditional families, were *more* likely to perceive their spouses as being stricter, and were *more* likely to report that their spouses felt they should be firmer with the children. The second trend for family-type by sex-of-parent interactions was that mothers in shared-caregiving families were *less* likely to report their spouses took charge when family problems arose and more likely to report that their husband volunteered to help when needed.

Table 22. Parental perceptions of differences in child-rearing practices

Item	Shared-Caregiving		Traditional	
	Father	Mother	Father	Mother
Agrees on what to expect from children	4.1	4.2	4.2	4.3
Thinks I'm too easy on children	2.3	2.6	2.2	2.4
Volunteers to help when I need it	4.1	4.3a	3.9	3.8
Lets the children do things I disapprove of	2.0	1.8	2.1	1.8
Approves of the way I handle the children	4.1	4.0	3.9	4.2
Is usually stricter with children than I am	2.4	3.2b	2.5	2.8
Pitches in willingly when I'm rushed	4.2	4.3	4.3	4.0
Tells me my rules for the children are too strict	2.0	1.6b	1.9	1.7
Takes charge when family problems arise	2.8	3.5ab	3.1	4.0
Backs me when I correct a child	4.3	4.3	4.3	4.2
Tells me I should be firmer with the children	2.1	2.4	1.9	2.1
Tries to be helpful when I'm busy	3.9	4.2	4.0	3.9
Thinks my standards for the children are too high	1.9	1.9	2.0	2.0

Scale: 5 = very much like; 1 = not at all like

aDifferences between family types $p < .05$
bDifferences between mothers and fathers $p < .05$
MANOVA – test of sex-of-parent differences $F_{(13,150)} = 3.29$, $p < .001$

Perhaps these findings can be interpreted as yet a further indication of responsibility and power being more evenly distributed between mothers and fathers in shared-caregiving families.

Finally, the two family types did not differ significantly on the following items: "agreement on what should be expected of the children"; "letting the children do things that the other parent disapproves of"; "approval of the way each parent handles the children"; and "backing each other when a child is corrected". Overall then, data on parental perceptions suggest that a shared-caregiving lifestyle has only a minor impact on conflicts between parents on child-rearing practices. These findings, it may be noted, are consistent with the finding reported in the previous chapter that shared-caregiving parents were not more likely to disagree about child-rearing.

Parent-Child Relationships

A change in parent-child relationships, but more particularly in the father-child relationship, may be another consequence of changes in child-care patterns. There are several possible ways of conceptualizing parent-child relationships: (a) time spent together, (b) frequency of interaction, (c) content of interactions, and (d) quality of interactions. Data have already been presented which indicate that shared-caregiving parents' relationships with their children differ quite markedly from those of traditional parents, on each of these four dimensions. For example, fathers spend much more time performing child-care tasks (content differences), and both fathers and mothers reported a significant change in the closeness of father-child relationships (qualitative differences). These findings, however, are based on self-report data, and on parents' own perceptions. Although fathers might feel differently about their children, it is an entirely different question whether this is reciprocated by the children or whether it is evident in the quality of father-child interactions. The purpose of this section is to review recent studies that have observed father-child interactions in families in which fathers were highly participant.

Field (1978) has investigated styles of interaction (videotaped observational session of three minutes duration) between parents and their four-month-olds in families in which (1) fathers were primary caregivers, (2) fathers were secondary caregivers, and (3) mothers were primary caregivers. Primary-caregiving fathers were found to be similar to primary-caregiving mothers and different from secondary-caregiving fathers on several features of interaction patterns (e.g., on the amount of smiling and imitative grimaces displayed), but different from primary-caregiving mothers and similar to secondary-caregiving fathers on others (e.g., game playing). Field has suggested that this pattern of findings, especially the similarity between primary-caregiving fathers and mothers, is likely to be related to the similar experiences they share in their day-to-day contact with their children. The finding that primary- and secondary-caregiving fathers also display similar patterns of interaction for play suggests that there are gender-based differences in parent-child interaction which are *not* influenced by changes in day-to-day experiences with infants. There are two major problems with this study, however; first, as was noted earlier, specific data were not provided on the level of father participation; and second, the study did not include a group of mothers who were the secondary caregivers of their children.

The second major study on the effects of father participation on father-child relationships is that conducted in Sweden by Lamb and his associates (Lamb et al. 1981, 1982). This is a longitudinal study of families in which fathers planned to take one or more months' leave (up to a possible six months in the Swedish system) to be the primary caregivers of their child — termed non-traditional fathers — and another group in which fathers planned to take less than one month leave — termed traditional fathers. Naturalistic observational sessions (forty-five minutes in duration) were conducted separately for mothers and fathers in their homes when their children were three months of age. In contrast to the findings of Field, differences between family types and between mothers and fathers were very small. Only one major finding emerged; this was that non-traditional parents, both mothers and fathers, interacted preferentially with daughters, a trend that is in the opposite direction to that found for traditional parents, where it is sons who are interacted with preferentially.

Although Lamb and his associates selected their sample on the basis of planned father-involvement, few fathers had actually taken over caregiving at the time of the initial observational session (Lamb et al. 1981). The researchers suggested that this was related to the high value placed on breastfeeding, and expected that when observational sessions were conducted at eight and sixteen months there would be a substantial number of fathers who were the primary caregivers.

When they returned at eight months, Lamb and his associates only found seventeen fathers had been primary caregivers for more than one month (the average was 2.8 months) (Lamb et al. 1982). Comparisons were made at this time between families in which fathers had been the primary caregivers for at least one of the three months immediately preceeding the observation (n = 14), and those in which fathers had not had this degree of recent involvement (n = 37). Mothers and fathers were observed interacting with their infants together in their homes for an average of 106 minutes.

In agreement with the observations at three months, father-involvement appeared to have little impact on the pattern of interactions. Mothers were found to be more likely than fathers to hold, tend to (i.e., engage in caregiving activities), display affection (kiss, hug, cuddle), smile at, and vocalize to their infants, irrespective of whether or not the father had been the primary caregiver recently. Also, non-traditional fathers were found to be the *least* likely of all parental groups to engage in play.

This study also involved the collection of data on security of attachment and infant sociability at twelve months, and the observation of parent-child interactions at sixteen months. Again, few differences were found between non-traditional and traditional fathers. The only hint of an effect was that at twelve months the children from families in which the father was highly participant were moderately more sociable towards a stranger.

These findings from the Swedish study suggest, therefore, that high father participation has little impact on observed patterns of mother- and father-infant interactions and attachment. Moreover, they could be interpreted as being at variance with the very strong findings from the self-report studies, that high father participation does have an effect on the time, frequency, content, and possibly the quality of parent-child interactions. There are, however, several limitations with the research of Lamb and his associates, which, when considered, suggest that there is a need to be somewhat cautious about their findings.

First, there is some question about the actual degree of involvement of these Swedish fathers, and whether they are *highly* participant. Few fathers maintained their high level of involvement throughout the course of the study, and the non-traditional classification at twelve and sixteen months was based on data collected at eight months. Moreover, the study (Lamb et al. 1982) did not provide data on specific levels of participation in either child care or play, nor on the amount of time fathers spent each day as primary caregivers. Given that at eight months of age, most infants are asleep for a significant portion of the day, differences in levels of participation between those classified as non-traditional and traditional might not be as great as we might expect. It is possible, therefore, that, as was found in the present study, these non-traditional fathers were less involved than their spouses. Nevertheless, even if they are more highly participant than either their spouses or traditional Swedish fathers, having only one month in such a family situation is obviously too brief a time to provide an adequate test of the effects of high father participation (note, this compares with eight months for the traditional mothers and seven months for the non-traditional mothers in this sample).

Second, it may be that the findings are an artefact of the particular observational situation employed (i.e., observing mothers and fathers together during the early evening). Lamb and his associates note that on five of their six major measures of parent-child interaction at eight months, non-traditional mothers scored the *highest* of all groups. This is consistent with the present findings that parents in shared-caregiving families reported mothers tended to take over when they came home; and that when both parents were at home, mothers were more involved than fathers in both child care and play. Observations of mothers and fathers alone, and together at different times of the day, might reveal entirely different patterns.

A final limitation of the Lamb et al. study is also applicable to the study by Field (1978). This is that the response measures chosen for study up to this point have been rather narrow in focus and have mainly examined the frequency and content of interactions (e.g., the frequency of different types of play). Yet, self-report data from the present study suggest that the quality of father-child relationships might be different too. Specifically, most fathers reported feeling closer to their children and deriving more satisfaction from the affection they shared with them, and a significant minority reported they understood their children better. This latter finding is consistent with the arguments of both Goldberg (1977) and Lamb and Easterbrooks (1980). Lamb and Easterbrooks have argued that "interaction facilitates the growth of parental sensitivity by providing practice differentiating among, interpreting, and responding to infant signals. Fathers who have more interaction with young infants may be better prepared for sensitive responding later."

Research is required, therefore, which employs measures of responsiveness and sensitivity similar to those already used in studies of mothers (e.g., Ainsworth et al. 1978), to investigate if highly participant fathers are more likely than traditional fathers to "provide contingent, appropriate, and consistent responses to infants' (or children's) signals or needs" (Lamb and Easterbrooks 1980). Other measures that need to be included in future observational studies are ones that examine more closely the affective nature of parent-child relationships, both from the parent's and the child's perspective. As has been pointed out already, however, particular care will need to be taken in such studies, as it may only be the already sensitive father who becomes highly participant.

Child Development Outcomes

Research on the influences that high father participation has on child development suffers from the same limitations as the studies already discussed on socialization practices and parent-child relationships. There are few studies; they have focused on a very narrow set of variables, and little data have been provided on the extent of father participation. The areas that have received the most attention to date have been sex roles, cognitive development, empathy, and locus of control.

Sex Roles

The hypothesis that fathers being more highly participant will effect patterns of sex-role development is probably one of the most obvious. Given that both mothers and fathers in these families adopt roles that are less sex-stereotyped, it might be expected that their children will be less stereotyped too. Three studies have assessed the effects of high father participation on children's sex roles and/or children's perceptions of parental roles (an important variable when considering the possible models parents portray in these families). Radin (1981), in her American study of highly participant fathers, administered the It-Scale (Brown 1956), a test of sex-role orientation, to the preschool-aged children in her sample. No significant relationship was found between paternal involvement and children's sex-role scores, either for boys or girls. In contrast, Sagi (1981) in his Israeli study found a relationship between scores on the It-Scale and paternal involvement for girls (again pre-schoolers); high father involvement was associated with girls scoring higher on the masculinity component.

Both Radin and Sagi have also investigated children's perceptions of their parents and their roles. Radin reports that high paternal participation is associated with children holding less stereotyped views of day-to-day parental roles (e.g., which parent uses the washing machine). Radin and Sagi, however, report conflicting findings for children's perceptions of the qualities associated with each parent. Radin reports that high father participation is associated with children perceiving their fathers as more punitive, whereas Sagi reports it to be associated with children perceiving their fathers as less punitive and more nurturant. The findings by Radin that highly participant fathers are perceived as more punitive is consistent with findings from the present Australian study. As was noted earlier, there was a trend for shared-caregiving fathers to be perceived as being stricter with their children than traditional fathers.

It is difficult to explain the different findings from the American and Israeli studies. Obviously the cultural differences must account for some of it. Neither study reports precise details on father participation, however, so this is a variable that may account for some of the differences as well. Finally, Sagi provides very few details of his sample (e.g., education levels, occupations); there may be differences here that would also help explain the discrepant findings.

In another American study, Braymen and DeFrain (1979) examined the sex-role attitudes and reported behaviours of children reared by parents defined as being androgynous (in DeFrain's terms they shared the caregiving responsibilities), and compared them with children raised by traditional parents. The children ranged in age from four to twelve years. Children of androgynous parents were found to have more flexible attitudes about parental roles, in assigning personality traits to the sexes, and in choosing peers of both sexes. No significant differences were found, however, on the expressions of masculine/feminine interests or on occupational interests.

Cognitive Development

Radin (1981) has examined the effects of high father involvement on children's cognitive development. Children were given the Peabody Picture Vocabulary Test — a verbal intelligence test

— and Raven's Coloured Progressive Matrices Test. Positive correlations were found between the degree of father involvement and verbal intelligence test scores for both boys and girls. Radin's findings also indicated that fathers heavily involved in caregiving spent more time in efforts to stimulate their children's cognitive growth, and that this difference between fathers who were highly involved and those who were not was more pronounced for sons than for daughters.

Empathy

Both Radin and Sagi have examined the relationship between father participation and their children's level of empathy, using the same test. Radin failed to find any significant relationship, whereas Sagi reported that higher levels of empathy were associated with higher father involvement. As before, because of the vast differences between these two studies, it is difficult to explain the discrepant findings. Sagi suggests that higher levels of empathy are related to highly participant fathers being more supportive, nurturant, sensitive and warm. The present study reported, however, that both mothers and fathers in shared-caregiving families were more likely to value interpersonal sensitivity and expressiveness; therefore it is possible that both parents have contributed to the difference noted by Sagi, and it may not be causally linked with paternal participation at all.

Locus of Control

Radin and Sagi have again both examined the locus of control variable. This time, more agreement is evident. Both studies report that high father participation is associated with higher levels of internality, or an internal locus of control (i.e., the feeling that the children have control over their lives). As Sagi also notes, this finding is consistent with other findings he discusses, which indicate that highly participant fathers encourage independence. This, in turn, is in agreement with the present finding that shared-caregiving parents placed greater value on independence in thought and action than traditional parents.

Conclusions

It is difficult at this very early stage of research into the effects of high father participation to be confident about drawing any conclusions. Findings discussed in this chapter are based on only five studies, and four of these were conducted in different cultures (the United States, Sweden, Israel, and Australia). Moreoever, few studies have provided adequate details either of the characteristics of the samples they have used or of the degree to which the fathers were participant in child care. There is some doubt, therefore, whether all studies could be considered to have provided adequate tests of the effects of high father participation. Despite these reservations, there are some findings which are sufficiently strong at this stage to warrant that they be investigated further.

Three studies lend support to the hypothesis that high father participation is associated with different socialization practices. Both the present study and that of Sagi in Israel report that when fathers are more highly participant there is greater emphasis on the encouragement of independence. Such a finding is consistent with the findings of both Sagi and Radin (in the United States) that high participation is associated with children who score higher on tests of internality or internal locus of control. Another emphasis in socialization found to be associated with high father participation was the encouragement of interpersonal sensitivity and expressiveness – again noted in the present study and that by Sagi. Nevertheless, findings from the present study did not lend support to the hypothesis that these socialization emphases are causally linked with the degree of father participation. Rather, the data supported the hypothesis that these families were different to begin with, and perhaps these socialization values were *antecedents* of this child-care pattern.

An area in which the findings are somewhat ambiguous at present, and therefore in need of more urgent attention from researchers, is the effects of father participation on the qualitative nature of the father-child relationship. Self-report data presented in this Australian study are quite strong in indicating there is an effect on the father-child relationship, particularly from the father's perspective. Yet observational studies in Sweden and the United States conducted to date reveal few differences between traditional and non-traditional fathers for father-child interactions or for infants' attachments to fathers. As was pointed out earlier in this chapter, we need additional observational research that focuses more specifically on the affective nature of the father-child relationship, as this was the aspect that was more commonly noted by both fathers and mothers in interviews as having changed. We also need to be more certain that the fathers being sudied are indeed highly participant.

Finally, if we ignore the limitations noted above and accept that all studies reported here included samples of very highly participant fathers, then we could conclude that the effects of this change are very minor indeed — a conclusion that agrees with parents' own assessments. Perhaps we need to be cautious about this conclusion, however, for a reason other than any of those already considered. All of the studies to date have been with infants or pre-school-aged children. It may be that the effects of non-traditional family roles will only become evident later in a child's life, and especially when they themselves become parents.

Would such a conclusion that high father-participation has a limited impact be very surprising? Perhaps not when all the other possible contributors to child development (e.g., peers, the media, schools) listed above are taken into account. Such an outcome would not be all that surprising either when the level of father participation is placed in perspective. In the present study, for example, fathers performed 44% of child-care tasks for thirty-one months out of the seventy their families had children, whereas the mothers performed 56% of child-care tasks for thirty-one months, and presumably 70–80% for the other thirty-nine months. Thus, even though in comparison to traditional fathers these fathers are highly participant, they have still not had the same degree of participation as their spouses or mothers in traditional families.

10

Shared-Caregiving — a Passing Phase?

One could not help but be impressed by the openness and enthusiasm with which the majority of shared-caregiving parents
spoke about their non-traditional family roles. There was even a
hint of missionary zeal in the way many advocated this should
be the normal family pattern, despite their having encountered
several problems with changing roles. The personal and family
benefits appeared to be more than sufficient to outweigh the difficulties and costs — or this is what the majority of parents said
when they were interviewed. It is possible, however, that this
initial enthusiasm clouded parents' assessments of this family
pattern and that at a later date they might perceive this balance
between benefits and costs very differently. This possibility was
examined here by following up and re-interviewing twenty-
seven of the families recruited in the early stages of this project
two years after their initial interview. It is this follow-up study
which is discussed in this chapter.

Rationale for a Follow-up Study

Most psychological and sociological studies of the family (and
other phenomena, for that matter) adopt static approaches by
studying behaviour or beliefs at only one point in time. When inferences are made about changes, this is usually done by
employing cross-sectional designs similar to those used in this
study. In this study, inferences have been made about a shared-
caregiving family pattern by (1) comparing this type of family
with the traditional family and (2) by examining the relationship
between the length of time a family had been in a shared-
caregiving lifestyle and variables of interest (e.g., marital
quality). This approach, however, can tell us little of how individual behaviour patterns change over the course of time, or

whether there are significant interactions between personal and family characteristics and peoples' reactions to this lifestyle. Also, given that shared-caregiving is radically different from the norm, and social support for it is lacking, it might be more susceptible to change than other patterns (e.g., the traditional family).

Answers to these questions of change are best provided by longitudinal studies — studies in which data are collected from the same families over an extended period of time — for example, before they adopted a shared-caregiving lifestyle, three months after, twelve months after, two years after, and so on. Such a sophisticated study was well beyond the bounds of the present program of research. By way of compromise, twenty-seven of the first thirty-three families recruited into the study were located and interviewed two years after their initial interview. And to provide a basis for comparison, a random sample of 31 of the 145 traditional families already described were also re-interviewed two years later. The aims of this follow-up study were (1) to investigate how stable this family pattern is (how long do people actually remain as shared-caregivers?) and (2) to explore whether people who remain in a shared-caregiving lifestyle change their perspectives of this family pattern and their assessments of the balance between benefits and costs.

Family Patterns Two Years Later

Only *ten* out of the twenty-seven shared-caregiving families were in exactly the same family organizational pattern two years later. In *four* families, all children were at school and both parents were employed full-time (the mothers, however, were carrying out the majority of child-care tasks). *Two* couples had separated; in one the mother had taken the children, while in the other, child care was still shared (see below). *Eleven* families (41%) had since changed back to a traditional lifestyle (here termed traditional-changed families), with mothers being the primary caregivers (although in three families the mother was employed either part-time or on a casual basis).

Things had not changed nearly so much in the thirty-one traditional families. Indeed, the striking feature of this sample, in comparison with what was found in the shared-caregiving group, was *how little had changed*. In *two* families the mother was now employed full-time, and *one* family had adopted a shared-caregiving lifestyle. But, in the other twenty-eight families (90%), the family organizational pattern was exactly the same as when the initial interview was carried out. So it seems that the shared-caregiving pattern is much less stable than the traditional pattern, with only 37% of shared-caregiving families remaining in the same family pattern over the period of two years.

Possible Explanations for Family Change

The families of most interest are those in which the parents had separated and those that had returned completely to a traditional lifestyle. Families in which both parents were employed full-time and all children were at school are of least interest. In three of these latter families the mother was employed as a schoolteacher, and it was her responsibility to care for the children of an afternoon. Although fathers were still highly participant, it was not the case that they shared child care equally.

Separated Families

Interviews were conducted with the father in one separated family and both parents in the other. These three parents were adamant that the adoption of a shared-caregiving lifestyle had not caused their separation; however, they did think that it had facilitated it in some way. In the first family, the father pointed out that two years before he resigned his job and stayed at home they had been separated for a period of six months. A major part of the "problem", he said, was the mother's frustrations at home and her strong desire to pursue her career. Adopting a shared-caregiving lifestyle with the mother employed and the father caring for the children was seen as a possible solution to the mother's difficulties and their constant arguments. The mother did extremely well in her job, gaining rapid promotion. Contrary to their expectations, however, little changed at home, and the level of conflict between the parents remained high. In the final event, the mother moved out, took the two children, secured a transfer in her job to another city where her parents were, and continued her career while her own mother cared for the children.

In the second separated family, the parents still shared the care of their two-year-old. The mother and father lived in the same street, and their child took turns at spending one week with each parent. These parents were also convinced that their separation was not caused by their shared-caregiving lifestyle. Staying at home, however, had given the father a breather from work and the associated career pressures, allowing him time to think about what he wanted to do. Having this time to sort himself out, the father said, meant the break-up had occurred sooner than it would have otherwise.

Rather than having a negative effect, both of these separated parents argued that the time the father had spent at home caring for the child had had a very positive effect on family relationships *after* they split up. Neither parent thought the father would have wanted to share child care had he not had the experience of staying at home. Fortunately, they still got along very well too, and this obviously had an important bearing on their decision to share child care. In the words of the mother and father:

"Until he stayed at home Michael wasn't aware of how close he could get to Andrew. It also gave him a lot of skills and understanding that are important now. If he hadn't had the contact he probably would only have a very minor involvement now – entertaining Andrew on weekends." (Mother)

"It brought me face to face with the realities of bringing up kids. I became fairly well versed in the little skills involved. It gave me competence and skills, and an appreciation of the nitty-gritty. If I hadn't this experience I wouldn't have entered into this arrangement, I don't think. As it was, the fifty-fifty arrangement became a very straightforward decision." (Father)

Both parents expressed concern about the possible effects the shared child-care arrangement might have on their child. The father worried that the child might be getting too much attention. The mother also said close friends and relatives were generally negative: "They all felt it wouldn't work and that it is especially unfair on Andrew, who wouldn't know whether he was Arthur or Martha." Despite these doubts, both parents thought their child had adapted extremely well. As the mother said: "Andrew has adapted well; indeed he benefits the most – he gets a lot more stimulation and a lot of different experiences. There is no evidence at all of him having problems; he seems secure and is very independent. He even takes pride in saying he has two homes."

Traditional-Changed Families

There were a variety of reasons given for changing back to traditional roles. In *two* families the decision was straightforward;

they wanted to have another baby. Neither of the parents from these families said they planned to adopt a shared-caregiving lifestyle again in the near future. *Five* families said they had changed back for employment or economic reasons. In three of these the father had recently found a job — they were all families who had previously said they adopted a shared-caregiving lifestyle because the father was unable to get a job. In another, the father had found a more highly paid and more demanding job as a sales manager. The final economic/employment reason given was that the family has decided to buy into a business which was run exclusively by the father. These five families were all better off financially *after* the change back to a traditional lifestyle.

Three families reported they changed back to a traditional pattern because the father had had enough of being at home. It was a novelty at first, and they enjoyed their new status and "intrigue value" in the neighbourhood; however, this soon wore off as the realities of their new *full-time* job became obvious. Two of these fathers also reported that the social disapproval from their male peers about their not having a "job" contributed to their dissatisfaction and their decision to revert to traditional roles. There was a sense of relief from these fathers; for example, one said, "I'm glad to have done it, but I'm also glad it's over."

The final couple who had changed back to a traditional lifestyle did so with a greater sense of achievement and fulfilment than most. Their initial reasons for changing lifestyles, however, were also more balanced than for most. It was for both the mother — she had a teaching qualification but had never taught, and the change in lifestyles allowed her to do this — and the father, who had been a teacher but wanted to change his occupation, which required him studying again. The father went to classes at night and studied during the day (when he had time), while caring for their children. It took the father three years to complete his course of study, a period of time that the mother also felt had been sufficient for her to gain the necessary teaching experience. It was then a question of *when* to revert to traditional roles. The timing was finally influenced by the mother, who felt she had missed out somewhat in her relationships with her children and had not had sufficient time to sit down and enjoy them during their early years. She argued that she would like to be at home with their youngest child in his last year before he went to school. They planned that the mother would return to teaching again when their last child went to school the following year.

Characteristics of the Traditional-Changed vs. Shared-Caregiving Families

Are there any differences between these families that might help us explain why some people return to a traditional pattern and others do not? There are several dimensions on which these comparisons could be made: (1) family characteristics – for example, families with more and younger children might be likely to change back, as child-care demands are likely to be higher in these families and therefore fathers might experience more difficulties with the child-care role; (2) personal characteristics of parents – it may be that the professional middle class group with higher incomes are able to purchase support systems (e.g., alternative child care) when pressures arise; (3) sex-role variables – those who continue might score higher on the opposite-sex sex-role scales, as it is they who will be more likely to feel comfortable in a non-traditional role; (4) initial reasons given for the change – families in which the initial reason was economic necessity might be more likely to change back when the economic situation changes; (5) family organizational pattern – perhaps it is the type of lifestyle that parents adopt that is the most critical variable (e.g., whether both parents are employed).

There are two possible hypotheses about the impact of the family organizational pattern. First, whether or not the family continues might be influenced by the amount of physical and emotional pressure generated by the family organizational pattern. Families in which both parents are employed, and therefore in which the rush and physical and emotional demands are likely to be higher, might be expected to be among the first to revert to traditional roles. Alternatively, families in which the lifestyle represents a more radical departure from societal expectations (i.e., families in which mothers are employed full-time and fathers are not employed) may be under more pressure to change. Finally, it is possible that these considerations are irrelevant and that the family financial situation is of primary importance. Families in which both parents are employed are obviously much better off than those in which only the mother is employed.

Family Characteristics

Families that continued as shared-caregivers tended to have older children. The average age of children in these families was

5.6 years, which compares with an average age of 3.6 years in the traditional-changed families. The two groups did not differ significantly on number of children (average 1.9 vs. 1.7), however. Thus, these findings lend partial support to the hypothesis that families are more likely to continue when child-care demands are lower. These findings also lend support to a social pressure hypothesis. A father caring for young children conflicts more with social expectations than a father caring for older children. The former group, therefore, would be expected to encounter more social disapproval and feel less comfortable in a non-traditional role.

Parental Characteristics

The two groups of families did not differ significantly on any parental characteristics. Of the families who remained as shared-caregivers, five could be classified as being more representative of the professional class, and five as more traditional working class. The same was true for the traditional-changed group — six of the eleven had parents with professional occupations.

Sex-role Variables

Fathers' femininity and mothers' masculinity scores were compared for the two groups of families. These variables appeared to be of little importance. In traditional-changed families the mean fathers' femininity score was 4.61 and the mean mothers' masculinity score was 4.53. The means for fathers and mothers who had continued in a shared-caregiving lifestyle was 4.68 and 4.55 respectively. Differences in beliefs about parental roles were also examined, and they were not found to be significant either.

Initial Reasons Given for Change

Of the traditional-changed families, six had given economic necessity as their major reason for changing when they were first interviewed, and five had said they had chosen to change family patterns. Two of these latter five had said they had changed because of their *strong beliefs* about sharing child-care responsibilities. Indeed, these were two of the most committed families. Both, however, were better off financially when in the traditional pattern than when they had shared child care. One of these families changed back to enable the father to buy into a lucrative business, and the other said the reversion was associated with the father's dissatisfaction with the child-care role. Nine of the eleven families who had changed back were also families who had previously said they experienced problems with a shared-caregiving lifestyle.

Of the families that remained in a shared-caregiving lifestyle, five had said previously they had chosen to adopt their lifestyle, and five that they had adopted it for financial reasons. Thus, an analysis of the initial reasons given for changing adds little to an explanation of why people change back to traditional roles. The final variable to be considered, family organizational pattern, does, however, appear to be important.

Family Organizational Pattern

An examination of family lifestyles showed that families were more likely to have changed back to traditional roles when fathers were *not* employed. In six out of the eleven traditional-changed families, fathers had not been employed. In contrast, families who had continued were evenly represented among the four major types of family patterns: two were families in which both parents were employed full-time; three were families in which mothers were employed full-time and fathers were employed part-time; and three were families in which the mother was employed full-time and the father was not employed. Thus, in seven of the continuing families fathers were employed in some way, and in only three was the father unemployed. These findings, therefore, do not offer clear support to the hypothesis that the physical and emotional pressures associated with both parents being employed are important factors in the decision to revert to traditional roles.

The conclusion to be drawn from this analysis is that families are more likely to revert to traditional roles when there is a more radical departure from traditional patterns and social expectations — that is, when the father is unemployed and caring for a relatively young child. Social pressure for a change back to a traditional lifestyle is likely to be much greater under such circumstances. Perhaps this is not the total explanation, however. In all but two of the traditional-changed group, the family was better off financially *after* the change. Although few parents placed a great deal of emphasis on this, it is obvious that it cannot be ignored as a possible highly significant contributing factor.

Consequences of a Shared-Caregiving Lifestyle

Did the experiences of a shared-caregiving lifestyle influence the roles and beliefs parents adopted when they reverted to a traditional lifestyle? In an attempt to answer this question, a comparison was made for divisions of labour for child care between families who had changed back to traditional roles and the random sample of traditional families also re-interviewed. In addition, parental evaluations of the effects shared-caregiving had had were examined.

Effects on Division of Labour

When asked about the effects of shared-caregiving, seven traditional-changed mothers said that fathers now spend more time on child care than they did when they had been in a traditional pattern before.

Support was given to the mothers' perceptions by a quantitative analysis of time spent on child-care tasks. Fathers in families who had once been shared-caregivers were spending an average of 4.2 hours a week in child-care tasks, which compared with an average of 2.6 for the traditional fathers who were re-interviewed. (This difference was statistically significant; $p < .05$). There were no differences between the groups for time spent on play and other activities. The traditional-changed fathers were also found to spend more time taking the sole responsibility for their children: 4.3 hours a week compared to 2.1 for the re-interviewed traditional families ($p < .05$). Combined with the reports of mothers, this seems reasonably strong evidence that indeed the experiences of a shared-caregiving lifestyle had had a significant impact on fathers' willingness to participate in child care. It should be remembered, however, that data are not available for the period before the beginning of a shared-caregiving lifestyle and that it is still possible that these fathers were more involved to begin with, and the experiences of these fathers at home has had little or no effect.

A Retrospective View of a Shared-Caregiving Lifestyle

Parents who had changed back were asked a series of questions about the effects of shared-caregiving, their perceptions of the advantages and disadvantages of the lifestyle, and which lifestyle they preferred. Although the responses were generally consistent with those noted in previous chapters, mothers especially were now less convinced about the advantages.

The overwhelming majority (82%) still felt fathers and children benefited most from the improved father-child relationship. This response was given as often by mothers as it was by fathers. Some examples of comments were:

"The benefits are fantastic for fathers; my relationship with my son improved out of sight. It made me aware of what fatherhood was all about." (Father)

"Keiran now has an easier relationship with the children, and could completely take over if the need arose. He also has an appreciation of the wear and tear of mothering (in the traditional sense)." (Mother)

"The children gained most — they had more time with their dad." (Father)

"He is now a lot closer to David than he would otherwise have been. He really enjoyed the experience. He liked the caring role and being involved in looking after a small baby." (Mother)

"I'm closer to my children, they now know their father and have two people with whom they feel equally secure." (Father)

An equally consistent response, but this time coming primarily from mothers, was that they and the family had benefited by fathers' increased understanding of mothers and the caregiving role. This response was given in some form by nine of the mothers and four of the fathers. Some examples of responses were:

"He now knows about all the work I have to do — he appreciates the housewife role a lot more, and he cooks a lot more, which is good." (Mother)

"It was a real eye-opener for me into the drudgeries of housework — it's such a repetitive way of life." (Father)

"He learnt how dreadful it was to be stuck at home, and appreciates my needs to go to work more now." (Mother)

"It helped us to develop more in an equal sense. We rely more equally on one another now for everything. We share in the decisions that involve the children right down to food they eat, and clothes they wear. I doubt that Michael would have become so involved had he never had this experience. For instance, if he doesn't like what Jason is wearing he will go in and change the trousers or jumper for another that is more suitable or attractive." (Mother)

"It helped me to understand the woman's role better." (Father)

"It gave my husband an appreciation of the stresses that are placed on a mother with a small child." (Mother)

All of these responses were given in answer to a question about what parents believed were the major advantages of a shared-caregiving lifestyle rather than to a specific question about changes in fathers' attitudes.

Six mothers also felt the change in fathers' attitudes had helped them cope with the demands of the child-care role, and that greater equality had resulted in their relationships with their husbands. Other advantages mentioned for mothers were their increased self-esteem and fulfilment derived from their employment, and their reduced child-care role. These were not mentioned very frequently, however.

Although there were many positive statements from parents who had changed back, there were also some very negative ones, particularly from mothers. They were not as positive about shared child care as they had been previously, and nine out of the eleven mothers (compared with seven out of eleven fathers) said categorically they would prefer traditional roles. The major reason why mothers were less positive about shared-caregiving was that they now placed a lot more significance on the negative effects of the rushed and physically and emotionally demanding nature of a shared-caregiving lifestyle. Mothers placed *overwhelming* emphasis on this aspect when they responded to questions about the disadvantages and the effects shared-caregiving had on them personally. Some examples of mothers' responses were:

"We never had time to do things as a family. I only had Sunday mornings to myself. I never had any privacy."

"Towards the end I felt I was doing two jobs, teaching and keeping house completely, washing, shopping, cleaning, etc. This period was physically very demanding."

"It was too demanding, and severely restricted our social life. We also tended to have a disorganized house. I would prefer to have it as it is now with the mother as the homemaker and the father as the breadwinner."

"I was always thinking work, it affected my attitude towards the kids. I used to get home tired and cranky from work and didn't really get to see the kids as babies; there was no relaxing motherhood."

There were five mothers in this group who only talked about the disadvantages; they felt the lifestyle had no significant gains for them personally at all (apart from indirect effects, like the fathers' changes in attitudes to the children and his greater willingness to participate in child-care responsibilities). These mothers also tended to emphasize their loss, and now gain, in their relationships with their children. These five came from families in which the initial change had been for financial reasons. The other six mothers, while being more negative about the demands of shared-caregiving, also emphasized the positive value of the experience too, and how they felt the entire family had developed and changed as a consequence.

The major disadvantages seen for fathers centred on the nature of the caregiving role – the constancy, boredom, and lack of adult company, the absence of support, and the criticism they received from significant others. For three fathers, constant questioning by others about their not having a job was a significant factor in their decision to revert to traditional roles. It was also interesting that fathers who were in a career framework (e.g., a schoolteacher and a lawyer) and who returned to employment said the period out of employment had not had a noticeable effect on their career prospects. They did not feel they had been discriminated against because of their absence from the work force.

Overall, then, it was these parents' views that a shared-caregiving lifestyle had more long-term consequences for children and fathers. The father-child relationship was perceived to improve, and fathers derived satisfaction from this. Fathers' attitudes towards women and the caregiving role appeared to be more egalitarian too, something most mothers perceived to be a gain for them personally. Mothers appeared much less convinced, however, about the advantages for them in adopting a lifestyle in which they were employed and still carried a major responsibility for children and housework.

An Updated View from Shared-Caregiving Families

The two most common responses from the families who continued in a shared-caregiving lifestyle was that either there was no change from when the initial interview had been conducted, or the parents had become more positive. Nevertheless, six families reported their problems and frustrations had changed somewhat. For example, in one family in which the child was six months when the initial interview was conducted, the father spoke about problems with adjusting to nappy-changing and feeding, and the mother spoke of her anxiety about her husband coping with a young baby. Indeed, she used to phone home every hour or so to check on him. When they were re-interviewed, the father concentrated on problems with his patience (e.g., "I don't seem to have enough patience and sometimes feel like hitting Brett."). Instead of worrying about how her husband was coping, the mother was more concerned about the nature of her job ("I hate having to get up early and follow the same routine every day."). A difference in other peoples' reactions was also noted by the father. Whereas in the initial interview he reported his mates thought he was funny and "they laughed their heads off", he now felt most people accepted him (e.g., "The neighbours think I'm doing a terrific job with Brett, so they all approve now. It was amazing to see the change in them."). This type of response, that other people were now more accepting of the fathers at home, was given by five of the fathers.

Four families also reported (and this was validated by responses to other questions) that fathers had now taken over more household responsibilities. One father said: "I think I'm probably doing more housework than when you were here before. Joanna used to get up early in the morning and run around and do a lot of things before she went to work — making beds and tidying up. I think she was reluctant to leave a lot of that to me before. Now she seems a lot happier about it. I'm not sure I'm so happy about it, but then, that's the deal we've got. I suppose you have to take the good with the bad. The good is the kids, the bad is the housework." Unfortunately, data were not collected on divisions of labour for household chores. A comparison was made, however, between divisions of labour for child care at the time of the two interviews. Fathers were found to be doing slightly more when re-interviewed (48% vs. 51%), but this difference was not statistically significant.

In agreement with responses given in the initial interview, 80% of these parents again spoke about the physical and emotional demands of their lifestyles, particularly with reference to the negative effects on women. Fathers obviously had not taken over the caregiving and housework roles to such a degree that women were now completely relieved of the problems of having dual roles.

Only one of these families had any immediate plans to return to a traditional lifestyle, although, when first interviewed, three of the ten had said they only expected to continue for another twelve months. Both parents in these latter three families were employed, and all had said they had changed for economic reasons. In one, it was the father who had become more positive about his role as caregiver, even though he was very reluctant to begin with; in another, it was the mother who argued more strongly in the second interview to retain their lifestyle, because she had done very well in her job as a public relations consultant and derived a lot of satisfaction from it.

The one family that indicated they were seriously considering changing back was again a family in which both parents were employed. The mother felt the pressures from her job were considerable and regretted not spending more time with her children. The children were at a more critical stage in their schooling (one was now in high school), and the mother felt they needed more time with her. She also argued that she was much more inclined towards helping with school work than her husband was. On the other hand, her husband was very happy and confident about his role with regard to the children and was keen for his wife to continue on in her career, as he thought her longer-term prospects for promotion, success, and satisfaction, were very good.

Conclusion

Two factors appear to be more critical for whether or not a family continues in a shared-caregiving lifestyle. First, the extent to which the family pattern is different from cultural expectations and norms. Families were more likely to return to traditional roles when there were younger children in the family and when fathers were not employed. A situation in which fathers are not employed and are caring for a six-month-old, it can be argued, is likely to generate more social disapproval than one in which a father has a job and cares for a four-year-old. A second factor that appears important is the family financial situation. In nine out of the eleven families who returned to traditional roles, the family was better off financially after changing back. It is difficult to know how much emphasis should be placed on this, as only four families gave this as the major reason why they changed back. Despite this, the family financial situation cannot be ruled out as a possible major contributing factor, and it is certainly one that needs to be explored in greater depth in future studies.

Although the majority of parents when interviewed initially were very positive about their lifestyles, the balance between the positive and negative aspects appeared to change by the time the second interview was conducted. Mothers who had changed back to a traditional lifestyle were much more likely to emphasize the demanding nature of their previous lifestyle, the problems involved in carrying out dual roles, and the lack of time they had with their children. As would be expected, families who continued in a shared-caregiving lifestyle appeared slightly more positive, and fathers reported having taken over more responsibility for housework, although this could not be supported by an analysis of actual time spent, as data on divisions of labour for housework were not collected here. Perhaps the two factors were linked, and those who continue are happier because fathers have taken over more of the responsibility for housework and child care. The evidence presented in the chapter on marital relationships indicating that fathers' involvement in child care is positively related to mothers' marital happiness adds further support to this interpretation.

This second look at the impact of a shared-caregiving lifestyle again emphasized the positive gain for fathers in their relationships with their children. Not one interview, either initial or follow-up, went by without some mention being made of how the father-child relationship had improved or how fathers now derived much more satisfaction from their interactions with their children. Fathers' more positive attitudes to their children and to child care and their greater participation in child care were also seen as benefits of the experiences of shared-caregiving for mothers. Nevertheless, the balance between mothers' and fathers' gains and losses from a shared-caregiving lifestyle appeared to favour fathers. The implications of this and other findings from the follow-up study for the longer-term possibilities for this lifestyle being adopted on a broader social scale are considered in the next and final chapter.

11
Conclusions and Policy Implications

The present book is probably best interpreted as a first attempt at describing and defining some of the possible antecedents and consequences of one type of non-traditional two-parent family — a family in which fathers are highly participant in child care and mothers are employed in the paid work force. This analysis has also involved a description of the nature and range of father participation in traditional families. There are obviously many unanswered questions about father participation in both traditional and non-traditional families, many of which have been discussed in preceeding chapters. This chapter summarizes these findings and examines the policy implications of the findings from this and other studies on fathers.

The chapter begins with an overview of the major findings reported here in terms of patterns of paternal participation and the antecedents and consequences of high levels of participation. What follows then is a discussion of what the prospects are for further changes in paternal participation. In particular, consideration is given to current barriers to change (e.g., beliefs about appropriate parental roles, the rigidity of the structure of employment), and recent and ongoing social changes that might facilitate father participation (e.g., the acceptance of fathers at child birth, unemployment, the women's movement).

The next section focuses on ways in which father participation could be encouraged by purposeful changes in social policies. The initiatives suggested are predicated on the assumption that fathers have equal responsibility for their children, and that they are equally capable of being warm and sensitive child-carers. Some of the areas in which proposals for policy changes are made are hospital practices and parent education classes, school curricula, parental leave, and the job structure. As well as suggesting policy changes that might lead to increased participation, this chapter examines the implications of recent findings on fathers for policies in other areas (e.g., for employment opportunities for men; for legal policies relating to custody and access).

An Overview of Findings on Father Participation

Patterns of Participation

It was suggested in chapter 3 that there are four different types of fathers, emphasizing the considerable range in levels of participation noted here and in studies conducted in other cultures. First, there was the *uninterested and unavailable father*, who was rarely at home and, when he was, spent little time with his children. The second type isolated was the *traditional father*, a father who had a strong but nevertheless traditional commitment to his family. It was this type of father who was associated with the modal pattern of participation: a father who took little responsibility for the day-to-day care of his children but who was available and played with his children regularly. Third, there was what was described by mothers as the *good father*. These fathers were more involved than traditional fathers, and it was more common for them to perform basic child-care tasks such as bathing, feeding, and changing nappies. The good fathers were members of traditional two-parent families and were seen as good because they were willing to help mothers. They were not considered to have equal status with mothers.

Finally, there was the *non-traditional, highly participant father* — the fathers from the shared-caregiving families. These fathers carried out 46% of child-care tasks each week, considerably more than the average for fathers in traditional families, which was 9%. On current standards, the fathers in shared-caregiving families were highly participant indeed. Nevertheless, on average they were not as highly participant as their own spouses and were significantly less participant than mothers in traditional families. There was little evidence of role reversal: of fathers taking on the same roles as traditional mothers, and mothers taking on the roles of traditional fathers. Many mothers and fathers in shared-caregiving families also agreed that mothers were still more likely to take overall responsibility for the children, even though fathers contributed nearly as much to their day-to-day care.

Antecedents of Paternal Participation

Implicit in the analyses presented in earlier chapters have been several hypotheses for the antecedents of paternal participation: family pressure, relative power and status of mothers and fathers, personal characteristics and socialization experiences of parents, and factors relating to the employment structure. The aim here is to consider the available evidence which relates to each of these possible general explanations.

Family Pressure

The hypothesis was put forward that father participation in traditional families would be higher when there was more pressure within the family situation, such as when there were more children and therefore the demands of child care were high, or when both the mother and father were employed. Findings from traditional families did not support this hypothesis at all. Father participation did not increase as a function of either the number of children or the number of hours each week a mother was employed. Instead, fathers were more highly participant when there were *fewer* children. This was interpreted as indicating either that there is a novelty effect for the first child or that a cultural change is in progress. Fathers who have had their first-child experience more recently are more likely to have been exposed to current knowledge about fathers, and therefore they are more likely to participate. Additional support is given to this latter hypothesis by the finding that father participation was also higher when couples had been married for fewer years.

In contrast to the above predictions for traditional families, it was hypothesized that an absence of high levels of child-care demands would be more likely to characterize shared-caregiving families. The argument was that fathers would be more willing to agree to take on the child-care role when it was less demanding. Support was found for this hypothesis: shared-caregiving families had fewer and older children than traditional families.

An entirely different form of family pressure was also found to be linked with shared-caregiving — economic pressure. Family changes, both from traditional to shared-caregiving and then back to traditional, were strongly associated with family financial factors. The explanations for family change given by thirty-one out of the seventy-one shared-caregivers involved financial considerations, and sixty-one were better off financially after becoming shared-caregivers. In addition, nine out of the eleven who subsequently changed back to a traditional family pattern were also better off financially after this second change. It seems highly unlikely, however, that economic factors can provide a sufficient explanation for all family changes. As we pointed out earlier, there are several alternative changes in family and employment patterns that could be made to overcome financial difficulties apart from the one chosen here of fathers taking on a major responsibility for child care (e.g., father taking a second job). Although economic factors might provide the initial impetus for a change to have fathers care for children, as is shown below, personal and social factors are important too.

Relative Power and Status of Mothers and Fathers

Australian society, like all industrialized societies, is patriarchal in nature; that is, it is male dominated. It might be argued, therefore, that a major reason why mothers carry the overwhelming burden for the lower-status jobs of child-carer and housewife is that they have less social status and less personal and economic power than their husbands. Fathers usually have higher-status jobs, are more highly educated, and control family income and overall family lifestyles. When this balance of social status and power is more evenly distributed between mothers and fathers, we might expect mothers to be in a better bargaining position with regard to divisions of labour for family and paid work. Support was found for this hypothesis here.

The analysis of divisions of labour in traditional families revealed that fathers were more highly participant when mothers were more highly educated. Furthermore, mothers in shared-caregiving families were more highly educated and had higher-status occupations than either traditional mothers or their own spouses. It can also be argued, of course, that higher-status jobs are more interesting, career-oriented, and potentially satisfying, and that the financial returns are likely to be greater, making the prospect of mothers in shared-caregiving families being employed more attractive.

Personal Characteristics and Socialization Experiences

It is possible that fathers who become highly participant are just different people — that they have different personalities, beliefs, and values and have had different socialization experiences. A degree of support was found for this hypothesis, although contrary to the suggestions of some (e.g., Curthoys 1976), father participation was not related to the traditional social-class variables of fathers' education level and occupational status.

Fathers and mothers in shared-caregiving families differed from traditional parents on sex-role personality traits. Shared-caregiving fathers scored higher on femininity traits, and shared-caregiving mothers scored higher on masculinity traits; both were more likely to score high on masculinity and femininity traits (i.e., they were more likely to be classified as androgynous). No relationship was found, however, between father participation and sex-role personality variables in traditional families.

Differences between shared-caregiving and traditional families were also found for beliefs about parental roles and child-rearing values. Shared-caregiving fathers were more likely than traditional fathers to reject the notion of a maternal instinct and more likely to believe that fathers do not differ from mothers in their ability to care for children. The rejection of the notion of a maternal instinct was also found to be associated with high father participation in traditional families.

Consistent with the differences noted for sex-role personality variables, shared-caregiving parents, when asked about child-rearing, were found to be more likely to value interpersonal sensitivity and expressiveness and independence in thought and action and less likely to value conformity to social rules of behaviour.

It is possible, of course, that these differences in personalities, beliefs, and values are not antecedents but rather are consequences of fathers becoming highly participant. Their personalities, beliefs, and values may have changed as a result of their experiences in this type of non-traditional lifestyle. Little support was found for this hypothesis in the analyses conducted for sex-role scores and child-rearing values. Neither of these variables was found to be significantly correlated with either the length of time fathers had been highly participant or the extent to which fathers participated in child care on a day-to-day basis.

Previous socialization experiences were also related to father participation. Highly participant traditional fathers as well as shared-caregiving fathers were likely to have attended the births of their children and ante-natal classes. In addition, shared-caregiving fathers were likely to have read books on child care and child-rearing. It is impossible to decide whether father participation is directly linked to these experiences, or whether this is simply an indication of these fathers being more committed to begin with. If the latter hypothesis is correct, then it may be that father participation is linked with socialization experiences from an earlier time in development. Both Radin (1981) in the United States and Sagi (1981) in Israel report findings that support the hypothesis that earlier socialization experiences are linked with father participation. Radin reports that a father having grown up in a family in which the mother was employed might be critical, whereas Sagi reports that fathers are more highly participant when their own fathers had been actively involved in child care.

There is yet another possible explanation for fathers' having attended ante-natal classes and the births of their children. Rather than this being an indication of fathers being more committed, it might be associated with the positions of relative power within families. Mothers may have persuaded or encouraged their husbands to attend, and as such, the experiences may have had a significant impact on fathers' willingness to participate later.

Nature of Employment

The nature of employment was found to be associated both with paternal participation in traditional families and with a shared-caregiving family pattern. Traditional fathers who worked fewer hours and were at home more often spent more time on both child care and play. Again, however, these fathers may have been more committed to their family role before and chose to adjust the demands of their job and their leisure interests to suit their family involvement.

Flexibility in hours of employment and/or fewer hours at the place of employment were characteristics of the jobs of most shared-caregiving parents; however, it is doubtful whether this can provide a sufficient explanation for the adoption of this lifestyle. Nearly 30% of these parents reported they had changed some aspect of their employment to enable them to adopt an alternative child-care pattern. Despite this, it is obvious that reduced hours and an ability to choose hours could facilitate the adoption of different types of family lifestyles.

An all-encompassing explanation of paternal participation is not immediately obvious from the above discussion, and perhaps this should not be expected to emerge either; different factors may be critical for different families. Although little support was evident for the family-pressure hypothesis, some support was obtained for the other three general explanations discussed. The relative power and status of mothers and fathers, the personal characteristics of parents and their previous experience, the nature of employment, and the family financial situation are likely to combine in complex ways to influence the degree to which a father participates in child care. Knowledge on just how much each of these factors contribute will have to await the outcomes of future studies.

Consequences of High Paternal Participation

The assessment of the consequences of high paternal participation made here relied entirely on the reports of mothers and fathers from shared-caregiving families. Although others usually focus on the effects family changes might have on children, shared-caregiving parents placed little emphasis on this possibility. Instead, the consequences that emerged here as the most significant concerned fathers, mothers, and their relationships with one another.

By far the most significant consequence evident for fathers was their improved relationship with their children. Nearly two-thirds of both mothers and fathers mentioned fathers had become closer to their children and that this was a major advantage of high father participation. On the negative side, fathers had difficulty adjusting to being at home and caring for children, especially in the first few months, and in adjusting to their reduced commitments to paid work.

Although mothers also thought the improved father-child relationship was a highly positive aspect of their lifestyle, and they reported being happy about not having the full responsibility for child care, the most commonly mentioned consequences for mothers focused on their paid work role. Increased independence and personal satisfaction derived from their jobs, together with the increased physical and emotional pressures associated with having dual roles and the reduction in contact with their children, were the most significant positive and negative aspects for mothers. Furthermore, the two-year follow-up study revealed that for mothers who returned to traditional roles the pressures associated with having dual roles represented an overwhelming negative aspect of a shared-caregiving lifestyle.

Parental reports both during the initial interview and at the time of the second interview also indicated that the experiences of adopting non-traditional roles had had a significant impact on parents' personal development and on their attitudes and beliefs.

It was common for parents to report they felt a sense of achievement and enhanced self-esteem as a consequence of having been successful in something that others thought they should not and could not do, and which they found difficult initially. Another consistent response was that fathers' attitudes to women changed; they were reported to be more sensitive to the difficulties experienced by mothers or others who care for children full-time.

The change in child-care patterns also had consequences for the quality of mother-father relationships. Shared-caregiving couples reported more frequent recent quarrels and irritability with one another and having considered ending their relationship more often, and they expressed less overall satisfaction with their marital relationships. Fathers were less satisfied when they felt they had little choice about whether they changed family patterns, whereas mothers were less satisfied when fathers spent less time on child-care tasks. Although shared-caregiving parents were found to have marital relationships of significantly lower quality than traditional parents, the difference was not sufficiently great to warrant a conclusion that these families constitute a high-risk group for marital breakdown.

A major limitation of this study, it could be argued, was its failure to assess consequences for children. This lack of emphasis, however, was with good reason. As was argued in chapter 9, launching into research at this stage of our very limited knowledge of high father participation is somewhat premature. Indeed, as the analysis of those studies that have involved the direct observation or assessment of children showed, very little could be concluded from the findings because of the inadequacies of the designs of these studies (e.g., few provided specific details on father participation) and because of our very limited knowledge of the antecedents of high father participation. However, as was noted in chapter 9 as well, given the multiplicity of contributors to parental socialization practices and child development, high father participation may not have as great an impact on children as some might expect.

Prospects for Further Change?

The analysis presented in chapter 3 indicated that families in which fathers are very highly participant constitute only a very small proportion (around 1–2%) of families with young children.

Additional support for this estimate comes from figures recently published by the Australian Bureau of Statistics. They reported that in 1979 of the full-time housekeepers in Australia, thirteen thousand (or approximately 2%) were male, whereas 2.5 million were female. The bureau also provided figures that suggested the number of full-time male housekeepers might be increasing, as there were only nine thousand in 1974. Unfortunately, because of the inadequacy of data collected in earlier studies on divisions of labour in families, it is impossible to say whether the 1–2% found here represents a significant change in the number of shared-caregiving families in the last ten or twenty years.

How likely is it that shared-caregiving families will become more prevalent in the future, and constitute 5–10% or even 20% of families? Some might ask, however, why should we be interested in such a question, and why would we want fathers to become more highly participant? This, of course, raises the very important question of values and research, and the ways in which a researcher's biases can intrude in the research process. A brief discussion will be presented of this issue as it relates to the present study before examining the possible barriers and facilitators to fathers becoming more highly participant in child care.

Bias in Research

One of the major issues with any form of research is the many different ways in which a researcher's own beliefs and values can intrude in the research process, at the level of the types of questions posed, in the method, or in the interpretation of findings. It is impossible to achieve complete objectivity, and therefore it should perhaps be mandatory that people state their biases so that others may better interpret and understand their work.

As was obvious from the way in which this study was introduced, my own involvement in a family like those described here provided the initial impetus for this research. When I started, my beliefs were: mothers and fathers have equal responsibility for their children; mothers and fathers are equally capable of caring for children; it is probably better for children to have close relationships with two adults than to have a close relationship with only one adult; and it is more *equitable* if mothers and fathers share in the care of their children and in their involvement in the paid work force. Although these are my biases, it is not my view that everyone should adopt the type of shared-caregiving family described here. Rather, I would advocate that people should be able to choose the type of family pattern that best suits their needs. At the moment, however, social expectations and social institutions tend to favour the adoption of traditional family patterns and traditional divisions of labour. The proposals considered below, therefore, should be seen as proposals to give more people the opportunity to *consider* adopting a family pattern in which fathers are highly participant.

That a shared-caregiving pattern would not work for everyone was clearly illustrated to me on several occasions during my interviews with traditional families. Some of the families that seemed the happiest (from both the mother's and the father's viewpoint) were those in which the roles and beliefs were extremely traditional. Both parents had clearly defined roles, both knew what was expected of one another, and both were highly satisfied. By way of illustration, consider the following statements made by the father and mother in one family:

"I am the head of the house. Being a father is a sacred responsibility. One of the things I have to do is train my wife."

"I tend to their basic needs, their emotional, spiritual, educational and health needs. My husband is the leader of the family, the patriarch, the strength. He could not stay at home and look after the children. He would be frustrated in his ambitions. It is his role to work and achieve his ambitions."

These views are obviously very different from my own. Both of these parents, however, were highly satisfied with their family roles and their own relationships; no hint of discontent or hostility was detected in the interview.

Barriers to Increased Father Participation

Beliefs about, and Attitudes to Sex-Appropriate Behaviour

The possibility that beliefs about differences between mothers and fathers and attitudes towards appropriate behaviour for males and females influence the roles parents adopt has been discussed on several occasions already. A father who holds strong views that mothers have a maternal instinct and that children need their mothers, for example, is likely to be difficult to persuade to take the sole responsibility for his six-week-old child for a day. And, even if he could be persuaded to, others who see this as inappropriate behaviour for a male would be likely to react negatively to him, making it less likely he would agree to do it again.

In strong support of this hypothesis, father participation was found to be associated with rejection of the notion of a maternal instinct and acceptance of the notion that both parents are equally capable of providing competent care for children. In addition, people who adopted non-traditional child-care patterns encountered considerable negative reactions from relatives, friends, neighbours and workmates, and this negative reaction was more common from males than from females. The hypothesis that the adoption of non-traditional roles is influenced by beliefs about appropriate behaviour was also supported by findings from the follow-up study. Families that had returned to traditional roles were more likely to be those in which conflict with accepted behaviour patterns was high – families in which the father was unemployed and in which he was at home caring for a very young child.

Barriers to fathers becoming more highly participant might also occur as a result of beliefs about the effects parents have on child development. One suggestion has been that increased father involvement will lead to an increase in incest between fathers and daughters. This kind of objection was raised by a Protestant religious group in an article on incest which appeared in Australia's largest circulation women's magazine. It argued:

> Working mothers may quite inadvertently contribute to the problem [of incest] by involving husbands more and more in the care of young and growing children. One of the very sad things which has become evident in research is the development of an incestuous relationship between a father and daughter which has its beginnings in the innocence and love of the child and the love and care of a father. Most incest begins for a child in the very tender years when its seriousness cannot be assessed or even guessed at by the child. A little girl who has been bathed and cared for by a loving father, whose nappies have been changed, and whose body has been handled lovingly and carefully by that same father is not in a position to realize or understand that the relationship has changed and is no longer innocent. [*Australian Women's Weekly*, 30 April 1980. Courtesy Australian Consolidated Press Ltd]

Significantly there was no mention of the mother-son relationship and the "dangers" there might be in this.

Beliefs about the development of sexuality could present another barrier to father participation. Probably the most direct expression of this came from an Australian television commentator before interviewing me in 1979 about my research on fathers. In the words of the commentator: "You know, I agree with a lot of what you say about fathers being more involved, but there are some things that worry me. Now, you take Australia; most of the best-known Australians, overseas — the entertainers — most of them are "poofs" and what you're advocating in getting men involved in child care will turn out more poofs. Australia certainly doesn't need any more of these." Although these doubts about the effects on incest and sexuality are rarely expressed, they are perhaps the bases of some very deep-seated fears many express about men having contact with young children, and therefore demand the critical attention of other researchers and policy-makers.

Beliefs about adult male-female relationships may also function to inhibit fathers becoming more highly participant. Close friendships or frequent interactions between adult males and females are usually looked upon with suspicion; people are reluctant to accept that these relationships exist without there being a sexual component as well. If fathers are to become more highly participant, more frequent day-to-day interactions between males and females in neighbourhoods will result. Visits to one another's houses to enable children to play and simply to maintain adult contact will become much more commonplace. Just what kind of reaction this might provoke can be illustrated by considering the following two situations:

Situation 1: The mother is at home with the children and the father is employed in the paid work force. The father comes home and says to the mother: "Hello, dear; did you have a good day? What did you do all day?" To which the mother replies: "Oh nothing much, we went up to Mary Brown's for lunch. The kids got on really well; they spent most of the time outside playing."

Situation 2: The father is at home with the children and the mother is employed in the paid work force. The mother comes home and says to the father: "Hello dear; did you have a good day? What did you do all day?" To which the father replies: "Oh nothing much, we went up to Mary Brown's for lunch. The kids got on really well, they spent most of the time outside playing."

Personal Identification with Roles

One of the major goals of socialization is the preparation of females to be mothers and housewives, and males to be employed and be the breadwinner. These goals are as evident in parental socialization practices (e.g., in the assignment of household chores for children on the basis of gender) as they are in the media and schools. Findings from a study of children's occupational aspirations (Russell and Smith 1979) discussed in chapter 1 indicated that identification with these adult roles begins very early indeed. A high proportion of seven- and ten-year-old girls aspired to motherhood, whereas most boys aspired to action-oriented and high-status jobs. Furthermore, the evidence presented in chapter 3 showed that over 50% of traditional fathers viewed their role as the breadwinner as being the most significant aspect of their father role.

Given the apparent strength of gender-based differences in identification with appropriate roles, an argument for a departure from these roles might be difficult to sustain. Moreover, mothers and fathers who adopt non-traditional roles might feel uncomfortable, depressed, and lacking in self-esteem. There is ample evidence from the recent literature on unemployment to indicate that men without paid work do experience identity problems. Further support for this hypothesis comes from the finding presented earlier that 32% of shared-caregiving fathers mentioned that the loss of status associated with their reduced commitment to employment was the thing they disliked most about their family pattern.

In the same way that fathers are likely to have problems changing roles because of their identification with the breadwinner role, mothers are likely to experience difficulties when they relinquish some of their power and responsibility in the child-care and domestic domains. For many women, success and control in these domains are their only sources of status, self-esteem, and satisfaction (e.g., children being well behaved; house being well kept; people enjoying a meal they have cooked). It is understandable, therefore, that many mothers will be reluctant to reduce their own commitment in this area or readily accept fathers participating too. The evidence from the present study discussed earlier again supports this hypothesis — for example, the reports by mothers that they felt guilty about leaving their children and that they regretted missing out in their relationships with their children. The finding that high father participation is associated with mothers who are more highly educated perhaps lends support to this identification hypothesis as well. Mothers who are more highly educated, because their socialization has been less traditional, might not identify as strongly with the mother-role and therefore will be more accepting of their husbands taking over some of the child-care and household responsibilities.

Lack of Skills and Knowledge

As well as being socialized in such a way that males identify with the breadwinner role and females with the mother/housewife role, this socialization process ensures that males and females have different experiences, develop different skills, and acquire a different knowledge base. Block (1979) discusses several studies which show that children from a wide range of cultures are assigned different tasks to prepare them for their adult roles. Females are, for example, more likely to be assigned the task of caring for young children; male "baby-sitters" are still rare in most cultures. At school, too, it is more common for girls to participate in home science classes and for boys to participate in woodwork or metalwork classes, again emphasizing differences in skills and acquired knowledge.

Gender differences in opportunities given to acquire skills and knowledge appropriate to the child-care role are obvious in other areas as well. It is mothers who are more likely to attend education classes centred on childbirth and child care. In hospitals, too, it is mothers who are shown how to care for their young infants, how to bathe them, and how to fold and change nappies. In a recent survey of twelve Sydney hospitals, only one was found to actively encourage fathers to learn these basic care-giving skills. Without these skills and knowledge, fathers might not have the self-confidence to become involved with their young children, even if they would like to.

Gender Differences in Employment Opportunities

At the same time as females are being socialized into the mother-role, males are busy acquiring other skills which will facilitate their success as the breadwinner. As a consequence, males are better educated and have higher-status jobs. This situation is likely to reduce the possibility that mothers will trade some of their child-care responsibilities for participation in the paid work force. As was noted before, a difference in status means that mothers are in an inferior bargaining position compared with their husbands, making it more difficult for them to seek employment even if they wanted to. A second reason why gender differences in employment opportunities might function to keep mothers in the home is that the jobs they could go to are less attractive as sources of either personal satisfaction or financial returns. Clearly, a mother would be more likely to return to a job as a lawyer than as a cog in a production wheel in a large factory.

Rigidity of Career Structures and Work Hours

Career structures and work hours are both characterized by considerable rigidity, making participation in child care less likely for fathers and participation in paid work less likely for mothers. For fathers, absences from the work force have the potential danger of affecting their careers in the way that women's careers are currently affected, for example, in the female-dominated occupation of infant school teacher, where women without children dominate promotional positions. On the other hand, women are more likely to be discriminated against by employers for promotion because they see them as being more likely to leave the work force or be absent from work because of the demands of child-bearing or child care.

The rigidity of work hours presents another barrier for mothers and fathers to share equally in child care and paid work. Having a nine-to-five job and an employer who has an expectation of total commitment to the company – and therefore an expectation of availability before and after work, either for work or for work-related social interaction – is clearly not conducive to parents arranging their work demands to mesh with alternative child-care patterns.

Current Social Changes That Could Facilitate Paternal Participation

There are three types of social changes currently in progress that could function to facilitate fathers becoming more highly participant.

Father's Attendance at Childbirth

Data presented here showed that fathers who attended the births of their children were more likely to be highly participant. Although, as has already been mentioned on several occasions, it is possible that this experience is not linked in a causal way with father participation, the expectation and encouragement of fathers to become involved in the birth at least gives greater recognition to the significance of fathers and it gives fathers more status. This more general change in views about fathers and the expectations that people have of them might therefore facilitate father participation in other areas too.

That a change in birth attendance has occurred in recent years is abundantly clear from the available figures. Alwyn (1977) reported that in one large Australian hospital in 1962 only 0.7% of fathers attended births. In a recent survey I conducted for one week in each of four of Sydney's largest maternity hospitals, the attendance rate ranged from 60 to 80% — quite a dramatic increase since 1962. On current indications, there are likely to be even further increases as more hospitals permit fathers to attend difficult births.

The Changing Nature of Employment and Career Values

A small group of families in the sample studied here had changed their child-care patterns primarily because the father was unable to obtain employment. With unemployment rates in Western societies likely to remain high or even increase, this could result in greater numbers of fathers spending time at home with their children, if only for short periods of time.

There is also a hint that male values towards careers and their identification with paid work are in the process of undergoing changes. Bryson (1974) has argued that men are becoming more openly critical of work values, and that as a consequence they will become more family centred. Although there is increasing anecdotal evidence of men becoming disenchanted with paid work as a source of satisfaction (e.g., the incidence of public figures resigning to spend more time with their families appears to be on the increase), and men's liberation groups are now much more common, there is little research data available at the moment to suggest that this change in values is widespread.

Another of the current social changes that could facilitate father participation concerns employment hours. Hours at the place of employment have decreased consistently over the last twenty years, and in Australia there is currently a concerted campaign to reduce them even further. Employment hours have also changed in another way. It is now much more common for employers to offer workers a choice of work hours — flexitime as it is usually referred to. The two most common ways in which flexitime operates are (1) people are allowed to choose their starting and finishing times each day within some limits (e.g., start up to two hours early) or (2) people are allowed to work longer hours on a number of days and take a complete block of time off (e.g., work longer hours for nine days and have the tenth day off).

Little research has been carried out on the effects of reduced hours or work scheduling on family participation. One major American study recently reported that flexitime had only a small and non-significant effect on the amount of time either fathers or mothers spent with their children. It is possible, however, that attitudes and beliefs about family participation are lagging behind these structural changes in employment. As beliefs and expectations about father participation change even further, then reduced hours and flexibility in hours at work might become instrumental in fathers increasing the time they spend taking responsibility for their children.

The Changing Roles of and Attitudes towards Women

Although the major thrust of the recent women's movement has been equality between women and men in employment opportunities and social status, and the provisions of more child-care facilities, a change to have fathers more involved in child care is entirely consistent with the basic aims of the movement – equality between males and females in *all spheres*. Indeed, as was pointed out earlier, there is some indication of a shift in emphasis in some quarters of the movement towards the role that men might play in child care. Perhaps this change has resulted from the lack of response that women have received from governments for the provision of child-care facilities, or it may be a consequence of the pressures women have felt from having dual roles. Although it seems inevitable that the push by women for equality in the paid work force must create pressures for changes within the home too, findings presented earlier suggested there was little indication of this having occurred to any significant degree as yet. It is also possible, however, that the full impact of the women's movement on family roles will be more evident in future studies. The most active in the women's movement are likely to be those whose family demands are lower – younger women and those whose children are no longer dependent. Perhaps as more of the younger women who have established careers begin to have children, the impact on divisions of labour for child care will be much more significant.

Policy Changes That Might Facilitate Father Participation

There are several implications for social policies when it is assumed that fathers have equal status as parents – equal responsibilities and equal capabilities. These include implications for hospitals and the medical profession, the general education process, and employment and industrial policies.

Hospitals and the Medical Profession

Father participation during infancy could be facilitated by policy changes during the period surrounding the birth and the first few days after. Even greater recognition could be given to the role of fathers at the birth (by permitting fathers to become more involved, e.g., in the delivery), in the first few days after (by giving them greater access to their child and placing fewer restrictions on visiting hours), and by actively encouraging fathers to learn basic caregiving skills (e.g., by providing classes or demonstrations for fathers during the evenings or on weekends). A change in policy to allow fathers to be present at the birth has been successful, and there is every reason to expect that additional changes, in time, will be accepted too. The potential effects on father participation are illustrated by findings from two recent studies. In one, a group of American researchers (Parke et al. 1979) made a film showing male caregivers engaged in play, feeding, and changing nappies, and showed it to fathers in the hospital in the first few days after birth. In a follow-up three months later these fathers were found to be more involved in caregiving tasks than a control group of fathers who had not seen the film. A similar finding was reported from a Swedish study (see Parke 1979), when fathers were provided with the opportunity to learn and practice basic caregiving tasks in the hospital.

The General Education Process

A change in the image of fathers through the media and schools, and the introduction of school curricula which assume males and females have equal responsibility for child care, would also help to facilitate changes in father participation. Currently there are few models of highly participant fathers portrayed in the media or in children's books, and school curricula are still by and large based on the assumption that females will have the task of caring for children and the house. Consideration could be given to the inclusion of child care and the teaching of home maintenance skills in general education courses, rather than have them covered by traditional home science courses which have become strongly sex-typed as only being appropriate for females. There is evidence to indicate, however, that, given different circumstances, boys could be very willing participants in child-care classes. An infant-care course was recently introduced for ten-year-old boys in an American school. Although there was some initial hesitation, the boys became very enthusiastic about it, and this is now the second most popular elective class in the school (just edged out by computers).

Paternity or Parental Leave

It is common for fathers to say that they would like to become more highly participant, but they cannot because of the demands of their jobs. One way of overcoming this problem, especially in the early days, weeks, and months of having a new child, would be to institute a paternity or parental leave scheme. A parental leave scheme has been in operation in Sweden for quite some time now. Under this scheme either parent is entitled to take six months' leave in the first nine months of a child's life and another six weeks which can be taken at any time up until the child is seven years. Parents are paid 90% of their normal salary for the duration of the leave. On current estimates, 10–14% of fathers take some part of this leave; however, it is usually much less than six months – the average in 1977 was forty-two days. Although some argue that this is a very small proportion and doubt the value of this policy, it is still quite a significant increase on the 2% of fathers who took leave in the first year the scheme was introduced, 1974.

In Australia at the present time, although social policy does not allow for fathers to take leave, a system of maternity leave is widespread. Unpaid leave is now the entitlement of all female employees; for some, part can be taken on full pay. Until four years ago, fathers employed by the federal government were entitled to one week's paternity leave; however, this was abolished. It is difficult to know why this occurred. Some reports suggested it was because of costs, and others that it was because fathers were not using the leave in the way that it had been intended. Perhaps this policy was before its time, and attitudes and values within the community were not consistent with it. Several

Australian employee groups are currently preparing cases for a system of parental leave similar to that in Sweden, indicating that changes in policies are likely to occur in the future. Nevertheless, they still have to deal with the patriarchal nature of society and the fact that it is probably traditional males who have the power.

Apart from the obvious advantage of allowing fathers to spend time with their infants if they want to, a proposal to institute a *parental* leave scheme has some other positive features. First it would eliminate a significant form of discrimination against men, which exists under the current policy of maternity leave. Second, if the leave can be taken by either males or females, then employers would be less likely to discriminate against women for employment and promotion. Finally, for the economically minded, given that maternity leave is already an entitlement, the broadening of this policy to allow either the mother or father to take the leave would not involve significant additional costs.

The ultimate success of these policies in terms of mothers and fathers both participating in these leave schemes will obviously depend on more general changes in social attitudes to male involvement in child care. Moreover, it may be that more success will be experienced if schemes allowed the leave to be taken at any stage during a child's pre-school years; as was noted before, a father caring for a four-year-old obviously conflicts less with prevailing social attitudes than a father caring for a six-week-old.

Changes in the Nature of Jobs

A suggestion that is often made is that changes in family patterns would be facilitated if permanent part-time work and job-sharing were more readily available. An attractive suggestion perhaps, but, from the experiences in other cultures, one that might not be as useful as expected. In Sweden, for example, where part-time jobs are prevalent, it has been women overwhelmingly who have taken these jobs, and they have usually taken them to fit in with child-care demands and household chores. This, it might be argued, has done little to enhance equality between the sexes and has increased the total amount of work done by mothers because they have dual roles.

Job-sharing has not been sufficiently widespread as yet for this to be subjected to detailed evaluation. As would be expected, it is difficult to find two people whose needs complement one another's, and many jobs do not lend themselves to this type of organization. Furthermore, this proposal has the same potential as permanent part-time work to maintain current divisions of labour between mothers and fathers.

Although changes in the nature of jobs to make permanent part-time work more readily available are unlikely to provide sufficient conditions for changing divisions of labour for child care, coupled with changes in attitudes and expectations about roles, however, they will increase the possibility that changes will occur. More importantly, they ensure a greater range of options are open to parents.

More Radical Changes in the Economic and Social Structures

An argument is sometimes made that current family patterns and the rigid divisions of labour for family and paid work are products of the industrial capitalist system, and that equality between the sexes can only be achieved if there is a radical change in the economic system. The evidence to support such an argument, however, is by no means clear cut. There is not space to go into these here. Suffice it to say that historical evidence does not offer conclusive support to the view that male participation in child care is causally linked to a change to industrial capitalism, and there is ample evidence from non-capitalist societies which shows that mothers have the major responsibility for child care and household tasks in these societies too (e.g., in Eastern Europe).

Another more radical suggestion for change is that child care should become the total responsibility of the community and that governments should provide child-care facilities. Although it is obvious that a shift to consider child care as more of a community responsibility would enhance considerably the options open to families, and particularly the options for women to participate in the paid work force, the recent experiences in Israel indicate that it may not necessarily result in equality in the public domain or higher father participation. The evidence indicates that it is *women* who provide the community care, and when the children are at home they are still seen as the woman's primary responsibility.

Neither of these radical proposals of themselves, therefore, are likely to generate equality between the sexes, and if they are to be seriously considered, then attacks would have to be made on other fronts as well – especially in the area of male involvement in child care. Currently, child care is seen very much as a women's issue; it is rare indeed to find any commentaries in Australia which frame the question of child care within the context of women *and* men. Perhaps while the question continues to be discussed as a women's issue, that is what it will remain.

Implications for Other Social Policies

An alternative view of the role of fathers and of male capabilities for child care and nurturance also has implications for policies in other areas. The two most significant of these are employment — what types of jobs are seen as appropriate for males — and legal policies relating to custody and access for fathers.

Employment

Just as females are discouraged from seeking more physically arduous jobs (e.g., labouring), males have been discouraged from seeking jobs that involve providing care for others (e.g., nursing), and those that involve the care and control of very young children. The evidence presented here indicates that males are likely to be just as competent in these types of occupations as women are, and there is no good reason why men should not be encouraged to seek employment in child-care centres, pre-schools, and infants schools.

Legal Policies

Even though there is some evidence of fathers getting a better deal from family law courts and being more likely to be awarded custody of children than they were five to ten years ago, it could hardly be argued that mothers and fathers have an equal chance of being awarded custody. Indeed, many cases fail to be even contested because fathers believe they have little chance at all. The evidence also indicates that fathers are treated differently from mothers in decisions about access. It is rare for a father to be given access to his pre-school-aged children overnight or for an extended period of time. The belief is still prevalent that because fathers are not biologically prepared for child care, they would not be capable of providing adequate care for their young children. Yet it is obvious that fathers will have difficulty either establibishing or maintaining a close relationship with their children without adequate contact. The type of limited access often awarded to fathers would only enable them to develop very superficial relationships with their children. Indeed, there is strong evidence that maintaining relationships with both parents after divorce is important. R.D. Hess and K.D. Camara, in a study of nine-to-eleven-year-old children, found that the negative effects of divorce were lessened when the children had positive relationships with both parents. In their words, "The child's relationship with the non-custodial parent [father] was as important as the continuing relationship with the mother" (Hess and Camara 1979, p. 80). From the evidence of the present study, it seems that time spent by fathers alone with their children is likely to be highly critical. Shared-caregiving fathers found that it was only when they began spending long periods of time alone with their children, having the sole responsibility for them, and being around at sensitive times, that they began to develop a very close and warm relationship with their children.

With the recognition that both mothers and fathers are competent child-carers, there is now a growing move in several countries for mothers and fathers to be awarded joint custody by courts, and for the two parents to share equally in the day-to-day care of their children in the way that one of the shared-caregiving parents who had separated did (see chapter 10). An argument for joint custody appears especially appropriate within the current climate of intense battles between parents for the sole custody of children. Today, a few fathers are prepared to fight extremely hard indeed to maintain their contacts with their children, and, as a result, several fathers' rights groups have emerged. The evidence reported here adds some weight to these claims of fathers. It is obvious that fathers can be competent child-carers and that many have high personal investments in their children and are strongly attached to them. As such, the battles between parents are likely to intensify even further in the future unless there is some change to the current system. At the theroretical level, joint custody appears to hold a lot of promise. However, the ramifications of such a change have yet to be explored either by the legal profession or by social scientists. Of particular importance here, it seems, is the likely impact it will have on the child (e.g., the difficulties a child might encounter going from one home to another; is this type of arrangement equally suitable for older and younger children?). Clearly, given the current climate of dissatisfaction with custody decisions, and fathers' increased commitments to children, the community, the legal profession, and social scientists will be forced to examine this issue in depth in the near future.

Conclusion

My own interpretation of the present findings on shared-caregiving families and the analysis of related social changes is that the future *will* see fathers being even more highly participant in child care. This change, however, is likely to be slow, as the forces to maintain the *status quo* are much stronger than those pushing for change. Another reason why it will be slow is because the widespread adoption of alternative child-care arrangements with fathers being equal participants is dependent on changes occurring at several different levels: changes in beliefs and attitudes, social policy, education, and the economic and employment and political structures. The area which is likely to provide both the greatest potential for change and the greatest potential for conflict and tension is the interface between the individual, paid work, and the family. It is the further exploration of this interface which should prove the most fruitful for our understanding of changes in family patterns. The conflicts and the tensions, however, are likely to be experienced differently by males and females. The prospects for future change and the different ways in which males and females view father participation in child care are well illustrated by the different perspectives a mother and father had about the ability of fathers to care for children:

Mother: "They could . . . if they had to."
Father: "They can . . . if they want to."

Appendix 1
Sampling and Sample Characteristics

1. Sampling

The aim in this study was to recruit as diverse a sample as possible of young families in which there was at least one child under ten years of age. The reasons for choosing to study young families are presented in chapter 2.

All of the traditional families (N = 145), the families in which mothers were employed part-time (N = 47), and the families in which mothers were employed full-time (N = 45), were recruited by approaching men, women, and men and women together, in shopping centres in seven Sydney suburbs (rated 1 to 7 on Congalton's status ranking scale) and in two New South Wales country towns (populations eight thousand and twenty thousand). Forty-five families were recruited from the country towns. Time-of-day and day-of-week for recruiting were systematically varied (i.e., recruiting was carried out on weekdays and on Saturdays; mornings, lunch times, afternoons, and late-night shopping times). People were approached who appeared to be in the age range twenty to fifty; the only criteria for inclusion in the sample were that the family lived in the suburb or town (or surrounding rural area) and that they had a child under ten years of age. Close to 50% of the people approached and who satisfied the criteria agreed to participate. The agreement rate across the nine shopping centres ranged from 70% to 30%, the highest being from a suburb rated 2 (i.e., high status) on Congalton's scale, and the lowest being from a suburb rated 6 (low status). The most frequently given reasons for not participating were: not enough time (51%); not interested (36%); father was rarely at home or mother thought he would not agree (10%); and that the father thought the mother would not agree (3%).

As was mentioned in chapter 2, this shopping-centre method

of sampling proved too time-consuming for the recruitment of shared-caregiving families, and so additional methods of recruitment were employed for this sample. Ten families were recruited from shopping centres; ten were obtained from information provided by traditional families who were recruited from shopping centres; thirty-one responded to notices placed on community and university notice boards; and twenty were recruited from approaches made to parents at play groups and pre-schools. There were only three shared-caregiving families with whom contact was made and agreement was not reached for an interview. In two of these it was obvious that the father had the strongest views about not participating, while in the other it was unclear which of the parents, or whether both, did not want to be interviewed. In all three families the father was not employed at the time contact was made.

2. Sample Characteristics

It is the 145 traditional families and the 71 shared-caregiving families that form the basis for the overwhelming majority of analyses described in the book, and thus complete sample characteristics will only be given for these two groups. A brief description of the other two sub-groups − mother employed either part- or full-time − is given in chapter 3.

Table 23 presents a summary of background and family characteristics for the two groups of families.

All but twenty-one parents in traditional families and thirteen parents in shared-caregiving families were either born in Australia or had been in the country for twenty or more years; only one father in one family was of Aboriginal origin. The majority of these thirty-four parents had come from English-speaking countries (especially from New Zealand and the United Kingdom). The sample, therefore, does not include large sub-groups of non-English-speaking ethnic groups.

The selection of the sample to include only a very narrow range of cultural backgrounds was intended from the beginning of the study. While accepting that this narrow perspective is a valid criticism, it was my view at the time that I neither had the necessary skills and knowledge of other cultures nor the resources available to employ other people who did have the knowledge and skills.

While the present sample does not include features of the

cultural diversity of Australian society, it does include a wide range in terms of traditional socio-economic status variables. Table 24 presents the distribution of suburb and occupational status ranking, and table 25 the distributions for the number of years of high school and tertiary education completed.

Table 23. Background and family characteristics of recruited families

	Shared-caregiving		Traditional	
	Mothers	Fathers	Mothers	Fathers
Years married	7.3		8.2	
Mean number of children	1.7		2.3	
Mean age of youngest child	2.9		2.3	
Mean age of oldest child	5.8		5.7	
Suburb status ranking[1]	3.91		3.96	
Age in years	30.9	32.9	30.6	32.7
Occupation status ranking[1]	3.8	4.2	4.7	3.9
Percentage completed high school	63	69	33	48
Percentage completed university	44	28	14	27

[1]Congalton (1969)

Table 24. Suburb and occupational status rankings[1] of recruited families (distributions in percentages)

	(High) 1	2	3	4	5	6	(Low) 7
Suburb of Residence							
Shared-caregiving	5	15	22	27	14	7	10
Traditional	15	11	18	17	12	12	15
Occupation							
Shared-caregiving							
Mothers	2	11	40	24	9	9	7
Fathers	4	13	20	17	18	18	10
Traditional							
Mothers	2	0	17	20	38	19	4
Fathers	10	15	12	24	18	16	5

[1]Congalton (1969)

Table 25. Educational standard of recruited families (distributions in percentages)

	Years of High School Completed		
	Twelve	Ten	Less than 10
Shared-caregiving			
Mothers	63	30	7
Fathers	69	18	13
Traditional			
Mothers	33	47	20
Fathers	48	36	16
	Tertiary Education			
	Higher Degree	Under-graduate Degree	College Diploma	Trade
Shared-caregiving				
Mothers	3	41	25	8
Fathers	8	20	7	19
Traditional				
Mothers	0	14	14	11
Fathers	4	23	10	31

Appendix 2
Methodology

1. Interview Procedure

Parents were interviewed in their own homes at a time convenient to them. Most interviews were carried out during the evenings, and *all* were conducted with both the mother and father present. Forty-five per cent of the interviews were conducted by men and fifty-five per cent by women. The interviewers' ages ranged from twenty-two to forty-two. There were two parts to the interview.

Part 1

The first part of the interview consisted of a series of structured questions covering background information, such as age, residence, occupation, and marital status; work and leisure patterns for parents and children; child-care patterns; children's attendance at school, pre-school, and playgroups; children's sleep patterns; the amount of time parents were available to their children; division of labour for child-care tasks; parent-child interaction and family activities; father's attendance at birth. Questions were asked in the same order as they are listed here.

The primary aim of the first part of interview was to obtain as accurate information as was possible about what the parents actually did. Each parent was asked separately (but in the presence of the other parent) how often or how much time each week he or she spent doing the following for or with the children: feeding, dressing, changing nappies, bathing, attending to during the night, reading stories to, helping with school work, and playing or interacting with. Play and other interaction were defined liberally to include both child- and parent-oriented activities such as cleaning and gardening.

The following interview strategy was adopted in an attempt to ensure that parents' responses reflected what they actually did, rather than their perception of what they did. Before asking the divisions-of-labour questions, information was sought on (1) the amount of time each parent spent at home, at work, and on recreational activities; (2) the amount of time the father spent taking complete care of the children; (3) the types of activities parents and children participated in together; and (4) the amount of time the children were at home (and awake). Fathers were asked each question first. After both parents had responded, the interviewer repeated their responses and asked them if they agreed that that was what they each did. The interviewer also pointed out any inconsistencies between these and earlier responses (e.g., if the father said that he bathed his two-year-old child four times a week but had previously stated that he arrived home from work at seven o'clock every night). In approximately 20% of the interviews at least one of the responses was modified, most commonly as the result of mothers providing further information about fathers' activities. This resulted in both increases and decreases in fathers' estimates. In several families, mothers and fathers resolved or avoided discrepancies by reviewing their own activities. However, because most fathers' involvement was so minor, there was little opportunity for major disagreement. In the interviews where parents were not able to agree, the interviewer reviewed their activities of the previous week. This was done by asking who had done the specific task the day before, the day before that, and so on.

This strategy of interviewing mothers and fathers together, and of asking fathers the questions first, was decided on after evaluating the results of a pilot study (N = 20 families). The major aim of the pilot was to examine four different methods of collecting data: (1) interviewing mothers and fathers together; (2) interviewing them separately; (3) using a diary (in thirty-minute intervals) of the parent-child activities for the day of the interview (filled out by the interviewer from information provided by parents); (4) using a diary of parent-child activities for a week (filled out by the parents). It was found that when mothers and fathers were interviewed separately, there were discrepancies (the criterion adopted here, and below, was a 10% difference) in approximately 50% of the responses. It was also found that diaries of the activities for the day of the interview corresponded closely (for 75% of the responses) with parental child-care estimates and information provided on parental activities (e.g., work patterns) obtained from the joint-interview technique. The major discrepancies occurred for estimates of play and other interactions. One of the problems found with using this diary technique was that it resulted in underestimates of fathers' participation. Most of the interviews were carried out on week nights, while much of the father-child interaction occurred on weekends. Finally, only nine of the sample returned diaries of a week's activities, and those that were returned were completed in varying degrees of detail. As such, no further analyses were carried out on these data.

Part 2

In the second part of the interview, mothers and fathers were interviewed separately. Here, questions were unstructured and open-ended and covered beliefs about parental roles and child development and about parental child-rearing values and aspirations, and, for shared-caregiving parents, their evaluations of their lifestyles. The complete list of questions is given below.

1. a. What do you see as being your *role/responsibilities* as a father/mother?
    b. How do you see your role in relation to your wife's/husband's? Do you see them as being the same, or do you see them as being different, in what ways do they differ? (Probe on similarities/differences.)
    c. What about discipline – do you see any differences here between mothers and fathers?
    d. Do you think you and your spouse differ in your approach to discipline? (Probe.)
    e. How important do you see consensus/agreement as being? (Probe.)
2. Do you think that there is something about a woman, something like a maternal instinct, that makes her more able to care for children? Something a woman is born with? Something biological?
3. Do you think a mother's place is in the home? (If yes; ask if there are any limits to this – e.g., one age/stage more critical than another.)
4. a. Do you think that a father could care for children as well as a mother? Why?/Why not?
    b. If *yes*, ask: Why do you think that so few men take on a caregiving role?

5. In what ways do you think you could change what you do now to improve your relationship with your children? (Probe – e.g., if say spend more time with them, ask *how* would spend time.)
6. I now want to talk about the influence you feel you have over your children. How much influence do you feel you have over each of the following? (Hand card.)

		A lot of influence	*Some* influence	*Very little* influence	*No* influence
1.	How well your children get along with other children	1	2	3	4
2.	Whether they are honest	1	2	3	4
3.	Their attitudes and morals	1	2	3	4
4.	Whether they are independent and stand up for themselves	1	2	3	4
5.	Whether they are co-operative and share things	1	2	3	4
6.	How they express love and affection	1	2	3	4
7.	What type of job they take up	1	2	3	4
8.	Their sense of humour	1	2	3	4
9.	Their financial security in the future	1	2	3	4
10.	Their ability to work things out, to think, reason and solve problems	1	2	3	4
11.	Their imagination and creativity (e.g., drawing, painting)	1	2	3	4
12.	How they go at school	1	2	3	4
13.	Their happiness	1	2	3	4
14.	Whether they are well behaved	1	2	3	4
15.	Their sensitivity to other people's needs and feelings	1	2	3	4
16.	Their self-control	1	2	3	4
17.	Whether they are well-mannered, and neat tidy	1	2	3	4
18.	Whether they try hard at things they do	1	2	3	4
19.	Whether they are curious or interested in how and why things happen	1	2	3	4
20.	How they act as a boy or a girl	1	2	3	4

7. Do you think there are any stages or ages in a child's growth and development that are more important than others? Specify.

8. *a.* (i) Is your role more important at any particular time?
   (ii) What about for sons/daughters? Do you see any difference there?
   b. (i) Is your husband's/wife's role more important at any particular times?
   (ii) What about for sons/daughters?

9. Now I would like to talk about the kinds of characteristics in children that you see as being important. (*Explain* and *show* card.)

		Very Important	Fairly Important	Fairly Un-important	Not Important at All
1.	Getting on well with other children	1	2	3	4
2.	Being honest	1	2	3	4
3.	Having good morals	1	2	3	4
4.	Being independent and able to stand up for themselves	1	2	3	4
5.	Being co-operative and sharing things	1	2	3	4
6.	Being able to express love and affection	1	2	3	4
7.	Having a good and secure job	1	2	3	4
8.	Having a good sense of humour	1	2	3	4
9.	Being able to work things out, to think and solve problems	1	2	3	4
10.	Having a good imagination and being creative	1	2	3	4
11.	Doing well at school	1	2	3	4
12.	Being happy	1	2	3	4
13.	Being well behaved; doing what they are told	1	2	3	4
14.	Being sensitive to other people's feelings	1	2	3	4
15.	Having self-control	1	2	3	4
16.	Being well mannered and neat and tidy	1	2	3	4
17.	Trying hard at things they do	1	2	3	4
18.	Being curious and interested in how and why things happen	1	2	3	4
19.	Acting like a boy or girl	1	2	3	4

10. What do you enjoy about being a father/mother?
11. What do you dislike about being a father/mother?

Questions related to Shared-Caregiving

12. How long have you been in this type of family organization?
13. How long do you expect to remain like this?
14. What were the major reasons for your changing. (Probe.)
15. Who do you feel was more influential in the decision – you or your spouse? Or was it fairly well a joint decision? (Probe.)
16. Have there been any problems or difficulties with changing roles/going back to work?
17. (Probe for personal problems in adjustment/getting used to change.)
    (Probe for problems of spouse.)
    (Probe for problems with children adjusting, etc.)
18. What do you feel have been the major advantages of changing? (Probe.)
    General.
    Personal.
    Spouse.
    Children.
19. What about family relationships? Do you feel they have changed in any way?
    What about your relationship with your spouse?
    Your relationships with your children?
    Your spouse's relationship with the children?
20. How have other people reacted to your changing roles/you – your spouse going back to work?
    General.
    What about your own and your spouse's parents or other relatives?
    What about your close friends? What do they think?
    What about your neighbours?
    The people you/your spouse work with?
21. Overall, what do you really enjoy about your current family organization?
22. What are the things you really dislike about it?
23. Why do you think that more people don't adopt the family organization you have?
24. What things do you feel need to be changed in society if more people are to change roles?

At the completion of the interview parents were asked to complete two inventories: the Bem Sex-Role Inventory and Spanier's Dyadic Adjustment Scale.

2. Bem Sex Role Inventory (BSRI)

The Bem Sex-Role Inventory (Bem 1974) consists of twenty masculine sex-typed adjectives and phrases (e.g., *dominant, aggressive, forceful, makes decisions easily*) and twenty feminine sex-typed adjectives (e.g., *affectionate, warm, understanding, compassionate*), each rated on a seven-point scale in terms of its self-applicability. An additional twenty adjectives which are neutral with respect to sex-typing are also included to assess the level of social desirability response set.

In contrast to previous sex-role scales, the BSRI therefore permits the *independent* assessment of masculinity and femininity. Indeed, the purported independence of masculinity and femininity provided the theoretical basis for the design of the scale.

The BSRI has also been put forward as a measure of androgyny. *Psychological androgyny* refers to the incorporation within the one individual both traditionally masculine and traditionally feminine traits. There has been some dispute in the literature about how to assess androgyny (see Russell, Antill, and Cunningham 1978). The method favoured here was that proposed by Spence, Helmreich, and Stapp (1975) — the median split method.

To use the median split method, the *median* masculinity and *median* femininity scores for a large representative group of individuals (males and females combined) are determined. The androgyny label is then applied only to those who are above the medians on *both* scales. Those who are below both medians are classified as undifferentiated. Those who are above the masculinity median but below the femininity median are referred to as masculine sex-typed, and those below the masculinity median but above the femininity median are referred to as feminine sex-typed. The medians used in the present analysis were those determined from a large sample of university students, which are reported in Russell, Antill, and Cunningham 1978.

Complete details of the properties of the BSRI for an Australian sample are reported in Russell, Antill, and Cunningham 1978. As can be seen from that analysis, the psychometric properties of the scale for Australian responses are comparable to those reported by Bem (1974) for an American sample.

Finally, it should be pointed out that there is some dispute about exactly what the BSRI and other similar scales are measuring. Bem has argued that the BSRI measures sex-role personality traits, and therefore can be considered to be an instrument that provides global measures of sex-roles and masculinity, femininity, and androgyny. Spence and Helmreich (1981), on the other hand, have argued that the scope of the BSRI and their own scale (the PAQ) are rather more limited. They argue that the two scales of the BSRI are best considered to be measures of *instrumentality* and *expressiveness* which are only minimally related to sex-role attitudes and gender-related preferences.

3. Spanier's Dyadic Adjustment Scale

Spanier's Dyadic Adjustment Scale (Spanier 1976) was designed to assess the quality of marriage and other similar dyads (e.g., unmarried cohabiting couples). It consists of 32 items, most of which are rated on a six-point scale. Spanier provides data which show that these items group into four reliable sub-scales:

1. *Dyadic consensus* (13 items): A scale which assesses a person's perception of dyadic agreement on items such as: "handling family finances", "religious matters", "friends", "making major decisions", "household tasks".

2. *Dyadic satisfaction* (10 items): A scale which assesses a person's satisfaction with his or her relationship. For example, items inquire about the frequency with which "divorce or separation has been considered", "one person leaves the house after a fight", "regret is felt about having married".

3. *Dyadic cohesion* (5 items): This scale essentially assesses the extent to which a couple engage in activities together or share experiences with one another (e.g., "laugh together", "calmly discuss something").

4. *Affectional expression* (4 items): These items assess the extent of agreement on and the occurrence of recent conflict in sexual relationships and the display of affection.

The final design of the scale and its reported psychometric properties were based on two American samples: (1) a sample of 218 married persons; (2) a sample of 94 people who had recently been divorced.

In an Australian study, Antill and Cotton (1980) administered Spanier's scale to 108 married couples and 68 cohabiting individuals. Although these researchers report some minor differences between Australian and American responses to the scale (e.g., in the Australian sample *consensus* and *satisfaction* tended to divide up into two or three smaller sub-scales when a factor analysis was performed), by and large psychometric characteristics were found to be comparable in the two studies. In particular, the means reported in the two studies were similar, and the total scale and the four sub-scales were found to be highly reliable. On the basis of these findings then, Antill and Cotton conclude that the scale "seems readily applicable to Australian samples".

Appendix 3
Data Analysis

1. Content Analysis

Most of the questions in part 2 of the interview were open-ended, and therefore techniques for coding and analysis needed to be developed for each. The technique adopted was the same for each question, and was a follows:

1. All responses on the question were read through and a list made of the different types of responses. At this stage the list was very extensive, and in some cases included as many as thirty categories.
2. A second person then worked on the extensive list and attempted to group the responses into a smaller number of meaningful categories (usually around five to fifteen).
3. An attempt was then made to code the responses into these categories. Further modifications were made to the categories according to the success/failure of this exercise.
4 . Another coder, who had not been involved in the process up to this point, was then asked to code the responses using the revised list of categories. Agreement with the other coder would then be checked and further modifications made where necessary.
5. The coding would then be done, with reliability being checked using a second coder. The percentage of agreement was found to vary between 84% and 100%, with the majority of questions having an agreement rate of higher than 90%.

2. Statistical Analysis

The type of statistics employed varied according to the nature of the response measure and the nature of the question of interest.

Table 26. Parents' perceptions of their roles and responsibilities (percentages of sample giving each response)

	Shared-caregiving		Traditional	
	Fathers	Mothers	Fathers	Mothers
Breadwinner	28	4	59	0
Care for day-to-day needs	41	56	23	59
General socialization	37	32	43	43
Discipline	7	11	14	13
Provide love and affection	21	34	18	33
Play	15	14	20	10
Head of the house	3	0	12	0
Housework	3	4	0	7
Provide stability/consistency	7	4	3	0
Be patient/tolerant	0	4	2	4
Encourage to achieve	1	2	5	5
Assist with education	7	4	13	8
Be there when needed	13	9	3	23
Ensure are well mannered	17	20	22	31
Look after health	4	13	10	28
Ensure have morals/values	6	6	18	17
Emotional stability	9	27	8	16
Ensure do well at school	4	4	6	2
Be a friend	4	13	10	8
Give varied experiences	1	3	5	3
Instil independence	17	11	9	13
Ensure are secure in future	4	0	2	2
Make sure are happy	9	20	14	19
Influence personality	2	3	0	3

In some cases, all that is presented are simple descriptive measures (e.g., means, percentages of people who gave one response or another). In other cases, highly sophisticated statistical tests have been employed (e.g., multivariate analysis of variance). These tests provide us with an indication of how likely it is that a difference we have on a measure (e.g., a difference between shared-caregiving and traditional fathers for perceived influence over sex-roles) is significant or important, or alternatively whether it is more likely to be due to something idiosyncratic about our response measure, or to a multitude of other factors. To help us make a decision about whether we should place any importance on a finding, we employ *tests* of significance, and report figures for the probability that our finding is in fact *not* important. For example, when it is reported that a finding is significant, with $p < .05$, this means that there is likely to be only five chances in a hundred that our finding is spurious. The .05 level has come to be accepted within social sciences as a reasonable level for us to conclude a finding is important. Note, however, that there is nothing absolute about this, and of course, there is still the possibility that our finding is spurious, even though our tests tell us that we can be fairly confident about it.

The level of significance accepted in the present study is .05, although at times, reference is made to the fact that there is a non-significant trend. The reason for pointing out these trends is that this study is best considered as exploratory. Some of the trends evident here appeared to *me* to be sufficiently important to warrant that they be given further attention in subsequent studies, and this is why attention has been drawn to them.

In some situations it was neither possible nor appropriate to carry out statistical tests, and therefore only summary descriptive statistics are given in the forms of means or percentages (e.g., in the case of many of the responses to the open-ended questions for shared-caregiving families). What importance to place on these means and percentages therefore is very open to the interpretation of the researcher and the reader.

References

Abrahams, B.; Feldman, S.S.; and Nash, S.C. 1978. Sex role self-concept and sex role attitudes: Enduring personality characteristics, or adaptations to changing life situations. *Developmental Psychology* 14: 393-400.

Adler, D.L. 1966. The contemporary Australiam family. *Human Relations* 19: 265-82.

Ainsworth, M.D.S., and Bell, S.M. 1970. Attachment, exploration and separation: Illustrated by the behaviour of one-year olds in a strange environment. *Child Development* 41: 49-67.

Ainsworth, M.D.S., Blehar, M.C.; Waters, E.; and Wall, S. 1978. *Patterns of Attachment.* Hillsdale, N.J.: Lawrence Erlbaum.

Aldous, J. 1974. The making of family roles and family change. *Family Co-ordinator* 23: 231-35.

Alwyn, J. 1977. Husband participation in childbirth. M.A. thesis. Australian National University.

Antill, J.K. 1981. Sex-role complementarity versus similarity in married couples. Unpublished manuscript.

Antill, J.K., and Cotton, S. 1980. Spanier's dyadic adjustment scale: Some confirmatory analyses. Unpublished manuscript.

Antill, J.K., and Cunningham, J.D. 1980. The relationship of masculinity, femininity, and androgyny to self-esteem. *Australian Journal of Psychology* 32: 195-208.

Australian Bureau of Statistics. 1977. *The labour force.* May.

Australian Family Survey. 1973, 1975, 1976. Australian Family Research Bulletins: 1, 2 and 3. School of Social Work, University of New South Wales.

Bailyn, L. 1978. Accommodation of work to family. In *Working couples,* ed. R. Rapoport and R.N. Rapoport. St Lucia: University of Queensland Press.

Barnett, M.A.; King, L.M.; Howards, J.A.; and Dino, G.A. 1980. Empathy in young children: Relation to parents' empathy, affection, and emphasis on the feelings of others. *Developmental Psychology* 16: 243-44.

Baumrind, D. 1980. New directions in socialization research. *American Psychologist* 35: 639-52.

Belsky, J. 1979. Mother-father-infant interaction: A naturalistic observational study. *Developmental Psychology* 15: 601-7.

Bem, S.L. 1974. The measurement of psychological androgyny. *Journal of Consulting and Clinical Psychology* 42, no. 2: 155-62.

_____. 1979. Theory and measurement of androgyny: A reply to the Pedhazur-Tetenbaum and Locksley-Colten Critiques. *Journal of Personality and Social Psychology* 37: 1047-54.

Bem, S.L., and Lenney, E. 1976. Sex typing and the avoidance of cross-sex behaviour. *Journal of Personality and Social Psychology* 33: 48-54.

Bem, S.L.; Martyna, W.; and Watson, C. 1976. Sex typing and androgyny: Further explorations of the expressive domain. *Journal of Personality and Social Psychology* 34: 1016-23.

Berger, M. 1979. Men's new family roles – some implications for therapists. *Family Co-ordinator* 28: 638-46.

Berman, P.W. 1976. Social context as a determinant of sex differences in adults' attraction to infants. *Developmental Psychology* 12: 365-66.

_____. 1980. Are women more responsive than men to the young? A review of developmental and situational variables. *Psychological Bulletin* 88: 668-95.

Berman, P.W.; Cooper, P.; Mansfield, P.; Shields, S.; and Abplanalp, J. 1975. Sex differences in attraction to infants: When do they occur? *Sex Roles* 1: 311-18.

Bernard, J. 1972. *The future of marriage.* Harmondsworth, Middx: Penguin.

Biller, H.B. 1974. *Paternal deprivation: Family, school, sexuality and society.* Lexington, Mass.: Heath.

Block, J.H. 1979. Another look at sex differentiation in the socialization behaviours of mothers and fathers. In *Psychology of Women: Future Directions of Research.* New York: Psychological Dimensions June.

_____. 1981. Personality development in males and females: The influence of differential socialization. Unpublished paper.

Blood, R.O., and Wolfe, D.M. 1960. *Husbands and wives.* New York: Free Press.

Bloom-Feshback, J. 1980. Data reported in Newsline section. *Psychology Today* 13, no. 11: 38.

Bowlby, J. 1951. *Maternal care and mental health.* Geneva: W.H.O.

_____. 1969. *Attachment and loss:* vol. 1. *Attachment* London: Hogarth.

Braymen, R., and DeFrain, F. 1979. *Sex-role attitudes and behaviours of children reared by androgynous parents.* Paper presented at the workshop on "Androgyny and children: Prospects in a Sexist Society", Groves conference on Marriage and the Family, Washington, D.C.

Brown, D.G. 1956. Sex-role preference in children. *Psychological Monographs* 70, (*14*, serial no. 287).

Bryson, L. 1974. Men's work and women's work: Occupation and family orientation. *Search* 5: 295-99.

————. 1975. Husband and wife interactions in the Australian Family: A critical review of the literature. In *The Other Half: Women in Australian Society*, ed. J. Mercer. Ringwood, Vic.: Penguin.

Carlsson, S.G.; Fagerberg, H.; Horneman, G.; Hwang, C-P.; Larsson, K.; Rodholm, M.; Schaller, J.; Danielsson, B.; and Gundewall, C. 1979. Effects on various amounts of contact between mother and child on the mother's nursing behaviour: A follow-up study. *Infant Behaviour and Development* 2: 209-14.

Cogswell, B.E.; and Sussman, M.B. 1972. Changing family marriage forms: Complications for human service systems. In *Non-Traditional Family Forms in the 1970's*, ed. M. Sussman. Minneapolis: National Council on Family Relations.

Congalton, A.A. 1969. *Status and prestige in Australia: Studies in Australian Society*. Melbourne: Cheshire.

Curthoys, A. 1976. Men and childcare in the feminest utopia. *Refractory Girl*, no. 10 (March).

DeFrain, J. 1979. Androgynous parents tell who they are and what they need. *Family Co-ordinator* 28: 237-43.

Ericksen, J.A.; Yancey, W.L.; and Ericksen, E.P. 1979. The division of family roles. *Journal of Marriage and the family*, May, pp. 301-13.

Fallding, H.J. 1957. Inside the Australian Family. In *Marriage and the family in Australia*, ed. A.P. Elkin. Sydney: Angus & Robertson.

Farrell, W. 1975. *The liberated man*. New York: Bantam.

Fein, R.A. 1978. Research on fathering: Social policy and an emergent perspective. *Journal of Social Issues* 34: 122-35.

Feldman, S.S.; and Nash, S.C. 1978. Interest in babies during young adulthood. *Child Development* 49: 617-22.

————. 1979. Changes in responsiveness to babies during adolescence. *Child Development* 50: 942-49.

Field, T. 1978. Interaction behaviours of primary versus secondary caretaker fathers. *Developmental Psychology* 14: 183-84.

Frodi, A., and Lamb, M.E. 1978. Sex differences in responsiveness to infants: A developmental study of psychophysiological and behavioural responses. *Child Development* 49: 1182-88.

Frodi, A.; Lamb, M.E.; Leavitt, L., and Donovan, W. 1978. Father's and mother's responses to infant smiles and cries. *Infant Behaviour and Development* 1: 187-98.

Frodi, A.; Lamb, M.E.; Leavitt, L.; Donovan, W.; Neff, C.; and Sherry, D. 1978. Father's and mother's responses to the faces and cries of normal and premature infants. *Developmental Psychology* 14: 490-98.

General Mills. 1977. Raising children in a changing society. *The General Mills American Family Report 1976-1977*.

Goldberg, S. 1977. Social competence in infancy: A model of parent-infant interaction. *Merrill-Palmer Quarterly* 23: 163-77.

Goodnow, J.J. 1981. Mothers' developmental timetables and associated ideas. Paper presented to the biennial meeting of the Society for Research in Child Development, Boston, April.

Greenberg, M., and Morris, N. 1974. Engrossment: The newborn's impact upon the father. *American Journal of Orthopsychiatry* 44: 520-31.

Gronseth, E. 1978. Work sharing: A Norwegian example. In *Working couples*, ed. R. Rapoport and R.N. Rapoport. St. Lucia: University of Queensland Press.

Harper, J., and Richards, L. 1979. *Mothers and working mothers.* Ringwood, Vic.: Penguin.

Herbst, P.G. 1954. Conceptual framework for studying the family. In *Social structure and personality in a city*, ed. O.A. Oeser and S.B. Hammond. London: Routledge & Kegan Paul.

Hess, R.D., and Camara, K.D. 1979. Post-divorce family relationships as mediating factors in the consequences of divorce for children. *Journal of Social Issues* 35: 79-96.

Hock, E. 1980. Working and nonworking mothers and their infants: A comparative study of maternal caregiving characteristics and infant social behaviour. *Merrill-Palmer Quarterly* 26: 79-101.

Hoffman, L.W. 1977. Changes in family roles, socialization and sex differences. *American Psychologist* 32: 644-57.

Hoffman, L.W., and Nye, F.I., eds. 1974. *Working mothers.* San Francisco: Jossey-Bass.

Hood, J., and Golden, S. 1979. Beating time/making time: The impact of work scheduling on men's family roles. *Family Co-ordinator* 28: 575-82.

International Labour Office. 1980. *Equal opportunities and equal treatment for men and women workers: Workers with family responsibilities.* International Labour Conference, 66th Session.

Jackson, B. 1980. Towards a sketch of the CHES father. Unpublished paper.

Josselyn, I.M. 1956. Cultural forces, motherliness and fatherliness. *American Journal of Orthopsychiatry* 26: 264-71.

Kelley, S. 1981. Changing parent-child relationships: An outcome of mother returning to college. Unpublished paper.

Klaus, M., and Kennell, J. 1976. *Maternal-infant bonding.* St Louis, Mo.: C.V. Mosby.

Kohn, M.L. 1969. *Class and conformity: A study of values.* Homewood, Ill.: Dorsey.

Kotelchuck, M. 1976. The infant's relationship to the father: Experimental evidence. In *The role of the father in child development*, ed. M.E. Lamb. New York: Wiley.

Lamb, M.E. 1976. Interactions between 8-month-old children and their fathers and mothers. In *The role of the father in child development*, ed. M.E. Lamb. New York: Wiley.

——. 1978a. Influence of the child on marital quality and family interaction during prenatal, perinatal and infancy periods. In *Child influences on marital and family interaction: A life-span prespective*, ed. R.M. Lerner and G.V. Spanier. New York: Academic Press.

———. 1978b. Qualitative aspects of mother- and father-infant attachments. *Infant behaviour and Development* 1: 265-75.

———. 1981. Fathers and child development. In *The father's role in child development*, ed. M.E. Lamb. 2nd ed. New York: Wiley.

Lamb, M.E. and Easterbrooks, M.A. 1980. Individual differences in parental sensitivity: Some thoughs about origins, components, and consequences. In *Infant social cognition: Empirical and theoretical considerations*, ed. M.E. Lamb and L.R. Sherrod. Hillsdale, N.J.: Lawrence Erlbaum.

Lamb, M.E.; Frodi, A.M.; Hwang, C.P.; Frodi, M.; and Steinberg, J. 1981. Attitudes and behaviour of traditional and nontraditional parents in Sweden. In *Attachment and affiliative systems: Neurobiological and psychobiological aspects*, ed. R. Emde and R. Harmon. New York: Plenum.

———. 1982. Mother- and father-infant interaction involving play and holding in traditional and non-traditional Swedish families. *Developmental Psychology* 18: In press.

Lamb, M.E., and Goldberg, W.A. 1982. The father-child relationship: A synthesis of biological, evolutionary, and social perspectives. In *Parental behaviour: Its courses and consequences*, ed. R. Gandelman and L. Hoffman. Hillsdale, N.J.: Lawrence Erlbaum.

Leibowitz, L. 1978. *Females, males, families: A biosocial approach.* North Scituate, Mass.: Duxbury Press.

Lein, L. 1979. Male participation in home life: Impact of social supports and breadwinner responsibility on the allocation of tasks. *Family Co-ordinator* 28: 489-96.

Levine, J.A. 1977. *Who will raise the children? New Options for fathers (and mothers).* New York: Bantam.

———. 1979. Everyman's blues: Harping on the male role crisis. *Psychology Today* 13, no. 6.

Mackey, W.C. 1979. Parameters of the adult-male-child bond. *Ethology and Sociobiology* 1: 59-76.

McGillicuddy-De Lisi, A.V. 1981. Parental beliefs about developmental processes. Paper presented at the biennial meeting of the Society for Research in Child Development, Boston, April.

Murray, A.D. 1978. Infant crying as an activator of altruistic and egoistic motives in adults. Doctoral thesis, Macquarie University.

Nash, S.C., and Feldman, S.S. 1980. Responsiveness to babies: Life situation specific sex differences in adulthood. *Sex Roles.*

Newland, K. 1980. *Women, men and the division of labour.* Worldwatch Paper, May.

Newson, J., and Newson, E. 1965. *Patterns of infant care in an urban community. Harmondsworth, Middx.:* Penguin.

Oakley, A. 1972. *Sex, gender and society.* London: Temple Smith.

———. 1974. *The sociology of housework.* London: Martin Robinson.

O'Brien, M. 1980. Fathers' perceptions of work-home conflicts. Paper presented at the British Psychology Society London Conference, December.

Parke, R.D. 1978. Parent-infant interaction: Progress, paradigms and problems. In *Observing behaviour*, ed. G.P. Sackett, vol. 1: *Theory and applications in mental retardation*. Baltimore: University Park Press.

_____. 1979. Perspectives on father-infant interaction. In *The handbook of infant development*, ed. J.D. Osofsky. New York: Wiley.

Parke, R.D.; Hymel, S.; Power, T.G.; and Tinsley, B.R. 1980. Fathers at risk: A hospital based model of intervention. In *Psychosocial risks in infant-environment transactions*, ed. D.B. Sawin, R.C. Hawkins, L.O. Walker, and J.H. Penticuff. New York: Bruner/Masel.

Parke, R.D., and Sawin, D.B. 1980. The family in early infancy: Social interactional attitudinal analyses. In *The father-infant relationship: Observational studies in a family setting*, ed. F.A. Pedersen. New York: Praeger.

Patterson, G.R. 1980. Mothers: The unacknowledged victims. Monograph of the Society for Research in Child Development, 45 (5), serial no. 186.

Pedersen, F.A., and Robson, K. 1969. Father participation in infancy. *American Journal of Orthopsychiatry* 39: 466-72.

Pleck, J.H. 1979. Men's family work: Three perspectives and some new data. *Family Co-ordinator* 28: 481-88.

_____. 1980. The work-family problem: Overloading the system. In *Outsiders on the inside: Women and organisations*, ed. B. Forisha and B. Goldman. Englewood Cliffs, N.J.: Prentice-Hall.

_____. 1981*a*. *The male role: Sex role identity and sex-role strain*. Cambridge, Mass.: M.I.T. Press.

_____. 1981*b*. Wives' employment, role demands and adjustment: Final report. Unpublished. Wellesley College, Centre for Research on Women.

_____. 1983. Husbands' paid work and family roles: Current research issues. In *Research on the interweave of social roles*, Vol. 3: *Families and Jobs*, ed. H.Z. Lopata. Greenwich, Conn.: JAI Press.

Pleck, J., and Rustad, M. 1980. Husbands' and wives' time in family work and paid work in the 1975 and 1976 study of time use. Unpublished manuscript.

Radin, N. 1980. Childrearing fathers in intact families: An exploration of some antecedents and consequences. Paper presented to a study group on "The role of the father in child development, social policy and the law". Haifa, Israel, July.

_____. 1981. Role-sharing fathers and pre-schoolers. In *Nontraditional Families: Parenting and child development*, ed. M.E. Lamb. Hillsdale, N.J.: Lawrence Erlbaum.

Rapoport, R., and Rapoport, R.N. 1976. *Dual career families re-examined*. New York: Harper & Row.

Rapoport, R.; Rapoport, R.N.; and Strelitz, Z. 1977. *Fathers, mothers and others*. St Lucia: University of Queensland Press.

Rebelsky, F., and Hanks, C. 1971. Father's verbal interactions with infants in the first three months of life. *Child Development* 42: 63-68.

Redican, W.K. 1976. Adult male-infant interactions in nonhuman primates. In *The role of the father in child development*, ed. M.E. Lamb. New York: Wiley.

Richards, L.L. 1978. *Having families*. Ringwood, Vic.: Penguin.

Robinson, J. 1977. *Changes in Americans' use of time, 1965 and 1975*. Cleveland, Ohio: Communications Research Centre, Cleveland State University.

Rodholm, M., and Larsson, R. 1979. Father-infant interaction at the first contact after delivery. *Infant Behaviour and Development* 2.

Rollins, B.C., and Galligan, R. 1978. The developing child and marital satisfaction of parents. In *Child influences on marital and family interaction*, ed. R.M. Lerner and G.B. Spanier. New York: Academic Press.

Rubin, J.Z.; Provenzano, F.J.; and Luria, Z. 1974. The eye of the beholder: parents' view on sex of newborns. *American Journal of Orthopsychiatry* 44: 512-19.

Russell, A., and Russell, G. 1982. Family versus teacher attitudes to child development. *New Education*, in press.

Russell, G. 1978. The father role and its relation to masculinity, femininity and androgyny. *Child Development* 49: 1174-81.

_____. 1979a. Fathers! Incompetent or reluctant parents? *Australian and New Zealand Journal of Sociology* 15: 57-65.

_____. 1979b. The role of fathers in child development — An Australian perspective. Paper presented to the 15th National Conference of the Australian Pre-School Association, Sydney.

_____. 1980. Fathers as caregivers: A preliminary study of shared-role families. *Australian Journal of Sex, Marriage and the Family* 1: 101-10.

Russell, G.; Antill, J.; and Cunningham, J. 1978. The measurement of masculinity, femininity and androgyny: A reply to Rowland (1977). *Australian Psychologist* 13: 41-50.

Russell, G., and Smith, J.E. 1979. Girls can be doctors . . . can't they?" Children's occupational aspirations. *Australian Journal of Social Issues* 14: 91-102.

Rutter, M. 1972. *Maternal deprivation reassessed*. Harmondsworth, Middx.: Penguin.

_____. 1979. Maternal deprivation, 1972-1978: New findings, new concepts, new approaches. *Child Development* 50: 283-305.

Safilios-Rothschild, C. 1969. Family sociology or wives' family sociology. *The Journal of Marriage and the Family* 29, no. 2: 345-52.

Sagi, A. 1981. Non-traditional fathers in Israel. In *Non-traditional families: Parenting and child development*, ed. M.E. Lamb. Hillsdale, N.J.: Lawrence Erlbaum.

Schaffer, H.R., and Emerson, P.E. 1964. The development of social attachments in infancy. *Monographs of the Society for Research in Child Development* 29 (serial no. 94).

Shorter, E. 1975. *The making of the modern family.* New York: Basic Books.

Spanier, G.B. 1976. Measuring dyadic adjustment: New scales for assessing the quality of marriage and similar dyads. *Journal of Marriage and the Family* 38: 15-30.

Spence, J.T., and Helmreich, R.L. 1981. Androgyny vs. gender schema: A comment on Bem's gender schema theory. Unpublished paper.

Spence, J.T.; Helmreich, R.L.; and Stapp, J. 1975. Ratings of self and peers on sex role attributes and their relation to self-esteem and conceptions of masculinity and femininity. *Journal of Personality and Social Psychology* 32: 29-39.

Staines, G.L.; Pleck, J.H.; Shepard, L.J.; and O'Connor, P. 1978. Wives' employment status and marital adjustment: Yet another look. In *Dual-career couples,* ed. J.B. Bryson and R. Bryson. New York: Human Sciences Press.

Stolz, L.M. 1967. *Influences on parent behaviour.* London: Tavistock.

Summers, A. 1975. *Damned whores and god's police: The colonization of women in Australia.* Ringwood, Vic.: Penguin.

Svejda, M.J.; Campos, J.J.; and Emde, R.N. 1980. Mother-infant "bonding": Failure to generalize. *Child Development* 51: 775-79.

Tolson, A. 1978. *The limits of masculinity.* London: Tavistock.

Tucker, N. 1976. John Bowlby on latchkey kids. *Psychology Today* 2, no. 11: 37-41.

Vanek, J. 1973. Keeping busy: Time spent in housework, United States, 1920 and 1970. Doctoral dissertation, University of Michigan.

Walker, K., and Woods, M. 1976. *Time use: A measure of household production of family goods and services.* Washington: American Home Economics Association.

West, M.M., and Konner, M.J. 1976. The role of the father: An anthropological perspective. In *The role of the father in child development,* ed. M.E. Lamb. New York: Wiley.

Young, M., and Willmott, P. 1973. *The symmetrical family.* Harmondsworth, Middx.: Penguin.

Index